DO NOT REMOVE
CARDS FROM POCKET

ALLEN COUNTY PUBLIC LIBRARY

FORT WAYNE, INDIANA 46802

You may return this book to any agency, branch,
or bookmobile of the Allen County Public Library

DEMCO

DATA PROCESSING DOCUMENTATION: STANDARDS, PROCEDURES AND APPLICATIONS

DATA PROCESSING DOCUMENTATION: STANDARDS, PROCEDURES AND APPLICATIONS

William L. Harper

Prentice-Hall, Inc.
Englewood Cliffs, N. J.

Prentice-Hall International, Inc., *London*
Prentice-Hall of Australia, Pty. Ltd., *Sydney*
Prentice-Hall of Canada, Ltd., *Toronto*
Prentice-Hall of India Private Ltd., *New Delhi*
Prentice-Hall of Japan, Inc., *Tokyo*

Library of Congress Cataloging in Publication Data

Harper, William L   (date)
   Data processing documentation.

   Includes bibliographical references.
   1. Electronic data processing documentation.
I. Title.
QA76.H284   029'.9'00164   72-6450
ISBN 0-13-196782-7

Printed in the United States of America
0-13-196782-7

About the Author

William L. Harper has had extensive experience in documentation, telecommunications and on-line communication systems, including 20 years with the Air Force. For the past six years he has been involved in systems analysis, systems documentation and EDP technical writing/editing for commercial and government data systems. He has been Systems Analyst for Amoco Production Corporation, Tulsa, Oklahoma, and is presently Data Communications Specialist with the Air Force.

The author is a frequent contributor of full length feature articles to such magazines as *Modern Data* and *Datamation*. Two typical articles have presented new insight into such subjects as documentation for application programming and digital switching. Mr. Harper has also completed more than 1,000 hours of classroom training in computer programming, systems analysis and design techniques.

Purpose and Benefits of This Book

This book is for the hurried EDP manager and busy analyst and programmer who are involved with management, design, and programming problems and have little time left for figuring out documentation principles that are best for their data processing needs.

One of the overriding needs in an EDP organization is the defining and establishing of documentation objectives. The primary purpose of documentation is to furnish information when it is needed, where it is needed, and in a form that is needed. Problems in developing, implementing, operating, and managing a data processing system can be lessened when sound documentation principles are used.

It is inconceivable that in this modern age of EDP there are still data systems being implemented without standards specifying user documentation. Experience has taught this author two fundamental lessons: first, that standards require full and active support from EDP managers; second, that certain definite functions must be assigned as the responsibility of designated individuals in order to achieve quality documentation.

In the beginning, EDP managers shunned documentation. They "believed" they had more pressing problems to solve than to worry about documentation. Documentation could be put off but the design and development of a new program, or keeping the on-going system on the air, could not. Even then, as now, part of the problem of keeping a system running was inadequate documentation.

When documentation standards were mentioned, programmers fought it. Some EDP managers fought it. Others viewed it passively. The passive documentation philosophy of many EDP managers has not changed to a great extent today.

The lack of a sound documentation policy eats away at profit as a result of program duplication. Some EDP managers "reinvent the wheel" in the design of a subsequent program or system because documentation standards are not established to make previously developed programs available for comparison.

Part I of this book is directed to the efficient and profit-oriented EDP manager who wants to become more efficient and more profitable for his company. It is directed to the busy system analyst and the creative programmer who desire to become more productive in the design and creativeness of their work.

It is the latter group that is struggling with documentation problems. The EDP manager looks to this group not only for error-free programs but also to provide proper documentation. EDP managers look to the analyst and programmer to provide documentation that will quickly and accurately define and clarify, and, when a program is in trouble, expose the area in need of attention. The EDP manager expects this same group to provide the user with documentation to explain the workings of the system.

Documentation and its preparation has become one of the annoying and nagging problems confronting EDP managers in recent years. Part II of this book suggests certain techniques that will aid data processing personnel who are struggling with the preparation of documentation. It is loaded with actual examples of poor documentation writing that is prevalent throughout the data processing field. It explains how good technical writing concepts can improve the quality of documentation.

Part II has as its main point the art of communicating clearly and accurately, in writing, an EDP technical concept or function in as few words as possible. It is predicated upon the belief that clarity, brevity, and accuracy of documentation are vital for EDP systems.

The underlying objective of this book is to present concepts, methods, and tested procedures that will aid the EDP manager, analyst, and programmer in establishing and implementing practices that will enhance the quality of documentation.

The documentation practices and standards advocated and exemplified throughout this book have proven to be valuable guides in certain commercial and military EDP systems. They are by no means exhaustive. They are appropriate to both small and large EDP operations. The profit-oriented EDP manager will study them and weigh their usefulness against his own operation. The prudent manager will adopt, modify, and incorporate those documentation practices that will aid his operation, and he will enforce them vigorously.

In the past few years, and for many diverse groups, the problem of documentation has been the subject of investigation and much concern. What is the problem? And why is it so? Why has concentration on the problem become so involved now? How *Data Processing Documentation* hopes to help by shedding light on this dark and nebulous corner of the EDP world is summarized below:

Chapter One: "The Key Ingredients for Success: Pre-Programming and Program Development Documentation"—Explains why the need for quality documentation is so vital to data processing, and why inadequate documentation can result in expensive reprogramming. Chapter One points out why documentation problems afflict all data processing organizations. It suggests methods of determining the documentation requirements and the type of documentation for a given system.

Chapter Two: "Setting Program Documentation Standards"—Suggests certain design and programming documentation standards that will aid commonality in data processing and minimize program duplication. Chapter Two explains techniques for setting up system design standards that will make possible the transition from one design phase to another without difficulty. It discusses program design concepts and techniques that can contribute to a reduction in programming manpower cost.

Chapter Three: "Preparing Feasibility Studies"—Tells EDP managers and system analysts how to plan and organize a feasibility study. It explains how to break a "total" system feasibility study down into individual functional areas for more precise analysis and how to put it all back together. Chapter Three points out important factors to consider in writing the feasibility study.

Chapter Four: "Decision Logic Tables: Their Potential for Relieving the Documentation Strain in Systems Work"—Presents a tutorial guide to understanding and use of decision logic tables (DLT's). It explains how a DLT forces the analyst to do complete analysis of a problem, and how to reconstruct an involved narrative procedure to DLT format. It explains how DLT's provide better communication between EDP and non-EDP people. Chapter Four explains why a DLT is self-sufficient, and complete documentation for a particular problem.

Chapter Five: "Preparing EDP Management Policy Manuals"—Defines the role of EDP policy and procedure manuals and explains the format for organizing them. Chapter Five suggests how sections can be laid out and identified so any section may be lifted from the manual without disturbing the layout and continuity of other sections.

Chapter Six: "EDP Forms Management and Design Considerations"—Deals with EDP forms management and explains methods by which to eliminate repetitive narrative paperwork. Methods are discussed that will provide EDP managers and other personnel with accurate data when needed without having to sift through irrelevant data. How to determine the need for an EDP form is discussed in detail. Guidelines for form analysis and form design standards are provided. Factors to consider in the control of EDP forms are brought out in this chapter.

Chapter Seven: "Forms as a Management Tool in Computer Center Operations"—Discusses various aspects of computer center operations and suggests certain EDP forms that can reduce operating cost and aid EDP managers in controlling the data processing operations. Specimens of certain EDP forms and an explanation for their use are given.

Chapter Eight: "Organizing and Maintaining Data Processing Documentation Libraries"—Explains why a properly organized documentation library can do more to further data processing techniques than any other single function of an EDP organization. Chapter Eight discusses in detail tested procedures for setting up and maintaining a documentation reference library. Procedures for documentation management and controlling changes to on-going programs are discussed.

Chapter Nine: "Documentation for Vendor-Provided Application Systems"—Suggests certain types of documentation that should be furnished with a vendor-provided system. It explains why the quality of documentation provided by a vendor is more critical than documentation developed by a user. Chapter Nine suggests certain procedures for testing a vendor-developed system.

Chapter Ten: "The Role of the EDP Documentation Writer"—Explains the role of the documentation writer and how he fits into the scheme of things. It explains why marshalling of data so that only relevant information may be documented, entered and retrieved from the system, should be a prime concern for EDP managers. Chapter Ten discusses the writing style and how to achieve quality documentation.

Chapter Eleven: "Planning and Organizing for Documentation Writing"—Explains why planning is the key to good documentation writing. It tells how to tackle large EDP writing jobs without getting "braincramped" at the outset. Chapter Eleven tells how to get started, how to avoid interruption, and how to produce a first draft. It tells how to revise in order to produce a clear and accurate document. Chapter Eleven shows how to avoid hedge words and deadwood in EDP documentation. It tells how EDP supervisors may review, edit, and critique subordinates' writing without offending the writer.

Chapter Twelve: "Effective EDP Documentation Writing"—Explains techniques of EDP documentation writing that will produce clear, concise, and quality documentation. Chapter Twelve tells how to avoid cluttering EDP documentation with nonessentials, or with verbose and abstract writing.

Chapter Thirteen: "How to Create a Written Piece"—Tells how to do it. It recaps and presents the theme of Part II in a simple and straightforward manner. This chapter is for the personnel in a company who provide administrative support for an EDP system but do not get involved in writing EDP documentation. It is for those individuals who seek information in capsule form to aid them in writing.

William L. Harper

ACKNOWLEDGEMENTS

This book would not have been possible without the cooperation and help of many people. Many individuals were asked to corroborate on certain ideas, concepts, and principles contained in the book; to them, I am appreciative.

I am indebted to John Culbertson, Robert Flechtner, and Anthony Stathopoulos for taking time to read certain chapters and for offering their criticism.

I am particularly grateful to my good friend, Joe Dorrough, for his patient reading of several chapters of Part I and Part II, and for his many suggestions for strengthening and making this a meaningful book.

I will always be indebted to my wife Mary and my daughter Robin for their part in making the book possible. Over the two years that I spent writing it, Mary gave up many evenings and weekends to type the manuscript. Robin did many of the household chores while the manuscript was being typed.

I am indebted to Donna Reed for typing and proofreading part of the manuscript. I am equally indebted to Marylene Zimmerman, EDP librarian, who read Chapter Eight and contributed valuable information for this chapter.

The opinions expressed in this book are those of the author and do not necessarily reflect those of his employer.

Table of Contents

PART II

DOCUMENTATION PREPARATION

DATA PROCESSING DOCUMENTATION: STANDARDS, PROCEDURES AND APPLICATIONS

Documentation Guidelines

1

The Key Ingredients for Success: Pre-Programming and Program Development Documentation

The present state of things is the consequence of the past. . . .

Samuel Johnson

The essential purpose of documentation is to provide information when needed, and where needed, and in a form needed, that will aid system and program development and minimize program duplication. The presentation of this documentation should be concerned with relevant and specific factual data that can be promptly found and used immediately.

In order that EDP managers may make sound data processing decisions that will be valid in the months and years ahead, they must have good recorded data processing "history." If this history (documentation) is ill defined and documented, EDP managers must rely on brainstorming sessions, memory, and a computer listing. All too often this method is a poor substitute for accurately recorded information.

One of the functions of EDP documentation is to collect, document, and arrange documentation in methods which will aid EDP personnel in understanding and developing subsequent systems.

Documentation should also serve to furnish EDP managers, as well as top company management, the specific information about data processing activities that a technical or administrative manager or his staff requires in the normal functioning of his duties. Documentation should be defined and recorded accurately, and retrieval of this information made routine and simple.

Leonard I. Krauss has this to say about good documentation:

Meaningful documentation, therefore, is vital to the continuance of the success of the EDP effort. Fast and accurate solutions to programming problems or data alterations arising in computer operations depend heavily upon good documentation. The efficiency and precision with which computer operations are carried out are often a function of how well the operating procedures have been spelled out.[1]

HIDDEN COST DUE TO INADEQUATE DOCUMENTATION

Poorly documented programs may not have immediate adverse effects on software performance, since the originating programmers can usually compensate for inadequate documentation. But the effects of poor documentation subsequently come to the surface when modification is necessary and the original programmer(s) is no longer available or has forgotten program details. Without adequate and controlled documentation, the task of updating the system, converting to newer hardware or higher levels of programming languages, becomes increasingly difficult and costly.

Dick H. Brandon says this about cost:

> A data processing manager who just lost his first programmer will readily testify to the costs which he has incurred in "taking over" the inherited program. . . . The language used may be highly individual; the symbology not standard, and inconsistent; the abbreviations and mnemonics absolutely not understandable. If changes to these programs are required, the problems to be faced are so severe that many programs are completely rewritten after the resignation of their authors.[2]

When matching hardware characteristics to software requirements, documentation on such variables as the appropriate peripheral devices and speeds, the volume of data to be processed, and the core capacity and speed of the computer must be accurately determined and documented. These factors are usually ruled on in the systems design study plan. It may be difficult to assess their true dimensions until documentation on data and programming requirements has been developed.

Unless managers are technically qualified to assess methods and needs for data processing, they must, in actual fact, delegate these important decisions to subordinate EDP personnel. Such decisions may be the result of compromise reached in conferences, or studies prepared in a joint effort by systems analysts and programmers. While delegation of authority and consultation with subordinates on such matters should not be discouraged, programmers and EDP managers must have adequate documentation to interpret correctly the information, advice, and opinions of systems analysts and programmers.

A system's size will determine the volume but not the methods of documentation applications required for an EDP operation. The size of the programming task should not affect such things as the scope and type of documentation, the need for standardiza-

---

[1] Leonard I. Krauss, *Administering and Controlling the Company Data Processing Function,* Prentice-Hall, Inc., Englewood Cliffs, N.J., p. 72.

[2] Dick H. Brandon, *Management Standards for Data Processing,* copyright 1963 by Litton Educational Publishing Inc., reprint by permission of Van Nostrand Company, Inc., 450 W. 33rd Street, New York, N.Y. 10001, p. 29.

tion of flowchart conventions, coding forms, and the various controls that are necessary for program maintenance and management. Much hidden cost exists in programming development due to program duplication when methods are not used for conveniently saving past and current programs for instant recall and use.

DOCUMENTATION PROBLEMS AFFLICT ALL DATA PROCESSING SYSTEMS

Documentation problems are present in all data processing systems. The problems are more prevalent in medium to large EDP systems. Even in some of the oldest applications, implemented in the days of the "green visor" and vacuum tube computer period, the documentation problem has not been solved.

It is not that these problems cannot be solved; rather, it is that we tend to postpone the problem of thinking by losing ourselves in other busy areas of data processing. Usually, documentation problems are postponed until all other EDP problems are in hand. And, of course, those of us who have concentrated on EDP documentation over the years know that this practice only compounds and aggravates other data processing problems.

It has been estimated that for certain EDP applications, e.g., payroll programs, more individual programs have been written to handle the automation of paychecks than the total number of computers installed.

Jackson W. Granholm, a noted EDP consultant and author who has more than 23 years of computing experience, was quoted in DATAMATION (April 15, 1971) as saying:

> Payroll has a near-universal application, since most everyone in the world is, hopefully, on some kind of payroll. Yet a close look at the real world of payroll programs reveals some interesting, if not provocative, facts.
>
> There comes a day in the life of every company (and this day is now pretty long ago in many instances) when the first computer is delivered, and the in-house crew is in business with their very own installation. What is the first program put on the air? You guessed it—Payroll. Management has a warm feeling that it is all going to be worthwhile when the machine-printed checks, with their machine-printed withholding stubs, roll out of the printer and are secretly embossed in the back room with the signature of the corporate treasurer.
>
> Since payroll is the first program written by the in-house crew, it is not too surprising to find that it is rather scantily documented. Of course, if it was first written 15 years ago, it may be a bit more distressing to find its documentation still scanty today, if, indeed, one can find the documentation at all.
>
> If one can find the documentation, one is not always sure of exactly what has been found. After all, payroll usually has to operate once every two weeks at minimum, and in some industries, like the motion picture industry, it has to operate daily. This makes changes to the payroll program assume the status of hasty patches, and the author of a hasty patch is all too prone to forget to write down what he patched. . . . Some of the more astounding examples of in-house-gener-

ated payroll software literature thus comes to resemble a battered shoebox full of notes of the type, "I changed the word in location 4632, and got back on the machine."

The frequent and extensive changes that are made to on-going systems eat into profit when documentation policies are not established to approve, direct, and coordinate the modification. Before setting up documentation policy, a clear understanding of each programming department's unique documentation problems must be studied.

PRE-PROGRAMMING DOCUMENTATION

One of the major functions of documentation is to identify and document programming objectives. Documentation applications fall into two major categories: pre-programming documentation and program development documentation. The majority of documentation applications discussed apply to the programming efforts while a system is being developed, after the system's pre-programming specifications have been determined. The system's specifications set out general programming objectives to satisfy data processing requirements of a user.

Pre-programming documentation policy and work procedures must be established early in the design and analysis phase. Pre-programming documentation falls into two areas: *problem definition* and *general program analysis*.

Problem Definition: In trying to determine methods for automation, it is important that the methods of operations of the existing system (manual or automated) be clearly identified and documented. The extra time it takes to write up clear problem definitions will be appreciated when documenting programming objectives. To isolate the problems, an in-depth analysis survey of the user's existing operation is required. This includes studying the many operational functions, manual as well as automated, and defining present applications and methods of doing business. The results of these studies should be documented in sufficient detail so as to enable others to complete preparation of programming objectives for the data processing system.

When making major modifications to an existing data processing system, changes in the internal and external documentation must be clearly defined. The establishment, clarification, and documentation of these changes cannot be postponed. If this is put off until programming has commenced, delays and temper flare-ups arise when trying to define the problem and identify programming concepts to satisfy the problem.

The documentation efforts in the pre-programming phase of system design should be devoted to problem definition and system analysis. These phases often overlap and vary with data processing applications; they should be documented separately. Problem definition is primarily concerned with the following factors:

- In-depth study and documentation of the user's present operations and procedures.
- Identification and documentation of certain related areas that influence data processing methods and applications for later analysis, but prior to final coding.

· Identification and documentation of alternate approaches and backup applications to satisfy the user's requirements.

These factors should be further defined by asking the following questions and documenting the answers:

· What are the environmental factors that may affect the system?
· What is the data to be processed?
· How does the data enter the system?
· How is the data recorded?
· What is the data used for?
· Who gets the data, for what purpose, and in what volume?
· What is the total data volume?
· What are the normal and peak load periods?
· What procedures must be used during system failure?

To find the answers to most of these questions, the analyst must go to the source—the facility where data processing services are required. The analyst must get firsthand information. He must observe the operation. He must spend time with the operations personnel; work with them for an extended period. This is necessary to make sure that all the details of the operation are documented for later analysis.

The movement and data processing functions should be charted and clearly documented. Determine what types of reports and format are required by EDP managers concerning the data processing operations. Note carefully the specially handled items, their volume, and how they differ from the normal flow.

Documentation of the problem definition should be thorough and concise. At this phase of pre-programming, it is too early to determine and define the details and precise composition of input/output formats, tables, files, and record layouts. The purpose of the documentation at this stage should be to identify the major programming features and their main functions. The main purpose of this pre-programming documentation is to serve as the source information for latter phases of program development for defining job specification, run time, setup instructions, operating manuals, and other documentation required by EDP management.

After the problem areas have been identified and documented, the analysis of these problems and the design phase of a data processing system is undertaken.

General Program Analysis:

The data processing specifications are analyzed, documented, and broken down into major programming segments. These segments are further segmented into programming functions or stand-alone programming features. This phase of pre-programming is concerned with documenting the general information required for programming and preparing documentation for operating procedures.

Here, the individual program applications are broken down into a series of functional programming features to satisfy the user's operational requirement. These functional features should include computer runs, general programming steps to achieve these runs, source data, equipment specifications, and other factors and procedures required to satisfy programming actions. The documentation for program analysis should include:

- General documentation on each programming feature of job runs, to include core storage, man-machine configuration, and interactions required to run the job. For batch-oriented applications, run time should also be specified.
- General layout of files, tables, and input/output records format.
- Semi-detailed flowcharts of each functional program.
- Documentation on the sequence in which the various programs should be developed, and what language should be used.
- A narrative giving an overview of the data processing specification, to include the purpose and function of each program that makes up a system of programs.
- Information on application requirements to include core size and other characteristics of equipment, the extent of conversion problems, the available resources to support the new or modified data processing activity, and the overall effect of computer use on the personnel and the organization.

This information should be documented according to the rules determined by the documentation policy established at the outset of the project. After the best methods and procedures for programming have been determined and the information documented, it should be turned over to a programming staff for coding.

After an individual programming application has been generally defined and documented, the application is ready for program development.

PROGRAM DEVELOPMENT DOCUMENTATION

The second major purpose of documentation is in the actual documentation of each program design and development. The analyst should turn over the proper pre-programming documentation in sufficient detail to the programmer to enable the programmer to design programming techniques. In many cases, the analyst will do the pre-programming as well as the program development work. This should not affect the documentation requirements as discussed under "Pre-Programming Documentation." The pre-programming documentation is a prerequisite for detail program analysis and clarification purposes in the program development phase. As a minimum of the pre-programming documentation that should be turned over to the programmer for each program application at the junction between pre-programming and program development, the following or its equivalent is suggested:

- Flowcharts showing the input/output areas, source and main flow of data, entrance and exit of subroutines, general processing functions and sequence of program operation.
- Documentation on computer jobs, run time, and core requirements.

- A general narrative describing the application.
- Card input and output layout, showing the arrangement of data in all input and output card format.
- Report layout, depicting the exact format and location of data.
- Specific job processing and run information.
- Documentation on file layout constants, showing parameters and variables to be maintained.
- Documentation describing tables and records format and data layout.
- System messages to the operator, cause and frequency of type-outs.
- Operator console commands, format and procedure for type-in.
- Documentation on other programming information required for program development.

Usually, many analysts and programmers are involved in the development of an EDP system comprised of many programs. Many of these programs must interface with each other and share the same boundaries. A tremendous amount of planning goes into program development.

In the pre-programming phase, specific information on each program application is collected, analyzed, and passed on to the programmer for program development. The programmer generates a great deal of additional material and information. It would be extremely difficult for the individuals who are involved in the program development phase to keep track of the details, material and information unless this information and material were recorded in a clear and orderly manner.

Information that will be needed in the coding of a program must be recorded in a clear and concise fashion. This documentation is not used only for program coding; it is the main source for debugging a program. It is essential for program testing and program maintenance after the system of programs is operational.

The documentation prepared during the program development phase should be reviewed by the lead analyst before programming starts. This will give the analyst and programmer a chance to detect careless preparation errors and errors in logic. The documentation should be revised and condensed until it is clear and accurate enough to serve as the reference during program development, debugging, conversion, testing, and program maintenance after implementation.

Much time must be devoted for planning, organizing, preparing and maintaining documentation for an EDP system. This documentation must be sufficient, accurate—and available when needed. The time and effort spent preparing quality documentation is justified when compared with the recoding efforts and other problems that may occur when complete documentation is not available.

Quality documentation is an essential and vital part of an EDP system. Documentation serves the following needs:

- It limits and clarifies the programming effort.
- It specifies methods used.
- It serves as the communication link among programmers, analysts and EDP managers, and user personnel.
- It serves as the official reference material for pre-programming and program development information.

· It aids training flexibility in programmer assignment.
· It provides programmer-to-programmer information about related programs or systems.
· It provides the communications necessary for keypunch operators, job control clerks, and computer operators when working with the program.
· It is indispensable in desk checking and debugging processes.
· It aids program and system modification.
· It provides historical data, and aids the development of subsequent programs.

DETERMINING DOCUMENTATION REQUIREMENTS

As mentioned earlier, much time is spent planning and organizing documentation applications in the program development phase. It is important at the outset to determine the general requirement for the type of documentation that will be needed for each program application. The lead analyst should have some idea of the type of documentation needed before programming starts. To aid him, the analyst should prepare a written outline identifying the type of documentation that will be required.

If a written outline for documentation is not prepared, and the documentation needs determined as programs are developed, previous documentation decisions and considerations may be forgotten. If this happens, the project may reach the completion stage without adequate documentation. This may hold up implementation until necessary external documentation (operations and run manuals) are available.

This could be costly in terms of an inordinate delay in system implementation and idle equipment and personnel. It could cost the software vendor penalty money for the delay in user acceptance of the system due to inadequate user documentation.

In the planning for documentation, it should be remembered that inadequate documentation may cause reprogramming when modification is required. On the other hand, too much documentation may prove inefficient and cause an undue burden on personnel in the preparation and upkeep of this information.

What is the right amount of documentation? There is no magic solution or answer to this question. Each program or system application may require different types of documentation. However, at the outset, if study is given to the documentation needs and standards defined and followed during the program development phase, it will make the task of answering this question easier. To aid in answering this question, the following is offered:

· Postponement of major portion of documentation until the program is developed may cause hasty creation of a large assortment, but inefficient documentation after the system has reached the operational stage. Documentation should be developed simultaneously with each program.
· The process of developing documentation should be concurrent with developing programs. Clarity and accuracy should be the main objectives in preparing documentation. To be of use, it should present the facts, depict special aspects, and provide procedures by which all functions of the program can be understood and followed.
· Modifications to programs are frequent during the program development phase and,

depending on the system, changes may occur often after the program is operational. An easy and simple method of making changes should be established so that the documentation will always be current. This will aid revising the documentation during conversions and major modifications, and will minimize the bulk of documentation.

TYPE OF DOCUMENTATION

During the *pre-programming documentation* and *program development documentation* phase, as discussed under these two topics, much documentation is created. This documentation falls in different categories, serves different purposes, and is directed to different people. What will be discussed in this section represents a typical requirement that can be adapted to the specific needs of an EDP system.

Information that is generated should be recorded and categorized to provide the proper reference material for the individuals who will be working with each program application. Normally, this type of documentation can be retained in an Application System Reference Manual.

Application System Reference Manual

The information contained in this manual is the byproduct of the pre-programming and program development phases of system development.

Carefully organized documentation concerning the program development efforts will permit EDP personnel to find what they need to know about a program. This information should be contained in binders with tabbed chapters or sections to identify the information contained in each section.

The Applications System Reference Manual will serve as the composite document for the system and should be developed concurrently with the system. The manual should contain a general narrative which gives a brief background of the system application. The authority that approved the system, the objectives, scope, and other pertinent information giving a clear and accurate understanding of the systems should be contained in the first section.

Also included in the first section should be a chart in block diagram depicting each program application by name. This chart (discussed more in detail in Chapter Two) would represent a general overview of the applications program that is needed to accept, process, protect, and output the data.

The following paragraphs will discuss the general type of information that should be contained in subsequent chapters of the Application Systems Reference Manual.

Narrative Description

For each application program or group of programs that are developed to do a particular job, a section should be provided to contain the following information:

- Program name or subject
- Description of the purpose, scope, and function
- Name of programmer or individual who is responsible for the program
- Description and sequence of input and output data
- Machine setup procedures, and disposition of output
- Console operator's procedures (type-ins and operator response to system commands)
- Restart procedures
- Test and implementation procedures
- Other information necessary for the processing and running jobs.

Flowcharts

This documentation provides a means of identifying input and output areas, programming functions, and sequence of operations to graphically and symbolically present the logic and the path of its flow in the solution of a problem. Generally, flowcharts fall in three categories: *first-level, second-level,* and *third-level.* These levels are discussed in depth in Chapter Two. The three levels of flowcharts should do the following:

- Give a general overview of major processing areas for system or program development and identify programming features required.
- Serve as a guide for system design.
- Show the main flow of data through the system or program.
- Give an idea as to the amount of time required for programming efforts.
- Identify the input and output areas that will be a data source.
- Show specific logic operations and decisions necessary for coding.
- Show and describe the sequence of one operation to another in graphic and symbolic notation.
- Identify the entrance and exit for subroutines.
- Identify error returns.
- Provide EDP personnel with a graphic means to review plans for program design.

Program Parameters and Record Layouts

Tables, records, and file layouts for each program application should be identified. This data should be laid out to contain sufficient information to identify and control data processing functions. This information should include the source for data input and output, format for tables or files, layout for reports, and arrangement for data contained in the report.

Examples of forms used for card and report layout should be part of each application program documentation. The carriage tape (or details for its preparation) should be contained with the documentation. A machine listing of the source and object program should also be included.

Operator's Console Procedures

From the type of documentation thus far discussed, certain information may be extracted to prepare the operator's console instruction. This information should contain sufficient information to permit the operator to run each job. This information may include a brief narrative giving the purpose and function of each program application. It should also contain the type-in and type-out commands, job setup instruction, disposition of the output product, carriage control tape information, etc.

The console operator's information should be organized and laid out in a convenient manner so the operator can readily locate the information he needs for job processing. A separate binder, with the various procedures and information separated and identified as suggested in Chapter Five, should be used. This information should be kept current and the binder kept at the console position.

ELIMINATION OF PROGRAM DUPLICATION THROUGH THE USE OF PROGRAM ABSTRACTS

Another important function of documentation is to provide an abstract on each program application of an EDP system. It would not be practical to assemble all information created during pre-programming documentation and program development documentation in a single binder and expect everyone to use this document as the sole documentation reference.

As mentioned earlier, different EDP people need different types of documentation to aid them in their work. In planning for the documentation requirements for a given EDP system, a method for extracting certain information should be established so that pertinent information about each program application can be made available to programmers, analysts, and EDP managers.

This information can be made available by a *program abstract*. After the coding of each program is complete, a program abstract (Figure 1-1) should be prepared. The information contained in the abstract can be extracted from the pre-programming and program development documentation.

Quite often, duplication of programming efforts occurs among programming groups because programmers have no quick reference to make them aware of each other's work. The program abstract would be primarily for EDP managers, analysts, and programmers. These abstracts should be contained in a binder and made available to all programming groups. The layout of this binder can be similar to that discussed in Chapter Five.

The abstract would provide pertinent information on various aspects of existing programs. The abstract would serve to limit program duplication because programming groups would have a compact reference describing the functional aspects on previously developed programs. As a system of programs is developed, a catalog listing of program

PROGRAM ABSTRACT

PAGE ＿＿＿ OF ＿＿＿
DATE ＿＿＿＿＿＿＿＿
REVISION DATE ＿＿＿

PROGRAM SUBJECT/NAME: (Meaningful and descriptive title/name)

SYSTEM: (Identify system)

PROGRAM CCN NUMBER: (This number is obtained from the Program Task Sheet.)

PROGRAM SOFTWARE NAME: (Alphanumeric mnemonic)

LIBRARY (SOFTWARE) RESIDENCE: (State the system's library in which the program resides and the amount of storage in bytes.)

LANGUAGE: (State language used.)

ENVIRONMENT CONFIGURATION: (Specify equipment configuration, the vendor's release number, e.g. IBM Release 18-MVT, UNIVAC Version Number, etc., under which the program was tested.)

PURPOSE: (What the program is designed to do)

FUNCTION: (Explain in detail how the program accomplishes the purpose.)

DESCRIPTION OF FILES, TABLES, ETC.: (Give example and usage.)

ENTRANCE AND EXIT RETURNS AND ERROR RETURNS: (Give entrance and exits, error messages, parameters default values, etc.)

OPERATING INSTRUCTIONS: (Give step-by-step operating instructions, if any, that are required for man-machine interactions.)

IMPLEMENTATION INSTRUCTIONS: (Special testing or implementation instruction)

PROGRAM HISTORY: (Give the date the program was developed and implemented and, over the life of the program, give dates of modifications. If the modification alters any features of the program that invalidate any of the above, the program abstract will be updated.)

PROGRAMMER: (Give the name of the programmer who either originated or is currently responsible for the program.)

(NOTE: The program abstract is presented with major captions that will aid in isolating pertinent information about the program/routine. An individual may be interested only in the "Description of Files, Tables." He can easily find it without reading through the abstract. Several pages may be required to provide the information of a particular caption, e.g., "Function.")

FIGURE 1-1

Program Abstract

abstracts by subject or name, and containing a brief description (one or two paragraphs) of each program, could be prepared. The catalog listing differs from the program abstract discussed above in that the program abstract contains all the pertinent information about the program while the catalog listing would only identify the various programs and briefly describe each program.

The catalog listing, identifying each program, would provide a quick program reference for the programming groups. After an individual finds a program in the catalog listing that he would like to examine, he then goes to the program abstract binder and reviews the various aspects of the program. If further review is desired, he may go to the Central Reference Library, as discussed in Chapter Eight, and examine the flowcharts, program listings, and other documentation associated with the program. In like or similar systems, many system concepts and much programming logic can be lifted from documentation on previously developed programs. (The binder containing the program abstract may become voluminous and discourage individuals from using it as a quick reference, while the catalog listing would be compact and easy to use.)

Such a system would extend control over programming efforts by making available an efficient and quick means of referencing a previously developed program. For example, if an EDP organization develops similar systems (e.g., message switching) which are comprised of programs with only minor differences, a decision can be made to consolidate certain programs, thereby eliminating duplication in programming efforts.

OFF-THE-SHELF PROGRAMS

When programs or a system of programs are developed to perform parallel or similar applications, this author is convinced that the acid test of a sound and economical documentation policy is its ability to provide off-the-shelf documentation for subsequent application programs or systems.

Consider a large department store retailer with several outlets in many states, but whose purchasing is done by the main corporate office. To aid in controlling this geographically dispersed firm, a corporate-wide on-line EDP system is installed. One of the requirements of this system is the provision of an application system to keep track and report the daily inventory status corporate wide. The regional and district offices are tied together with an on-line EDP system. The district offices report to the regional office, and the regional offices consolidate the reports and transmit a composite report to the main corporate EDP office.

Suppose also that the design and program development to satisfy the inventory and reporting system for each district and regional office is left up to the individual EDP manager. No programming or documentation standards were established by the corporate office. The only systems requirement levied upon each regional EDP manager is that the composite report must reach the main EDP office by a certain time each day. (After one more assumption, the point of this hypothesis is made clear.)

Now, suppose that the hardware for the corporate-wide EDP system is of one manufacturer. Here, we have a large EDP system with each user of the system developing application programs that perform basically the same function (inventory control), and these programs are run on basically the same equipment. There are no corporate-wide documentation standards set up to insure program commonality or compatibility in application design. The only restraint is in "reporting on time."

The Point:

Many users of "real" EDP systems are developing programs for *like* systems, but each EDP manager is free to develop programs without any documentation restraints. This is a costly process in "reinventing the wheel."

Commercial and military batch-processing systems are giving way to, or incorporating, on-line EDP functions. The federal government, particularly the military, is the perpetuator and biggest user of on-line systems. The military's SAGE (Semi-Automatic Ground Environment) system of the 1950s and early 60s, the global AUTODIN (Automatic Digital Network) and its interface systems, and the Automated Weather Communications Network, coupled with the World Wide Military Command and Control System (WWMCCS), attest to the military involvement in on-line systems.

Considerable savings could be realized in data processing systems by adopting documentation procedures for the standardization of system and program design. *For example:* If it takes a given number of manhours/months to develop a system employing data communication techniques, then a subsequent system requiring similar or parallel techniques, e.g., computer-to-computer interface, queuing and switching, data protection and accountability, buffering and file/record/table build, etc., can be developed with fewer individuals, and in less time, by using or modifying previously developed programs and techniques. When systems are configured of like hardware and the software performs the same or similar functions, commonality in program design standards for off-the-shelf programs would be a logical follow-on in system development.

Batch processing lends itself more to off-the-shelf programs than on-line data communications systems. Each step or feature of a programming job should be indexed by subject. Each stand-alone feature or routine of a major program, or each stand-alone program of an application system, should contain an abstract stating its purpose and function.

When developing documentation policy, EDP managers should keep in mind the commonality of programming efforts and establish or recommend guidelines and procedures that will lend themselves to documentation standardization for off-the-shelf programs. Documentation commonality in the design and programming concepts of batch or on-line data systems can contribute to profits by permitting a reduction of programmers.

Off-the-shelf programs will facilitate future design and program development. It is very expensive in personnel salary, which eats away profits, to "reinvent the wheel" for a customer who wants a software inventory or an automated payroll system, or an on-line communications message switching system.

Off-the-shelf programs would not be "canned" ready-to-use programs. Changes or even major modification may be required. But a considerable amount of time would be saved by not having to reinvent completely each new program or system. To make off-the-shelf programs available, library procedures, as discussed in Chapter Eight, for both administrative and software storage and retrieval would have to be implemented for cataloging, indexing, and updating these programs.

DOCUMENTATION IN INTEGRATED VS. NON-INTEGRATED EDP ORGANIZATIONS

Documentation requirements are less confusing in EDP organizations where the design, development, and maintenance functions are performed by the same people, under the direction of a single EDP manager, than in organizations where these functions are performed and managed separately.

Recorded cases reveal that the separation of design, development, and maintenance is an unwise practice as far as harmonious relations and documentation are concerned. All of these groups rely upon each other's documentation as a major input to their own activities. In non-integrated EDP organizations, documentation becomes the cohesive element and gives viability to the EDP organization.

Unless there are strong management influences, friction and ill feeling may occur between separate EDP groups because of the lack or the condition of documentation that is passed from *design to development,* and from *development to maintenance.* If something goes wrong in the program development group, they may blame poor design work or inadequate documentation. The maintenance group could use a similar excuse.

Small batch-oriented EDP organizations may function satisfactorily with non-integrated functions. But in medium to large on-line systems much confusion would exist and sound documentation practices would become impractical. In on-line systems, there are numerous features that interface and overlap each other. This would require maintenance programmers to have an in-depth working knowledge of the design and coding of these programs.

Integrated organizations lend themselves to good documentation concepts, while non-integrated organizations compound documentation problems. When one department is responsible for the design, development, implementation and maintenance, and documentation, the communications problems among analysts and programmers are minimized. They all have, to some degree, been involved in all these areas of system installation.

Generally, integrated EDP organizations will have:

- fewer documentation problems
- higher user satisfaction with documentation
- less cost and time expenditure in providing documentation
- better quality and less quantity of documentation
- less difficulty in meeting documentation requirements
- less need for formal and detailed documentation in certain areas of documentation, e.g., detailed flowcharts can be eliminated
- less confusion in communications among programmers and analysts
- better coordination and control over documentation.

When an EDP organization is integrated, documentation applications are difficult enough. But in non-integrated organizations, meaningful documentation could become unmanageable. An integrated organization would enjoy fewer documentation problems and lower documentation maintenance than a non-integrated one.

In a non-integrated EDP organization, more documentation is required and more attention must be given to the preparation of documentation. Why is this so? Because:

- Each phase of installing a system is developed by an autonomous group: design, development, or maintenance. These groups usually work independently of each other.

· Precise program design specifications and associated narrative description, general flowcharts, record/table layout and file descriptions must be passed on to the development group.
· Detailed logic flowcharts must be passed on to the maintenance group, along with user documentation, i.e., job setup and computer run instructions, etc. Job specification (operating procedure) is usually the weakest area of documentation under a non-integrated organization.

The need for formal, detailed, and complete documentation in non-integrated organizations is vital because documentation and communication needs cross departmental boundaries.

2

Setting Program Documentation Standards

If you think of "standardization" as the best that you know today, but which is to be improved tomorrow—you get somewhere.

Henry Ford

Documentation policy should be written before detailed programming objectives are defined. This will provide data processing managers with guides which they can use in making decisions. But equally important, managers will have a tool upon which to base programming documentation standards. Written policy should set out definite work objectives and responsibilities for the data processing organization.

Policy may be revised as the need arises, without affecting the standards to any degree. The objectives set out for the various sections under the data processing department should be in sufficient detail and clear enough so these sections may comply with the standards with minimum difficulty.

Programming groups within a company should not operate in a vacuum. That is, they should not operate as an autonomous group, defining and establishing their own documentation standards. All groups that share interface boundaries influence and are influenced by other programming groups.

When rational standards are not established for EDP documentation, much of the documentation that is voluntarily generated is, too often, meaningful only to the author. Paraphrasing a classic statement by Mr. Churchill, one of the greatest English language practitioners: "Never in the history of human communications has so much been written by so many which is of use to so few."

Here is what Leonard I. Krauss says about standards:

Since the very nature of data processing implies uniformity of some kind, it is not particularly surprising that certain standards are needed to make the installation efficient, if not workable. From the standpoint of being able to readily understand the work of any programmer in an installation, there must be a commonality of expression within this specialty group. Moreover, the work of this group may have to be interpreted, for various reasons, by someone who may not have an intimate knowledge of programming.[1]

It is of primary importance that standards be determined prior to the start of programming. The ideal situation would be to establish standards for a given system before a programming staff is chosen because standards would most likely be accepted by programmers as a job requirement. However, this may be difficult to do because the system specifications must be known before sound and realistic documentation standards can be determined. Certain documentation prerequisites must be determined in the pre-programming phase so that standards may be determined for program development.

DOCUMENTATION STANDARDS ARE ILL DEFINED OR NONEXISTENT

Modern computers and more sophisticated input/output devices have increased the scope and complexity of the manufacturer's software (supervisor and utility) systems. This has made the interface of application programs more difficult and certain aspects of programming, i.e., multiprogramming, multiprocessing, access and linkage, program modularity, file organization, and man/machine interactions more exacting. If coordination and controls over the development and life of an application program or system are to be effective, and optimum utilization of man and machine is to be realized, documentation standards and guidelines on all programming facets must be defined and formulated in the initial stages of program analysis and development.

Dick H. Brandon has this to say about standards:

> Many experienced personnel argue against the establishment of standards, much as they might argue against the benefits of documentation, or the value of "closed shop" program testing. A common myth among "creative" people is their feeling that creativity is inhibited by rules and regulations. This is entirely false. Good standards and good practices never inhibit creativity; creativity is greatly enhanced by good operating procedures. . . . Channeled and controlled by effective rules, the programmer will increase his productivity and his own understanding.[2]

Success of a data processing system is directly dependent on the policy and standards established to direct and control the actions of the employees. Documentation standards will vary considerably from system to system. Each data processing system is

---

[1] Leonard I. Krauss, *Administering and Controlling the Company Data Processing Functions,* Prentice-Hall, Englewood Cliffs, N.J., p. 73.

[2] Dick H. Brandon, *Management Standards for Data Processing,* copyright 1963 by Litton Educational Publishing Inc., reprint by permission of Van Nostrand Company, Inc., 450 W. 33rd Street, New York, N.Y. 10001, p. 29.

unique to some degree. They vary in size as well as application, and the overall environment in which they operate can be unusually different. Some factors of EDP documentation may be unique to a peculiar application but certain aspects of documentation are common to all. But in many data processing systems, documentation standards are ill defined or nonexistent.

Documentation principles must be adjusted and tailored to satisfy the particular needs of a given system. Because of the differences in data processing systems, types of application, and organization philosophy, it would be presumptuous to prescribe documentation policy that would serve as a panacea for any system. Nevertheless, experience has taught this author two fundamental lessons. The first is that documentation standards require full and active support from data processing managers. The second lesson is that within data processing organizations, certain definite functions must be assigned as the responsibility of designated individuals in order to achieve quality documentation. For some reason, certain EDP managers are about as reluctant to pursue these two lessons as programmers are to sufficiently document their work.

EDP managers have hardware costs documented to the decimal point, and they can quote the dollar cost for their personnel—but they have no way of knowing how much of personnel cost is spent for program duplication. Duplication can be measured only by a documentation policy that requires standards and guidelines for program design, development, storage, and retrieval of this documentation in a form immediately usable.

Documentation standards must be established at the outset of a project if EDP managers want to optimize program design and development and minimize program duplication. Standards should be flexible because documentation requirements vary from job to job.

ACTIVE PARTICIPATION BY EDP MANAGERS

The active participation of top EDP managers in the standardization efforts is what makes the difference between good and poor documentation policy. The phenomenal growth of data processing systems has reached a point where documentation applications must be reckoned with. Managers can no longer look upon documentation with apathy, or view documentation as a passive thing.

Many EDP operations are totally void of any written programming documentation standards. These EDP activities *seem* to manage fairly well without written standards, according to some managers. They get programs developed, tested, and implemented. And EDP managers will say that their operations are saving the company money. But these same EDP managers do not know how much money they are costing the company because of program duplication.

EDP managers look to the computer vendor for certain techniques in the technical design of application programs. The vendor is very efficient in this area. But the vendor leaves the documentation standards and procedures to the EDP manager. When a documentation problem arises the EDP manager blames the programmer's "poor" attitude for documentation and his reluctance to document his work. The programmer blames the EDP manager for not specifying a sound documentation policy. Herein lies the crux of the documentation problem that is prevalent in many EDP organizations, large or small. This has become the Achilles' heel of an EDP organization.

The problem of documentation often lies in the failure or inability of EDP managers to correctly define their documentation requirements. Where poor documentation exists, factors other than the programmer's biased attitude against documentation may be responsible. The problem can usually be traced to the default of EDP managers in not providing a sound documentation policy.

Programmers would be willing to document their work if they only had documentation guidance that explained *how* and *what* to document. EDP managers have failed sadly in this area, and because of it, their EDP organization is less efficient and their company is less profitable than it could be.

Many EDP managers are proud of their data processing systems; they have a right to be proud because they spend many long hours, night and day, designing, debugging, and installing their systems. They are eager to "show and tell" the attributes of systems to top company executives.

The executive is impressed by the marvels of computer technology before him; he has difficulty in understanding the programming endeavor that makes the computer run. He walks away feeling that the annual report will look better because of these machines —and the EDP manager dreams of a larger paycheck.

But the balloon bursts the first time the system gets into trouble and requires a modification, and the lead programmer is no longer with the company or cannot recall the details of the program due to the passage of time. The executive is pressing the EDP manager for the computer-generated weekly inventory report. The EDP manager is red-faced because he must tell the executive that the report will be delayed a few days, since the program that produces the report must be recoded because the programmer who wrote the program is no longer with the company and did not document the program very well.

When the EDP manager was building the total management information system, he was able to hire experienced analysts and programmers and buy the latest EDP equipment. He has all the tools available and was using the latest state of the art techniques in building a system of which he could be proud. But the documentation procedures were prehistoric or non-existent and proved the EDP manager lacking in management concepts.

EDP managers and specialists are constantly studying system design and programming techniques to improve the efficiency of their machines. But in the pursuit of system design and programming excellence, documentation and standardization of programming techniques suffer. The quest for this excellence is hindered when standards for documentation and its preparation are neglected.

Clearly defined documentation standards and guidelines should be a vital concern for EDP managers. An EDP system comprises three material elements: (1) hardware, (2) software (supervisory and application programs), and (3) documentation. Documentation is for human consumption. It defines and specifies the interactions, controls, and relationship between the hardware and software, and between the human and the total EDP system.

The basic principles and concepts discussed in this chapter are suggested as guidelines for documentation policy, standards and procedures for application programming. These principles and concepts promote commonality in system design and program development in an EDP system. This chapter will not discuss methods or explain the various techniques and logical details of the language syntax for program coding. Standards and constraints to handle these techniques are discussed in the vendor-supplied programming document. What is discussed in this chapter are methods, concepts, and guidelines for documenting the program development efforts involved in system installation.

The intent of this chapter is not to suggest or imply that the creativeness of the programmers should be restricted, nor is it intended to discourage originality among programming individuals. But with the standardization of certain programming methods and policy for their documentation, the analysts and programmers can direct their attention to the most important aspects of their jobs—problem definition, problem program analysis, and synthesis for a problem solution.

Chapter One identified the general functions of documentation and discussed the various types of documentation required for a given EDP system. For the rest of this chapter, certain areas of program documentation will be presented in detail.

DEFINING PROGRAMMING OBJECTIVES

To preclude unnecessary backtracking or needless expenditure of debugging time, it is recommended that the following approach be used in developing a program:

- Analyze and determine the programming features.
- Research environmental and operator interface/factors.
- Define methods and determine feasibility.
- Determine the most efficient programming techniques.
- Establish criteria, priorities, and parameters.
- Determine what sub-routines and linkage techniques are to be used.
- Determine core requirement, to include external storage requirement.
- Determine requirement for I/O devices.
- Define the source and frequency of data input requirement.
- Define layout and format of printed documents, punch cards, paper tape, and other data that will be outputs of the program.
- Determine file, table, and record format; controls and bookkeeping functions necessary to accept, process, and protect data.
- Determine restart and recovery procedures.
- Define message storage and retrieval techniques during system overload or circuit outage.

Depending on the complexity of a programming task, all of the above may or may not be relevant factors in defining program objectives. However, those factors that are relevant should be well documented. From the above conclusions and from additional data as required, the programmer plans his program and prepares the systems flowcharts.

SYSTEM FLOWCHARTS

Flowcharts provide a means of identifying programming functions and visualizing the logic and the path of its flow in the solution of a problem. Flowchart documentation should be a series of flowcharts which identify the application programs and depict the processing being performed, the sequence of operations, and decision points.

Generally, three levels of flowcharts should be prepared: *first-level, second-level, and third-level.* Standard flowchart symbols as recognizezd by the International Organization for Standardization (ISO) and American National Standard Institute should be used. Appendix A contains standard flowchart symbols. In developing the MACRO and MICRO level flowcharts, too much time should not be spent on keeping the flowcharts neat while changes are being made. But when the program is ready for implementation, flowcharts should be neatly drawn, or reduced, on 8½ × 11, or 8½ × 13 inch sheets, suitable for binders or reference manuals.

First-Level—System Flow:

The first level should be a general system flow or diagram, giving an overview of the major processing areas and programming requirements (programs) that will be required for system development (see Figure 2-1). This flow should identify the programs and the programming path necessary to accept, process, and output data. The general system flow should also show any overlay programs such as support and common routines that are required for system development. This diagram should identify the application programs by grouping them within a block to show in which processing area the program belongs in the systems programming path. The blocks of the general systems flow should be identified as follows:

· Each block should be designated alphabetically or numerically. Each program or routine within a block should be given a symbolic name, or plain subject, and designated alphabetically or numerically. (See Block B of Figure 2-1.)
· All references to a program should contain the block alpha or numeric designator plus the alpha or numeric program designator. *Example:* BF—where B = Block B of the first-level flow, and F = a program designator for magnetic tape validation of Block 'B' (see Figure 2-1).
· Overlay programs should be identified by name and designated alphabetically or numerically.

Second-Level—Macro Flow:

The programming functions identified in the first-level system flowchart should be developed into MACRO flow (semi-detailed) diagrams (Figures 2-2(a), 2-2(b), and 2-2(c)). The MACRO Flowchart (program) should be identified by the alpha or

CORE RESIDENT MODULAR PROGRAMS

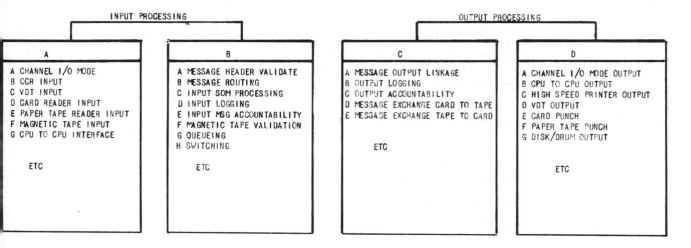

INPUT PROCESSING

A

A CHANNEL I/O MODE
B CCR INPUT
C VDT INPUT
D CARD READER INPUT
E PAPER TAPE READER INPUT
F MAGNETIC TAPE INPUT
G CPU TO CPU INTERFACE

ETC

B

A MESSAGE HEADER VALIDATE
B MESSAGE ROUTING
C INPUT SOM PROCESSING
D INPUT LOGGING
E INPUT MSG ACCOUNTABILITY
F MAGNETIC TAPE VALIDATION
G QUEUEING
H SWITCHING

ETC

OUTPUT PROCESSING

C

A MESSAGE OUTPUT LINKAGE
B OUTPUT LOGGING
C OUTPUT ACCOUNTABILITY
D MESSAGE EXCHANGE CARD TO TAPE
E MESSAGE EXCHANGE TAPE TO CARD

ETC

D

A CHANNEL I/O MODE OUTPUT
B CPU TO CPU OUTPUT
C HIGH SPEED PRINTER OUTPUT
D VDT OUTPUT
E CARD PUNCH
F PAPER TAPE PUNCH
G DISK/DRUM OUTPUT

ETC

NON-CORE RESIDENT OVERLAY MODULAR PROGRAMS

OPERATING SUPPORT PROGRAMS

O

A ALTERNATE MSG ROUTING
B SERVICE MSG GENERATION
C HISTORY STATISTICS
D DEVICE MSG STATUS
E LINE CONTROL AND MONITOR
F TAPE ASSIGNMENT
G DISK ASSIGNMENT
H MESSAGE ADDRESS BUILD
I MESSAGE RETRIEVAL

ETC

SYSTEM SUPPORT PROGRAMS

S

A SYSTEM RECOVERY
B TRAFFIC ANALYSIS
C CORE DUMP AND DEBUG AIDS
D HISTORY TAPE/DISK SEARCH
E MESSAGE RETRIEVAL BACKUP
F MESSAGE MICROFILMING
G STATION LOG

ETC

COMMON SUBROUTINES

Z

A CODE CONVERSION
B BUFFER GET AND RELEASE
C NUMERIC CONVERSION
D OVERLAY CONTROL AND RELEASE
E CHARACTER PACKING AND UNPACK
F CONSOLE PRINTOUTS (CANNED)
G BINARY TABLE SEARCH

ETC

FIGURE 2-1

First Level Flowchart

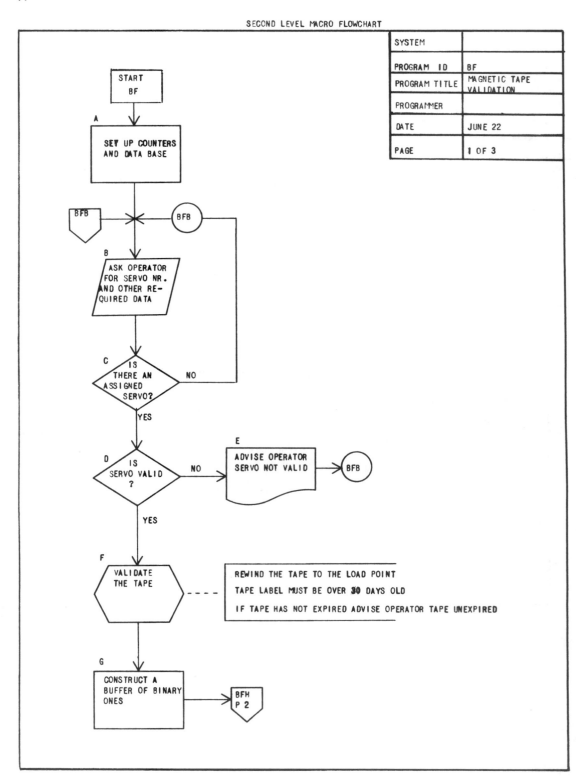

FIGURE 2-2(a)

Second Level Macro Flowchart

SECOND LEVEL   MACRO FLOWCHART

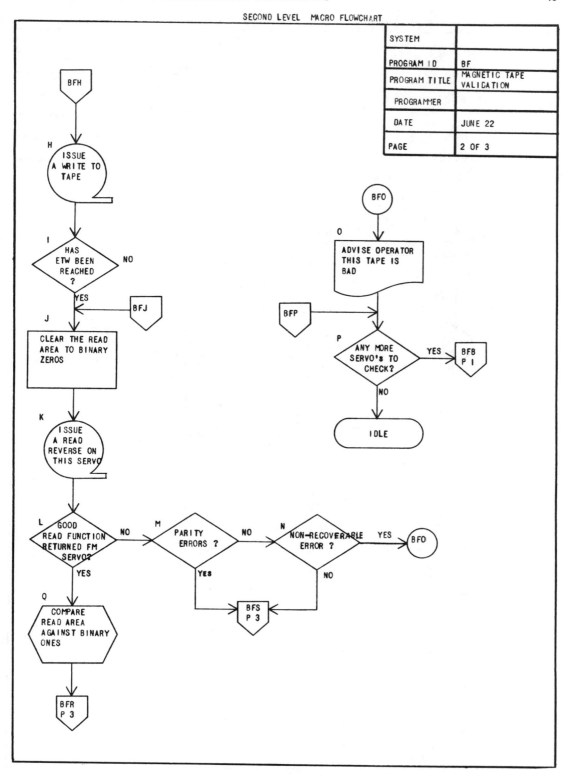

SYSTEM	
PROGRAM ID	BF
PROGRAM TITLE	MAGNETIC TAPE VALICATION
PROGRAMMER	
DATE	JUNE 22
PAGE	2 OF 3

FIGURE 2-2(b)

Second Level Macro Flowchart

SECOND LEVEL MACRO FLOWCHART

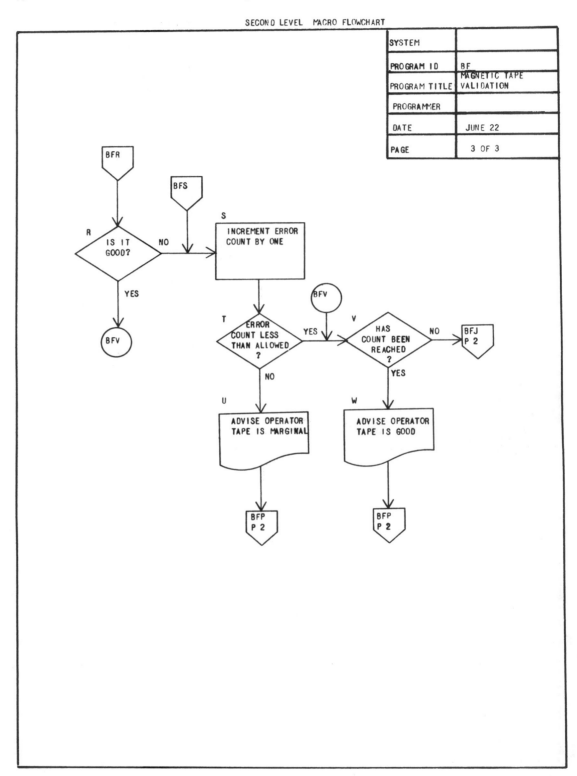

FIGURE 2-2(c)

Second Level Macro Flowchart

numeric assigned to the block and the alpha or numeric assigned to the program. Descriptive symbology used in applications programs should relate to the program listing by use of unique statements or tags (names). Each functional symbol or block of the MACRO flow should be assigned an alpha or numeric character. This will give each block or symbol a unique identification. The following is an example of the alpha-naming convention for the MACRO flow:

B F B
    ↑   ↑   ↑ A processing function of the second-level MACRO flow
    | Program Name—"Magnetic Tape Validation"
    Block B of the first-level general flow.

The purpose of the MACRO flowchart is to depict the input/output functions, general processing areas, subroutines, logical sequence in processing relationship, and decision points of a program. The MACRO flowchart expands the program or major processing function of the first level into semi-detailed component blocks or programming symbols. The MACRO flowchart should be machine and language independent.

Figures 2-3(a) and 2-3(b) illustrate a flowcharting technique with an alpha-numeric cross referencing method to relate to each symbol. A striped symbol (see shaded area, F4) indicates that a more detailed flowchart of that programming function exists (see Figure 2-3(b)). Identification of that programming function may be placed above the stripe and the function placed below the stripe. This technique can be traced by observing the shading areas on Figure 2-3(a) and noting the Chart ID of Figure 2-3(b) and the start of the flow.

MACRO Page Connectors: On-page and off-page connectors for a MACRO flow-chart should contain the alpha or numeric character assigned to the block of the first-level flowchart, the alpha or numeric assigned to the program within the block, and the alpha assigned to the symbol or block of the MACRO flowchart to which the connector is pointing.

EXAMPLE: (BFD) = On-page connector

BFH
P2 = Off-page connector

Third-Level—MICRO Flow:

As the second-level flowcharts are reviewed by the lead analyst, processing errors and omissions should be detected prior to developing the third-level flowcharts. Using the MACRO flowchart and the narrative, a detailed MICRO flowchart should be drawn (see Figures 2-4(a) and 2-4(b)).

The MICRO flow should depict, in graphic and symbolic form, each logical step and the processing sequence for the coding of a program. Each symbol or processing

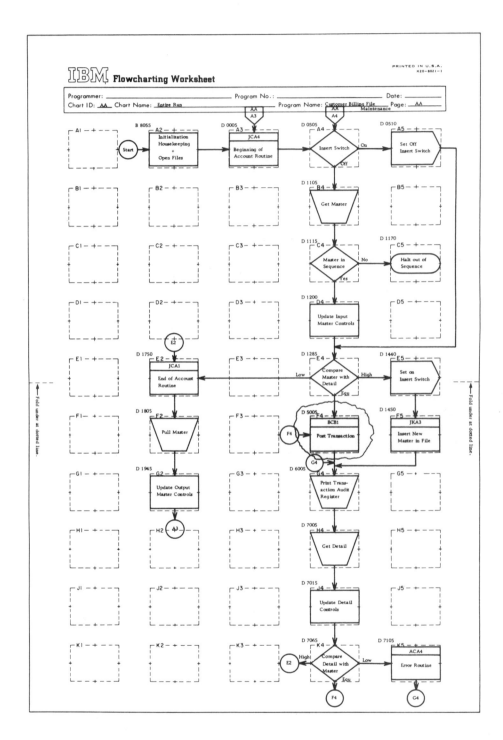

Reprint by permission from Flowcharting Techniques (Form C2908152), by International Business Machines Corporation.

FIGURE 2-3(a)

Flowcharting Worksheet

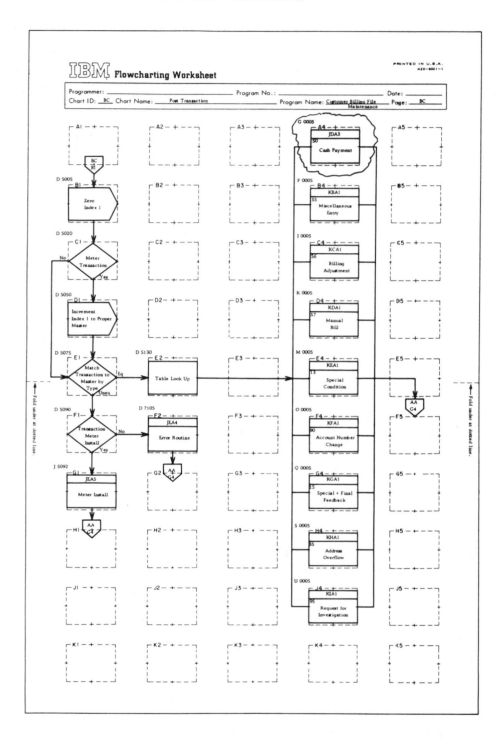

Reprint by permission from Flowcharting Techniques (Form C2908152), by International Business Machines Corporation.

FIGURE 2-3(b)

Flowcharting Worksheet

THIRD LEVEL MICRO FLOWCHART

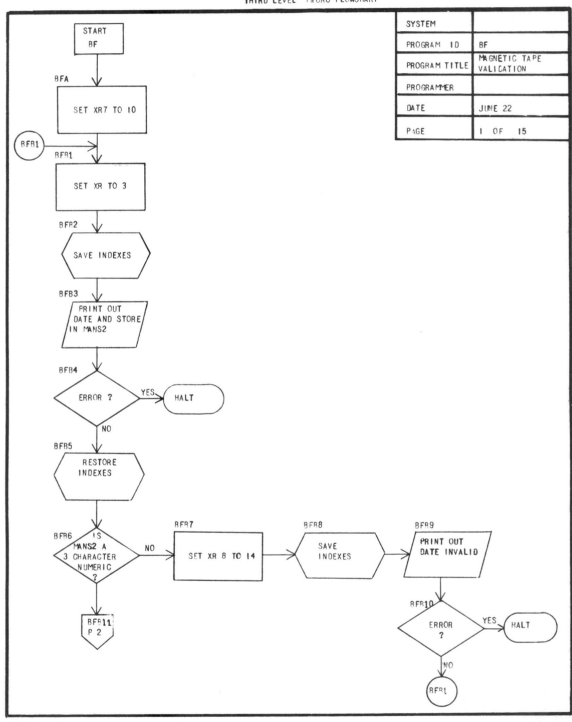

FIGURE 2-4(a)

Third Level Micro Flowchart

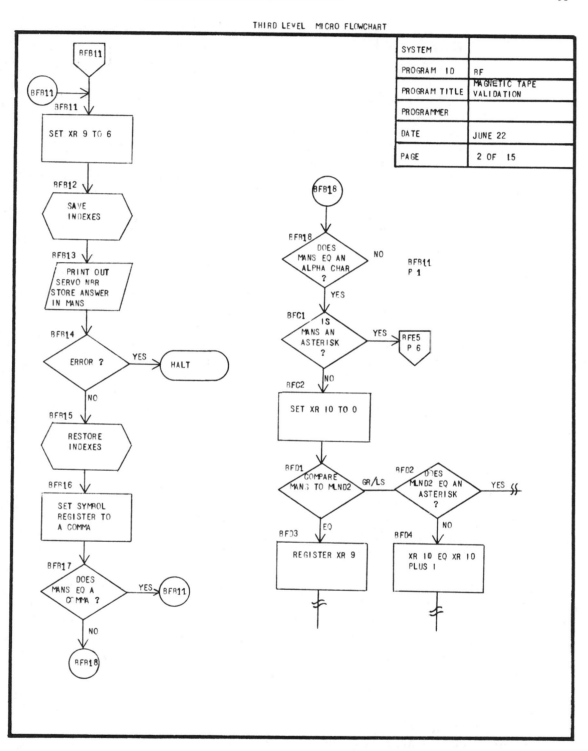

FIGURE 2-4(b)

Third Level Micro Flowchart

step should be assigned a numerical number, in addition to the naming convention suggested for the functional blocks or symbols of the second-level flowchart.

MICRO flowcharts should be prepared along the following lines:

· Build a detailed flowchart showing each computer process, each decision, all peripheral and manual input/output processing, and the relationships of all the preceding and subsequent processing steps that are necessary to perform a required function.
· Begin with the MACRO flow and narrative description, the programming objectives and analyses derived from the pre-programming and program development discussed in Chapter Three, and flow the processing steps from initial input of date to output.
· Flow should be from top to bottom.
· When subroutines are not part of the mainline program, they should include entrance and exit requirements, such as which general registers are expected to contain predetermined values, the exit status, and which registers were changed.

MICRO-Page Connectors: Off-page and on-page flowchart connections should be used when the normal flow is broken to point to the next functional block or symbol in the program's flow. The connector should contain the following:

· The alpha or numeric assigned to the block of the first-level flowchart.
· The alpha or numeric assigned to the program of the first-level flowchart.
· The alpha or numeric assigned to the symbol or processing block of the second-level flowchart.
· The numeric assigned to the symbol or processing step of the third-level flowchart.

Example:

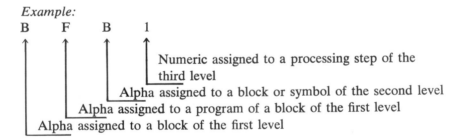

The salient features of the naming conventions suggested for the MACRO and MICRO page connectors are: (1) easy identification of misplaced or out of sequence flowchart pages; for example, when debugging or making reference to a program, isolation of the problem or finding the referenced area can be facilitated by using the alphanumeric characters of the page connectors to "trace" backward or forward in the flowcharts; and (2) the ease with which debugging can be accomplished.

All mnemonic tags or codes used to identify certain blocks or symbols in the second and third-level flowchart should be identified on a separate sheet of paper or contained in a document.

In large and complex programming tasks, the programmer should plan the modularization and concatenation of the program and what, if any, precoded routines or MACRO instructions are to be used. The MICRO flowchart should be sufficiently detailed to support the actual coding of the program. After the flowchart is complete, the programmer should:

- Verify logic used in the flow process.
- Construct the coding.
- Use maximum "English" comments to explain source language.
- Translate coding to input media, i.e., card, paper magnetic tape, or optical character recognition input.
- Assemble or compile program.
- Obtain machine listing.
- Desk check and debug.
- Prepare appropriate documentation for inclusion in the job setup procedures, computer run instructions, system reference manuals, etc.
- Implement program.

PROGRAM MODULARITY AND OVERLAY TECHNIQUES

It is generally agreed that there is no "perfect" or exact method that dictates the logic construction for a program. To promote efficient computer utilization through optimized programming practices, certain concepts for standardization of program design are suggested.

An EDP system will comprise many programs. Several subroutines that are not part of the mainline programming will be required. A system of programs should be built on a functional basis. That is, each program or functional feature, e.g., validate message header or compute withholding tax for individual payroll, should be specified and developed in modular segments.

Coding should not be started until the program has been carefully defined and all formats for files, tables, records, items, I/O functions, etc., have been established.

In addition to core resident, certain nonresident programs should be developed as overlay modules. Program modularity is very desirable in developing overlay programs. It is conducive to program and system flexibility, and reduces the effort to maintain a given system. Modularity permits modification to a particular program segment without reaccomplishing the entire source program.

Modularity is a design technique used to divide a system of programs or a program into separate job functions and to program and test each module separately. This technique provides a program design standard that will aid programming and maintenance. A module may consist of a subroutine, a program, or an entire application. Some applications may be programmed as one module, but developed according to modular programming techniques. Nonresident overlay programs may be classed as *support programs* and *common subroutines*. A combination of these programs may be called upon in the execution of a task.

- *Support or specialized program routines* are those routines which are restricted to a given program or system, e.g., Device Message Queue Status or Systems Recovery.

These programs aid day-to-day operations and system functioning, and compile certain daily, weekly, or monthly reports and statistics.
· *Common routines* should be developed for general use by any program in the system, e.g., Binary Table Search, Translate Routines. These programs should be generalized in nature and made available to the system by the calling program.

Generally, there are three types of program structures available to the programmer: *simple, overlay,* and *dynamic.*

· *Simple structured program routine* contains sufficient coding to complete a job without having to link to or obtain the services of another program. *Example:* A routine to check End of Message (EOM) could be considered a simple structured routine. However, many features could be coded into a major program, executed to do a series of functions without being aided by other programs, and still be a simple structured program.
· *Overlay structured program routine* may be coded as a simple structured program, but may or may not be called upon in the execution of a task. Overlay programs are not core resident. Developing program modules as overlay programs conserves core memory and optimizes programming efficiency.
· *A dynamic structured program routine* has the attribute of being relocated without the programmer being aware of its location in memory. A dynamic structured program may be a series of simple structures programs, but calling of the modules is under the control of the machine rather than the programmer. The value of each module location would have to be passed as parameters between the various modules being used. Dynamically structured programs may be reused in a processing step, whereas in a planned overlay structured program they cannot be reused within the same processing task. They must be recalled by the programmer.

SELECTING THE TYPE OF CODING FOR PROGRAM DEVELOPMENT

Coding used in either type of program structure may be *reentrable, serially reusable,* or *non-reusable.*

· *Reentrable* coding is that which does not modify itself in any way during execution. All manipulations are done in general registers or in a work area which is conveyed to it by the calling program. Reentrable coding can be shared in core by two or more tasks which are being executed concurrently.
· *Serially reusable* coding is that which will completely revitalize itself after being executed. The same coding may be used repeatedly. Although it cannot be shared concurrently by other programs, request for the same coding may be queued. This allows the same copy to be reused, and a fresh copy need not be brought in to satisfy each request.
· *Non-reusable* coding can be neither shared nor reused. A fresh copy of the coding is required each time it is requested.

Each of the three types of coding has attributes which affect its availability for use at a given time. In general, all coding that is not reentrable should be serially reusable.

It takes just a small amount of effort and planning to make a program serially reusable.

PROGRAM PARAMETERS

To provide for maximum program flexibility and data protection, files, tables, and records should be stored externally from core memory. Parameters such as dates, factors, constants, etc., should be entered by means of the input job procedure and not through operator intervention, when time permits. Accessing and maintaining these parameters should be through the use of utility and support programs.

Files/tables (queue, output, input, records) should be described and formats laid out to contain sufficient information to identify and control data processing functions. If tables are parameterized to allow on-line changes, operator commands and procedures for making changes should be specified. Tables and other parameters should be identified and explained in the narrative description of the program they are associated with. Data buffers should be specified and formatted to contain sufficient control information to protect and secure data while it is being processed.

PROGRAM-NAMING CONVENTIONS

When EDP systems are configured of like hardware designed for similar application, e.g., digital message switching, program names can be standardized for programs performing the same communications function. This would facilitate developing programs for "off-the-shelf" use.

Example:

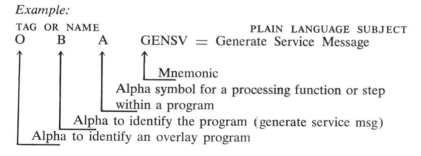

TAG OR NAME   PLAIN LANGUAGE SUBJECT
O   B   A   GENSV = Generate Service Message

Mnemonic
Alpha symbol for a processing function or step within a program
Alpha to identify the program (generate service msg)
Alpha to identify an overlay program

The flow and logic for a program to "generate service message" should be fairly standard for a given message-switching system. All labels and tags in tables and buffers used in a program should be given a unique name.

PROGRAM "DESK CHECKING"

Regardless of the experience level of programmers or how much study and meticulous coding attention are devoted to developing a program, some design and coding errors will exist.

Each program should be carefully desk checked prior to assembling or compiling. Desk checking should be done by someone other than the programmer who wrote the program, or by a team of programmers, one of whom may be the originating programmer. The following approach to desk checking is recommended:

· Prior to keypunching:

1. Carefully proofread the handwritten symbolic coding to eliminate any ambiguities or transposed alphanumeric characters.
2. Insure that all constants and records are defined and given the correct value.
3. Make sure that all branches or transfers of control (jumps) in the program are accounted for.
4. Check for proper data and record format.
5. Keypunch and interpret source cards.

· After keypunching:

1. Make a machine listing of source cards and verify listing with the handwritten source program for keypunch errors.
2. To avoid duplicate program documentation maintenance, the original handwritten copy may be destroyed.
3. Check coding and sequence of coding with the program flowchart for:
   a. error in logic
   b. closed loops
   c. errors in program branching
   d. correct definition and use of source language
4. Simulate the computer by stepping sample data through the program in sufficient areas to check all branches, transfer of controls, and the simplest and most complex logic facets of the program.

· Modification and updating should be done directly to the program card deck and the machine listing.

· Implement program.

PROGRAM DOCUMENTATION CHECKLIST

The appropriate documentation created during the pre-programming and program development phases for each application program, as discussed in Chapter One, should be identified on the program documentation checklist (Figure 2-5) and made available to the documentation management control group discussed in Chapter Eight. The purpose of the program documentation checklist is to serve as a quick reference for the types of documentation created for each program.

The checklist (modified to fit the particular EDP documentation needs), along with a copy of each type of documentation, would be routed to the Documentation Library for cataloging and filing. The librarian, after filing the documentation, would

Documentation	Required	Available	Individual Responsible	Library File No.
Analysis Studies				
General Systems Flowcharts				
Semi-Detailed Flowcharts (MACRO-level)				
Detailed Flowcharts (MICRO-level)				
Test Deck Prepared				
Test Procedures Prepared (quality controls)				
Computer Run/Console/Procedures				
Job Set-Up Instructions				
User/operating Procedures/Manuals(field)				
Program Listing				
Program Abstract Prepared or Updated				

PROGRAM DOCUMENTATION CHECKLIST

System:

Programming Division:

Program Number:

Program Name:

Equipment Configuration:

Implemented Date:

Approval (Lead Analyst/Supervisor):   Date:

Remarks:

FIGURE 2-5

Program Documentation Checklist

record the file number in the appropriate column of the checklist and catalog, and file the checklist in a convenient reference file or binder associated with the system.

The checklist (one for each "stand alone" program) would identify the documentation and its library file number associated with the various types of documentation created for a particular program. The checklist would aid in retrieving documentation for off-the-shelf programs discussed in Chapter One.

The program documentation checklist, or a similar one, should be required for the vendor-provided documentation. The vendor-supplied documentation should be cataloged and filed in the documentation library in the same manner as user-provided documentation. (Vendor-provided documentation is discussed in Chapter Nine.)

DOCUMENTATION CONTROLS FOR MAGNETIC TAPE LABELING

Another significant area of documentation is controls and standards for tape labeling. In large systems with a high volume of tape files, proper tape labeling of file identification should be a primary concern for EDP managers. The EDP manager or lead analyst, in setting up the documentation requirements for pre-programming and program development, should specify the format for the label and information to be contained on the label. Information for tape labeling is usually classified in two categories: *external* and *internal*.

External labels should have adhesive backing. These are visible labels that are physically affixed to the tape reel. Information will vary depending on the systems applications, but the following is suggested information for external labels:

- Reel serial number
- Length of tape
- File number
- Date of run
- Output tape unit number or address
- Number of runs (jobs) the tape is used on
- Scratch date (date the tape may be available for other jobs)
- Description of file contents—brief statement (optional)

A color code for tape labels will help to identify files belonging to different system applications, i.e., inventory, payroll, etc. The examples in Figure 2-6 and Appendix B to Chapter Five are typical labels for a given application.

Internal labels contain information similar to that contained on external labels. Internal information consists of programmed header and trailer data. This information is usually written at the beginning and end of each magnetic tape file. Checking and verifying of this header and trailer information is accomplished by programmable means and console type-outs.

The header information should be the first record written on each magnetic tape. The record should contain all or part of the information suggested for extenal labels. When writing (by software) header information onto a magnetic tape, the information

PLACE ON TAPE REEL	PLACE ON REEL CONTAINER
RUN INVENTORY	RUN INVENTORY
GROUPING	GROUPING
WRITE DATE	WRITE DATE
TAPE UNIT ADD.	TAPE UNIT ADD.
TAPE UNIT NO.	TAPE UNIT NO.
REEL OF	REEL OF
CONTENTS	CONTENTS

EXAMPLE 1

FILE NO.	USED ON	
	RUN NO.	TAPE ADDRESS
REEL OF		
DATE OF RUN		
DATE OF WORK		
OUTPUT		
TAPE		
ADDRESS		
SCRATCH DATE		

EXAMPLE 2

Reprint by permission from "Planning for an IBM Data Processing System," by International Business Machines Corporation (F20-6088-2).

FIGURE 2-6

should be printed on the console printout so that the operator or librarian can compare the information on the internal label with that on the external label.

The trailer information usually contains such information as:

· Reel serial number
· File number
· End of file (if not the last tape file)
· Record count
· End of job (if the last tape file for that job)
· Other control information as needed.

Internal labels are not required on all magnetic tapes used in an EDP system. Tapes used for system testing purposes, sorting jobs, etc., would not require an internal label. Tapes used for certain memory dumps should be assigned an internal and external label to identify their purpose; otherwise, they may be used as scratch tapes.

The control of file and scratch tapes should be a function of the documentation library, under the supervision of *Documentation Management and Program Control* discussed in Chapter Eight. (The library should provide a good storage facility with proper temperature and humidity conditions.) Because of the vital information contained on tapes, coupled with the frequent use by many users, it is important that efficient records be maintained and procedures for the use of tape be established. Chapter Seven will present certain forms that would be helpful in establishing a filing and record-keeping system for magnetic tapes.

APPENDIX A

BASIC SYMBOLS

INPUT/ OUTPUT

PROCESS

ANNOTATION, COMMENT

FLOWLINE

CROSSING OF FLOW LINES

JUNCTION OF FLOWLINES

PROCESSING SYMBOLS

DECISION

AUXILIARY OPERATION

PREDEFINED PROCESS

EXTRACT

PREPARATION

SORT

MANUAL OPERATION

COL-LATE

MERGE

ADDITIONAL SYMBOLS

CONNECTOR

TERMINAL

OFFPAGE CONNECTOR

TRANSMITTAL TAPE

PARALLEL MODE

SPECIALIZED INPUT/OUTPUT SYMBOLS

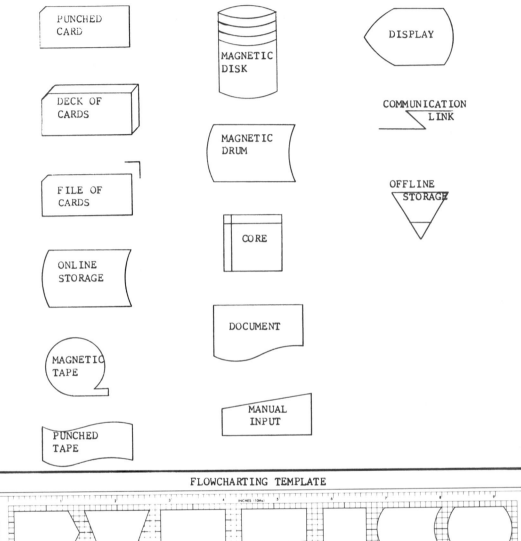

FLOWCHARTING TEMPLATE

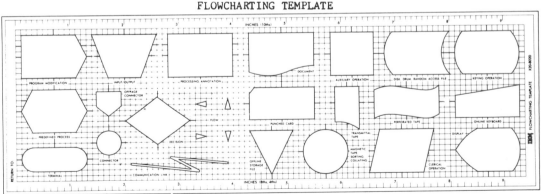

Template reprint by permission from Flowcharting Techniques, Form C208152, by International Business Machines Corporation.

APPENDIX A1

SYMBOL USE IN FLOWCHARTING [3]

SYMBOL SHAPE: The actual shapes of the symbols used should conform closely enough to those shown in Appendix A to preserve the characteristics of the symbol. The curvature of the lines and the angles formed by the lines may vary slightly from those shown in this standard so long as the shapes retain their uniqueness.

SYMBOL SIZE: Flowchart symbols are distinguished on the basis of shape, proportion, and size in relation to other symbols. Proportion of a given symbol is defined by the rectangle in which that symbol can be inscribed. Dimension and relative size of these rectangles are given with each symbol by a pair of numbers (width: height).[4]

The size of each symbol may vary, but the dimensional ratio of each symbol shall be maintained.

Flowchart symbols are formed by straight and curved line segments. When prepared automatically by machine, they may be formed by patterns of successively printed graphic symbols (asterisks, periods, and so forth) which exhibit the characteristic shapes.

FLOWLINE: Normal direction of flow is from left to right and top to bottom. When the flow direction is not left to right or top to bottom, open arrowheads shall be placed on reverse-direction flowlines. When increased clarity is desired, open arrowheads can be placed on normal-direction flowlines. When flowlines are broken due to page limitation, connection symbols shall be used to indicate the break. When flow is bidirectional, it can be shown by either single or double lines, but open arrowheads shall be used to indicate both normal-direction flow and reverse-direction flow.

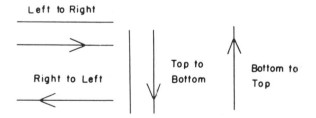

[3] SYMBOL USE IN FLOWCHARTING: This material is reproduced from the American National Standard "Flowchart Symbols and Their Usage in Information Processing," Number ANSI X3.5–1970, copyright 1970 by the American National Standards Institute at 1430 Broadway, New York, N.Y. 10018.

[4] The dimensions are given in Section 3 of the American National Standard Flowchart Symbols and Their Usage in Information Processing (ANSI X3.5–1970) for sale by American National Institute, 1430 Broadway, New York, N.Y. 10018.

COMMUNICATION LINK: Unless otherwise indicated, the direction of communication link flow is left to right and top to bottom. Open arrowheads are necessary on symbols for which the flow opposes the above convention. An open arrowhead may also be used on any line whenever increased clarity will result.

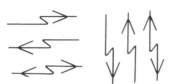

FLOWCHART TEXT: Descriptive information with each symbol shall be presented so as to read from left to right and top to bottom regardless of the flow direction.

SYMBOL IDENTIFICATION: The identifying notation assigned to a symbol, other than a connector, shall be placed above the symbol and to the right of its vertical bisector.

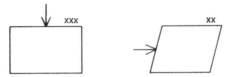

SYMBOL CROSS REFERENCE: Identifying notation(s) of other elements of documentation (including this set of flowcharts) shall be placed above the symbol and to the left of its vertical bisector.

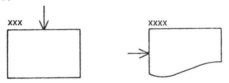

CONNECTOR COMMON IDENTIFICATION: A common identifier, such as an alphabetic character, number, or mnemonic label, is placed within the outconnector and its associated inconnector.

CROSS REFERENCE CONNECTORS: Additional cross referencing between associated connectors is achieved by placing the chart page(s), coordinates, or other identifier(s) of the associated connectors above and to the left of the vertical bisector of each connector.

SYMBOL STRIPING: Striping is a means of indicating that a more detailed representation of a function is to be found elsewhere in the same set of flowcharts. This representation differs from a predefined process symbol which need not be represented in detail in the same set of flowcharts.

STRIPED SYMBOL: A horizontal line is drawn within, completely across, and near the top of the symbol, and a reference to the detailed representation is placed between that line and the top of the symbol.

FIRST SYMBOL OF DETAILED REPRESENTATION: The terminal symbol shall be used as the first and last symbols of the detailed representation. The first terminal symbol contains an identification which also appears in the striped symbol, as indicated in paragraph above.

CROSS REFERENCING OF STRIPED SYMBOL AND DETAILED REPRESENTATION: A reference to the location of the detailed representation within the flowchart is placed above and to the left of the vertical bisector of the striped symbol. A reference to the striped symbol is placed above and to the left of the vertical bisector of its associated terminal symbol.

Example: Striped Symbol and Detailed Representation

Striped Symbol   *Detailed Representation*

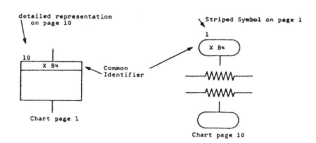

MULTIPLE EXITS: Multiple exits from a symbol shall be shown by several flowlines from the symbol to other symbols or by a single flowline from the symbol which branches into the appropriate number of flowlines.

MULTIPLE LOGIC PATHS: Each exit from a symbol shall be identified to show the logic path which it represents. The logic paths may be represented by a table that indicates their associated conditions and the inconnector references.

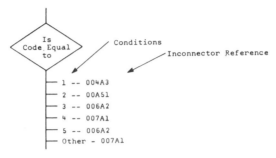

BRANCHING TABLE: A branching table may be used in lieu of a decision symbol to depict a decision function. The table is composed of a statement of the decision to be made, a list of the conditions which can occur, and the path to be followed for each condition. The terms "Decision Statement" and "Paths" are not part of the standard. The "Go to" section contains either an inconnector reference or a single flowline exiting to another symbol. Examples of branching table formats are shown below.

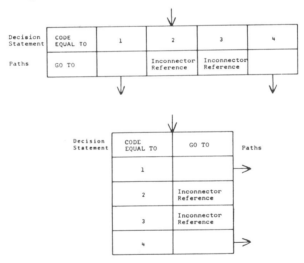

MULTIPLE SYMBOLS: As an alternative to a single symbol with appropriate text, the same input/output symbols may be shown in an overlay pattern to illustrate their use or creation of multiple media or files: for example, number of copies, types of printed reports, types of punched card formats, multiple magnetic tape reels.

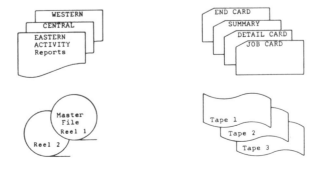

OVERLAY PATTERN: The overlay pattern must be drawn from front to back with the first symbol as the entire I/O symbol. The center line of the second symbol must be offset up or down from the horizontal center line and to the right or left of the vertical center line of the first symbol. Similarly, the third symbol must be offset in the same direction from the second symbol, the fourth from the third, and so on for any remaining symbols.

PRIORITY REPRESENTATION: When the multiple symbols represent an ordered set, the ordering shall be from front (first) to back (last).

FLOWLINES WITH REPETITIVE SYMBOLS: Flowlines may enter or leave from any point on the overlay symbols. The priority or sequential order of the multiple symbols is not altered by the point at which the flowline(s) enters or leaves.

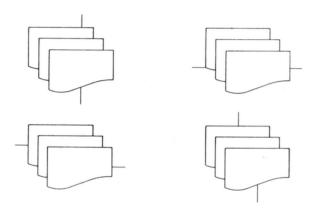

3

Preparing Feasibility Studies

Desultory studies are erased from the mind as easily as pencil marks; classified studies are retained like durable ink.

Peter Cooper

Feasibility studies are usually one-time requirements. The goal is to provide certain analyses and methods of how an objective may be accomplished. The study may require various combinations of data, and often the results of the study are unpredictable.

The primary objective of the study should be to examine the present methods of operation and recommend applications that will improve efficiency through computer automation. The study team or individual should not let "political" ramifications interfere with the objective of the study or the recommendation that will be drawn from the investigative analysis. Only the benefits of an automated system should be considered.

Political or parochial views may hinder or delay the implementation of the recommendations made in a study. Machiavelli reminds us in *The Prince* of the difficulty of implementing a new system:

"It must be remembered that there is nothing more difficult to plan, more doubtful of success, nor more dangerous to manage, than the creation of a new system. For the initiator has the enmity of all who would profit by the preservation of the old institutions and merely lukewarm defenders in those who would gain by the new ones.

Before management decides to undertake an in-depth feasibility study, they may require certain preliminary information about the project to make a judgment as to the need, approximate cost factors, and benefits derived from altering the present structure of doing business.

PRELIMINARY STUDY

A small team or an individual may be asked to prepare a preliminary study based on general objectives specified by management. This study would determine and provide management with the general application and benefits derived from implementing a new program, system or modification to an on-going system.

This study would also indicate if a comprehensive and detailed study is warranted. Based on the result of a preliminary study, the EDP manager determines the need for an in-depth analysis, areas of concentration, and factors to be considered in the feasibility study. The manager can clarify the general objectives and identify the type of information and actions required in the feasibility charter. A designated team can then set about to do the research for an in-depth feasibility analysis on a particular subject or project.

ORGANIZING THE FEASIBILITY STUDY

EDP managers should state in a memorandum the need for the study, and identify:

- The purpose of the study—Why and what.
- Brief background of the project—Brief information leading up to the study.
- Scope of feasibility study—Activities, and limit of study.
- Team leader or chairman and members—The leader should be brought in on the planning at the outset.
- What information and actions are needed—Statistics and parameters should be considered.
- Problem or problems to be solved—What functional areas or how efficiency will be improved.
- Progress reporting—Reporting schedule and procedures to follow.
- Completion date—Realistic, allow sufficient time.

There are several types of feasibility studies and several approaches to conducting studies. The feasibility study has taken on a different function than it had in the early days of computer automation. At one time, a feasibility study covered the complete system analysis—from site location to determining the cost of all resources for developing, implementing, operating and managing a data processing activity.

Some feasibility studies may require background analysis, study of the present method of operation of an on-going system, and the future implication of implementing a new or modified system.

The charter for directing a feasibility study may require the team to define problems, study new applications, and determine the cost for equipment, communications facilities, personnel requirements, and the site or location for EDP installation. This type of "total" system feasibility study would take months to complete.

This type of feasibility study would require a team of experienced system analysts, operations analysts, and management talent. This team would function as a working group. It would study all aspects of system design, software development, and implementation. This type of study would consider economic factors, such as personnel and material resources, i.e., hardware and environmental factors, tariff considerations; Federal and State regulations would be looked into also. The feasibility study prepared by this group may be a large document with volumes relating to different subjects. This represents a total system design approach for a major modification or a new EDP installation requiring long-line data communications and common carrier services.

BREAK THE FEASIBILITY DOWN TO FUNCTIONAL AREAS

One approach to the total systems study would be to segregate the study into functional or classified studies. For example: problem definition for a new computer installation survey would be assigned to one or two individuals. This team would study the present manual and clerical functions to be automated. After documenting the problem as suggested in Chapter One, the team would render the report or study to the chairman of the feasibility study. Investigation of the proper computer selection may be assigned to another team or an individual.

Periodically, the chairman should meet with his team members and review the overall progress of the feasibility study. This would ensure progress and the completion of the study on time.

Members of a study team should have a current background and experience in the functional areas in which they are to study. The team or the individual should be skilled in systems work, and understand methods and techniques presently in use. Individuals should also possess mature judgment, be expert in the subject matter they are studying, and have technical and working knowledge of computers. The team members' overall background should be heavy in operations rather than technical or programming oriented. The team may be comprised of members from various departments of the company. The members would be "on loan" to the feasibility efforts until the project is finished.

The personnel selected to conduct a study should be dedicated and loyal employees who plan to remain with the company. Regardless of how well a study is documented, invariably many questions arise that only the author of the study can answer. It is important that the team leader, or individual who did the study, remain with the project until it is implemented.

The trend in system studies now seems to be moving away from the total system study approach. Usually, when a total system approach is undertaken, two or more individual studies may be made. These studies may appear as a feasibility or applications requirement study, or equipment specification study, or may carry some other similar title.

Leonard I. Krauss says: "One of the most critical weaknesses of the vast majority of studies is that they [management] assume highly competent systems and programming people are available, or will be made available. Such assumptions can and do lead to worthless systems, not to mention completely unreliable time and cost estimates." [1]

Mr. Krauss also suggest that a total or "full systems study" should be separated into three parts:

Part 1. Learn and Understand the Present Methods

· What are the weaknesses and strong points?
· What are the functional tasks and activities involved?
· How are the tasks now performed?
· What time constraints exist?
· Where are the tasks performed?
· What inputs and outputs are involved?

Part 2. Conceptual Design of the New System

· Determine the present and foreseeable future requirements and objectives.
· Combine the requirements of the old system with new concepts.
· Work out the design concepts of the new system.
· Analyze the design for workability, see if it meets intermediate and longer term requirements, and look for possible alternate approaches.

Part 3. Economic Analysis and Work Plans

· Cost out the new system including costs of personnel, training overhead, EDP equipment, and supplies. Amortize conversion expenses and costs of study.
· Cost out old system on comparable items. Project for three years or more.
· Use discounted cash flow method for evaluations.
· Set up a schedule for the work to be done, showing cost incurred at the various stages.

Some military departments of the Department of Defense have moved away from the total system feasibility study. They do not consider EDP equipment a part of a system study. A system study is made to determine or satisfy certain applications for a computered system. This type of study will normally specify the characteristics and type of equipment needed, i.e., core size, speed, peripherals. A centralized and specialized activity of the military department will incorporate these equipment specifications in a "request for bid" and send it to selected equipment manufacturers.

THE CLASSIFIED STUDY

The total system approach to analyzing the requirement for an EDP installation is usually directed by top company management. It requires, as noted earlier, a large amount of time, personnel and talent to complete this type of feasibility study.

---

[1] Leonard I. Krauss, *Administering and Controlling the Company Data Processing Functions*, Prentice-Hall, Englewood Cliffs, N.J., p. 11.

The total system approach will not be discussed in this chapter. Only that portion or feature of the design, development, or implementation of an EDP application that requires a detailed analysis, which a small team or an individual may write, will be discussed. *For example:* A requirement is received in an EDP organization to incorporate an additional feature into an existing system. It may be a manual function which is part of the total system, e.g., replacing the manual keypunch function with an automated input function (optical character recognition [OCR] input); or it may be a requirement to automate the manual processing function of distributing messages to the addressee (by messenger or pneumatic tube) in a message-switching environment. The analyst would be asked to write a study to determine methods and feasibility. This may require that the analyst do certain background research, study present administrative and software procedures, and develop or recommend methods and procedures to implement the new requirement.

This type of study is defined as a classified study. What is meant by classified is a complete analysis of one subject. This subject or study may be part of the feasibility study for a total system. But an individual will normally be assigned to do the feasibility on a particular subject.

The feasibility study will be a single written document concerning a single subject. It may be combined with other studies which will comprise the total system approach in the design, development, and implementation of a new EDP system or modification to an existing system. The methods and concepts recommended in the study should satisfy the user's immediate needs and be compatible with the long range needs of the user.

THINGS TO CONSIDER IN WRITING FEASIBILITY STUDY

The efforts here are directed at the individual who has the responsibility for writing studies and doing analysis for a programming requirement. The efforts will deal with the approach, consideration, techniques, and method of writing and presenting a feasibility study.

A feasibility study may be required because of the following:

- changes in the hardware or software techniques
- an obsolete system or procedure
- converting from a manual to an automated system
- updating an automated system
- recurring software, hardware, or operational problems
- changes in operational philosophy
- new requirement from user/customer, or management.

Before the analyst starts his study, he should understand well the purpose of the study. Planning is an important aspect of research. Planning what to write and preparing an outline, as suggested in Chapter Eleven, will save much time and will ensure the ultimate success of the feasibility study. After the analyst has determined what he is to write about and why the study is necessary, he should ask himself the following questions:

- What is the study about?
- What is the purpose of the study?
- Do I understand clearly the objective for the study?
- What additional research material or documentation do I need?
- Who will read the study?
- What is the reader's background and experience level?

Unless the analyst has a background in the system in which he is to write a feasibility study, he may have difficulty in answering the above questions. The analyst may have to do considerable reading of existing documentation to get himself "on-board." He will find it necessary to talk with analyst and operational personnel who are involved in the software and operational management of the present system.

Until it is clear to the analyst what he is to do, he should seek help through existing documentation, and consult with analyst and operations personnel. He must know what he is to accomplish in order to write a meaningful feasibility study. The analyst must know the following:

- what he is going to do
- what he wants to do
- how he can do it
- the documentation or where to find the material that he needs to do his study
- the reliability of the source
- how it is to be done
- his time period to complete the study
- the individual that he wants to have review and critique the study
- where to find help in answering questions
- the readers of the study.

If these things are understood by the analyst, he will have no difficulty in writing a meaningful feasibility study. He will not have to spend needless time rethinking, reorganizing and rewriting his drafts in the development of a feasibility study.

WRITING THE FEASIBILITY STUDY

If the analyst has answered the above questions satisfactorily, he should not have a problem in writing his feasibility study. As previously mentioned, the analyst will be concerned with writing a feasibility study for a particular problem of an EDP requirement.

The analyst presents data and facts, and makes recommendations for a solution to the problem. As mentioned in the beginning of this chapter, management will identify the major problems, determine the scope and the general type of information and actions needed. The team leader will determine the subject or problem to be studied by an individual. The analyst will concern himself with the research and identify methods and procedures for the application of a solution to the problem.

The feasibility study should be prepared in an easy reading format. The study should have a title page, giving the subject of the feasibility, the author, and date. There should be a table of contents containing major topic subjects and sub-topics, and a list of appendixes, if any. The title page and table of contents should be prepared after the body of the feasibility study has been typed in final draft copy.

The feasibility study may be required by the parent company or a higher echelon of your company, or your boss may ask you to do a feasibility study on a particular subject. Before the feasibility study has been officially assigned, correspondence may have been received concerning the feasibility subject.

The body of the feasibility study should contain the following major topics as a minimum:

1. Introduction Statement
2. Problem
3. Purpose of Study
4. Factors Bearing on the Problem
5. Discussion
6. Conclusion

1. *Introduction Statement* should be the opening topic of the feasibility study and should identify the office that required the feasibility study. The correspondence that tasked your organization to conduct the study and other correspondence relating to the subject should also be identified in the introduction statement.

2. *Problem,* the second topic of the study, should consist of one or two short paragraphs stating the problem in concrete terms, with no discussion. The analyst should restate briefly the problem which has been identified by management. The problem statement reacquaints management (or the boss) with the problem.

3. *Purpose of the Study* should be the third topic of the study. Here, the writer should restate briefly the purpose of the feasibility study. This should be a brief statement to clarify what the study is about. The writer should identify his solution of the problem in two or three sentences. The details should be saved and discussed under the major topic, *Discussion.*

4. *Factors Bearing on the Problem,* the fourth topic of the study, is the section that supports the writer's solution to the problem. It contains the pertinent *Facts, Assumptions* and *Standards* used to guide the writer in developing the feasibility study.

The writer's *facts* are most important. The writer should research available material on the subject and extract facts that will lend support to his solution to the problems. The writer should list those facts that can be proved, and other supporting evidence that is recognized as customs or practices commonly accepted. The analyst should do his own research. He should not rely on the "swivel chair experts." A writer who misinterprets the facts or lists something that is not factual is committing a serious error. The reader, after discovering an incorrect statement or unsupported evidence, will lose faith in the validity of the study, and the competency of the writer will be questioned.

The analyst should not be too eager to accept the *printed* facts. He should weigh the facts against his experience and observations. He should not let his mind become cluttered with *other people's* facts and logic. The analyst should take the time to research and *think through* the validity of his own logic. He should identify the source of his facts and supporting evidence. Here is what John Luther has to say about facts:

> Most people, simply by applying a few sound principles, could THINK more effectively than they do. Too many of us are awed by the experts, preferring to let them do our thinking for us. We fail to realize three fundamental principles about thinking, which, if recognized, will strengthen our confidence in our own ability to think:
>
> 1. Knowledge doesn't come from books—it comes from human observations and deductions. That's how it got in the books in the first place. The most important knowledge we possess comes from observing and thinking, not from reading books or listening to professors.
>
> 2. It's ALWAYS worthwhile to try to think for yourself. Study the available facts and apply your own imagination and logic. Sometimes you can find the right answer —or a perfectly good answer—despite lack of experience.
>
> 3. Be wary of the "expert." If what he says doesn't agree with what you have seen and deduced for yourself, make allowances for the fact that he may be wrong. Books and experts often are.[2]

Assumptions are the opinions of the writer. His opinions should be based on experience, research, and on observation. Assumptions may or may not be true. But for the purpose of the feasibility study, the assumptions must be accepted as the basis for the writer's reasoning, and they should be considered as true assumptions. The analyst should be careful not to use generalizations. He should present assumptions that are plausible. Too many generalizations in a feasibility study will invalidate the study and degrade the competence of the analyst.

Standards, or company policy, that are binding upon the analyst and have a bearing upon his solution should be identified. Standards or policy guides that the analyst used to test the validity of his study should be identified also.

These three sub-topics—"Facts," "Assumptions" and "Standards"—should be written in separate paragraphs in sufficient detail to identify the criteria used as the source for the writer's rationale in developing the feasibility study. In presenting facts, assumptions, and standards, the analyst should make sure of the following:

· that the facts are true and can be proved
· that the facts are pertinent
· that facts are distinguished from assumptions

---

2 "Bits and Pieces," Vol. B, No. 3, 1970, published by the Economics Press, Inc., 12 Daniel Road, Fairfield, N.J., 07006.

- that assumptions are logical rather than generalized in nature
- that the company standards were accurate and current
- that all standards and policy guides have a bearing on the subject
- that the source and authority for the facts, supporting material, and standards are identified.

5. *Discussion* should be the fifth major topic of the study. Under this topic, the analyst presents his solution to the problem. He outlines his approach and elaborates on the solution that he feels will resolve the problem. He should weigh the solution that he proposes against the facts, standards, and policy guides which the writer should have identified under "Factors Bearing on the Problem."

If the analyst presents several solutions, he should identify the one that he feels most logically would resolve the problem. He should give reasons as to why he chose a particular solution. The writer should use analogies and show how he weighed one solution against the other.

In the majority of feasibility studies, the analyst will not be asked to consider several different solutions to a particular problem. He will be asked to provide only one solution—the *best* solution to a problem.

This topic *Discussion* will, no doubt, be the longest section of the study. It may be desirable to give some background information. This may help to clarify and identify the problem. Although management may have previously identified the problem, due to the time that has elapsed since the feasibility study was assigned and during the period required to complete the study, management may not readily recall the details of the problem. Depending on the nature of the problem, several paragraphs may be required to give sufficient background information.

The *Discussion* topic should be written in a positive and straightforward manner. The writer should sound convincing. His facts should back him up. He should write as if he were an expert or an authority on the subject of which he writes. If the analyst has done adequate research, he will be able to do this. The analyst should not use hedge words, or verbose or pompous writing. The analyst should keep in mind the following:

- Make the *Discussion* as brief as possible but not to the point that clarity is sacrificed.
- Maintain a coherent and logical thought process throughout the writing.
- Explain the rationale used by showing the reader how you reasoned the problem through.
- Let the logic of your argument and facts, rather than your emotions or personal convictions, convince the reader.

If the suggestions contained in this chapter and Chapter Eleven are followed, the analyst will be able to write a factual, convincing, and meaningful document. To know if he has followed good writing techniques, the analyst should ask himself the following questions:

- Is the material well organized?
- Does it follow an easy reading format?

· Are the paragraphs short and confined to one topic?
· Are there transition sentences or words from one paragraph to another?
· Are the sentences concise, clear, and short?
· Are the modifiers placed close to words they modify?
· Is the study free of generalizations and prolix writing?
· Are the sentences logically constructed?
· Is the punctuation adequate?
· Are the facts true?
· Are the assumptions based on experience, research, and observations?
· Are terms and abbreviations defined in a glossary?

6. *Conclusion* is the caption of the final topic. This topic would be the writer's summation. Here, the analyst would restate in concise language a workable and realistic solution to the problem, and should not present new facts or alternate solutions. The writer should simply restate the solution and arguments presented in the feasibility study, being careful to limit the conclusion to a few short paragraphs.

ILLUSTRATIONS AND APPENDIXES

The analyst should use supplemental material to support his feasibility study. If he feels that quotation and footnotes will not support his study, the writer should attach supporting evidence as appendixes and illustrations to the feasibility study. Illustrations such as tables, graphs and diagrams are helpful in clarifying a certain portion of the text, and should be placed close to the text that they support. The text should refer the reader to the illustration that supports the text; otherwise, the reader may not associate the illustration with the text.

If appendixes or illustrations are placed outside the body, they should be identified with tabs. The tabs should be affixed to a plain sheet of paper and placed ahead of the appendix or illustration. In preparing appendixes it may be necessary to extract information from bulky documents and use this information as the appendix. The documents that the material was extracted from should be identified. The tabs should be positioned so that they are visible. This can be accomplished by staggering them on separate sheets of paper; then when the feasibility study is presented, all the tabs can be seen.

If the feasibility study contains terms, abbreviations and acronyms, the analyst should prepare a glossary to define those terms used in the study. The glossary should be included as an appendix.

REVIEWING AND CRITIQUING THE FEASIBILITY STUDY

After the final revision (but before the final typing) of the feasibility study, the analyst should ask someone to review the study. The purpose for the review is to correct misleading or incorrect facts and to test the soundness of opinions and assumptions and the logic of the concepts as presented in the study.

The document should be reviewed by another analyst or a person knowledgeable on the subject. The writer soon gets to know individuals who "nit-pick" a document and play on words. Such people overlook completely the purpose for the review. They suggest semantic changes that do not change the concept or meaning of a sentence or paragraph.

Corrections to obvious grammatical errors and constructive comments on an awkwardly worded sentence or paragraph are appreciated by the writer. The analyst should shun individuals who try to engage him in a dialogue about semantics. Selfappointed experts of the English language should be avoided also. The English language is not static—it is constantly changing. The language is for communicating ideas. If it does this, it has served its purpose.

DISPOSITION OF THE FEASIBILITY STUDY

After the final typing, the feasibility study should be placed in a manila folder containing a transparent window. The subject should be typed on the title page of the study so that the typing can be seen through the window of the folder. When the manila cover is opened, all tabs (if any) should be visible (see Figure 3-1). The feasibility study is then ready for presentation.

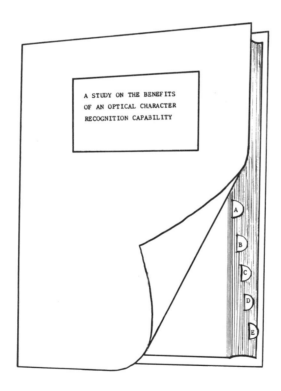

A STUDY ON THE BENEFITS OF AN OPTICAL CHARACTER RECOGNITION CAPABILITY

FIGURE 3-1

If the study is to be sent to another department or organization, a transmittal letter will be necessary. The letter should be typed on company stationery and addressed to the office requesting the study.

The transmittal letter, which should be two or three paragraphs long, may serve as an abstract for the study. It should identify the subject of the study, who authorized it, and explain what the document is about. The explanation can be accomplished by briefly stating what is discussed in the study.

4

Decision Logic Tables: Their Potential for Relieving the Documentation Strain in Systems Work

Logic is the science of the laws of thought as thought, that is, of the necessary conditions to which thought, in itself considered, is subject.

Sir W. Hamilton

Our association with decision tables over the years has been with train schedules, airline schedules, IRS tax tables, mortgage repayment schedules, and so forth. These tables are two dimensional in that two variables will give a certain result. The result is the outcome of an *if then* relationship. Examples: *If* your income is a certain amount, *then* your tax is also a certain amount; or *if* your mortgage loan is a certain amount, *then* the monthly repayment rate is also a stated amount. Two-dimensional decision tables are also called result tables. They give one result obtained from two variables.

The tables that are discussed here are referred to as Decision Logic Tables (DLT). DLT's are more powerful than result tables. DLT's give more than results; they give a course of actions required of a single variable or condition. The *if then* relationship is used in DLT's, but used differently than in result tables. In DLT's the *if* represents a stated condition, and the *then* represents an action or a variety of actions required to solve or satisfy that condition, whereas in result tables there can only be one action or result, and this is the result of two variables. An example of an *if then* relationship as used in the construction of a DLT follows:

If the alarm clock goes off and *if* it is a work day, *then* get up, get dressed, get your breakfast; and *if* it is raining, and *if* you have a raincoat, *then* get your raincoat and kiss your wife and *then* go to work.

Decision logic tables force the analyst to do complete analysis in the problem solution in system work. They can play an important role in the documentation and understanding of system problems, and in reducing narrative procedures to a table format. Some major advantages of DLT's are:

- They are useful in detecting errors in omission because the nature of DLT's forces complete analysis of a problem.
- They lend themselves to review by management, subject matter specialist, and non-EDP personnel.
- DLT's provide a standard format that is easy to follow, while a flowchart may contain personal reference and technical jargon that is hard to understand.
- The "English" columnar table format and the compactness of DLT's allow a complex problem or procedure to be easily grasped.
- DLT's provide better communication among the manager, analyst, programmer, and user; they permit the individual with the problem to review and evaluate the proposed solution.
- A DLT becomes a stand-alone, self-sufficient, and complete documentation for a particular problem.

The examples and explanations used here may tend to oversimplify DLT techniques. The main purpose is to explain DLT's, how to prepare them, and how they may be used in documenting systems work, particularly in reducing narratives and work procedures to DLT format. For the reader who wishes to study DLT techniques in depth and learn how they may be applied to programming, the references at the end of this chapter are recommended.

NARRATIVE PROCEDURES PRESENTED IN DLT FORMAT

DLT's may be used extensively in writing operating procedures for manual aspects of a systems work. With the use of DLT's, the analyst is forced to consider every detail, while in flowcharting and written procedures, individual discretion is followed in determining the degree of detail.

A DLT is a work procedure presented in a narrative and columnar table layout form giving the *conditions* (if this is present) and *actions* (then do this) of a given problem. DLT's are easy to construct. They are a proven method for documenting procedures in easy-to-read-and-understand format. Individuals involved in the documentation of procedures will find a DLT an invaluable aid.

One disadvantage of a narrative procedure is that sometimes the narrative does not describe the complete procedure. Some conditions may be left out. Other conditions may be implied but not specifically stated. Too often, those "in-between-the-line" conditions are overlooked by the individual who is to take the action specified in the procedure. The possibility of overlooking a condition and the actions to satisfy that condition is eliminated when the procedure is described and presented in DLT format.

The following is an example of a narrative procedure reduced to DLT, as shown in Figure 4-1:

The Assistant Secretary of the Air Force for Financial Management (SAF/FM) . . . will approve the selection and acquisition of EDP contractual services, including software and related services, which have an anticipated development cost greater than $200,000. The approval authority is paragraph 13a(5) of AFM 300-2.

The Director of Data Automation, Hq USAF, will . . . approve the selection and acquisition of EDP contractual services including software development cost for projects ranging from $100,000 up to and including $200,000. The approval authority is paragraph 13b(6) of AFM 300-2.

The Directorate of Data Automation or comparable activity at Major Command . . . will . . . approve the selection and acquisition of EDP contractual services, including software development, when the cumulative costs do not exceed $100,000 per contract. The approval authority is paragraph 13d(4) of AFM 300-2.

	EDP CONTRACTUAL SOFTWARE DEVELOPMENT COST	RULE		
		1	2	3
A	COST > $200,000	Y	N	N
B	COST < $100,000	N	Y	N
C	OFFICE OF APPROVAL SAF/FM	X	-	-
D	OFFICE OF APPROVAL HQ USAF/ADC	-	-	X
E	OFFICE OF APPROVAL MAJCOM	-	X	-
F	APPROVAL AUTHORITY PARA 13a(5), AFM 300-2	X	-	-
G	APPROVAL AUTHORITY PARA 13b(6), AFM 300-2	-	-	X
H	APPROVAL AUTHORITY PARA 13d(4), AFM 300-2	-	X	-

FIGURE 4-1

DECISION LOGIC TABLE DISCIPLINE

In DLT's the analyst is not limited to two variables and one result. There can be as many variables and as many results as necessary to solve a problem. A DLT is limited only by the size of the problem and the creativity of the analyst. However, there are certain disciplines and standard symbols that the analyst must use.

A DLT is partitioned into four parts called quadrants. These quadrants are separated by a set of double lines or heavy lines, as shown in Figure 4-2. Each quadrant has a name. The upper left quadrant is the condition stub; the upper right quadrant contains the condition entries; the lower left quadrant is the action stub; and the lower right quadrant contains the action entries.

The condition stub contains the *if* statements or conditions that must be considered in solving a problem. The action stub contains the actions to be taken to solve a problem.

The upper right quadrant (condition entries) and lower right quadrant (action

QUADRANT (Condition Stub)	QUADRANT (Condition Entries)
QUADRANT (Action Stub)	QUADRANT (Action Entries)

FIGURE 4-2

entries) are divided into vertical columns. These columns are referred to as rules. The squares of the upper right quadrant contain a Yes (Y) or No (N) response to indicate if the condition exists or not. The squares of the lower right quadrant contain an $\times$ or a dash (—). The $\times$ indicates that the action must be taken. The dash means that no action is required.

In preparing a DLT there should not be any blank areas or squares in a rule. If a blank exists, it may cause someone to wonder if the DLT is complete.

After the DLT is drawn in quadrant format, it should be given a name. The rules should be sequentially numbered. And for each condition and each action contained in the condition and action stubs, an alpha character should be assigned for row identification. The basic format for the makeup of a DLT is illustrated in Figures 4-3 and 4-4.

	(TITLE)	1	2	3	4	5	6	7	8
A									
B									
C									
D									
E									
F									
G									

FIGURE 4-3

The permissiveness of DLT's do not limit them to a given format. Analysts or documentation writers may develop variations in DLT makeup as to need, type, and size as the procedure or problem may suggest. However, the four quadrants of a DLT are basic. The order of the conditions, actions and rule columns may be arranged as shown in Figure 4-4. This type of format is often used for DLT's with extended entries. Extended entries are discussed later.

DLT's are not complicated. They are action oriented and easy for non-EDP people to interpret and comply with. Figures 4-2, 4-3, and 4-4 illustrate the components, format, and makeup of a DLT.

(TITLE OF DLT)						
R U L E	A	B	C	D	E	F
1						
2						
3						
4						
5						
6						

FIGURE 4-4

Every rule of a DLT should exit to another table or terminate in some type of action that makes the rule complete. A DLT should not have any loops. The reader should be able to go from a starting point (a condition) through the table or a network of tables to an action terminal point. A network of tables is discussed later. The DLT or a rule of a DLT should be traced through without any feedback information. This does not mean that the same table cannot be referenced a number of times. However, it does mean that if the same DLT is referenced a number of times and the same rule is traced, an error exists in the logic of the DLT and it should be investigated.

BIFURCATED FORMULA AND 2^n FACTOR IN DLT CONSTRUCTION

As conditions increase, the rules will have to be extended to accommodate for the Yes and No responses. There are two mathematical conventions that can be used to aid in this process. One is called the two to the nth (2^n) factor. What this means is that given the number of conditions in a DLT, the number of rules will always be two to the nth power. Example: A one-condition table has two rules, a two-condition table has four rules, a three-condition table has eight rules, a four-condition table has 16 rules, and so forth.

When the number of rules has been determined, the other convention can be applied. This convention is referred to as a bifurcated formula. Bifurcated means two-pronged or divided into two branches or parts: the yes and no branch. This formula is applied in this manner: Regardless of the logic in the condition entries, start with the bottom row of the condition entry and alternately write in Y and N responses for all rules for that condition entry row.

Move up to the second row and write Y and N in pairs for all rules of that row. Next, move up to the third row and write Y and N in groups of four. Continue doubling the Y and N responses until all rows of the condition entries rule columns have been filled in. The bifurcated formula and 2^n factor are to be used with limited entry DLT's such as the format illustrated in Figure 4-5. Limited entries are discussed later.

When the bifurcated formula and the 2^n factor are used, every condition and action rule are visible. As many actions as needed may be added to the action stub without adding any rules columns. Remember, the adding of conditions will require the adding of rules. Remember also that a condition or conditions can have any given number of actions. Actions may be arranged in the order in which they are to be performed. Sometimes this brings about quicker understanding of the procedure or steps of a procedure which are contained in the DLT.

Illogical Rules: When using the bifurcated formula, it is possible to have conditions agreeing with each other that cannot possibly exist in the real world. For instance, a traffic light cannot be green and yellow and red at the same time as Figure 4-5 suggests.

TRAFFIC LIGHT		1	2	3	4	5	6	7	8
A	Light Green	Y	Y	Y	Y	N	N	N	N
B	Light Yellow	Y	Y	N	N	Y	Y	N	N
C	Light Red	Y	N	Y	N	Y	N	Y	N
D	Proceed	-	-	-	X	-	-	-	-
E	Slow Down	-	-	-	-	-	X	-	-
F	Stop	-	-	-	-	-	-	X	-

FIGURE 4-5

When an illogical rule exists, remove that rule from the DLT. This will compress the table down to the logical rules. This is known as DLT compression. Figure 4-5 has been compressed to three rules, thereby eliminating the illogical rules, as illustrated in Figure 4-6. When a table is compressed, renumber the rules.

Negative Conditions: Another way to compress and reduce a table is to avoid creating any negative conditions. Now, what is meant here? Simply this: a negative condition exists when a condition is entered in the condition stub for both the Y and N responses. For instance, if we stated the two following conditions in a DLT, one would

TRAFFIC LIGHT		1	2	3
A	Light Green	Y	N	N
B	Light Yellow	N	Y	N
C	Light Red	N	N	Y
D	Proceed	X	-	-
E	Slow Down	-	X	-
F	Stop	-	-	X

FIGURE 4-6

be unnecessary, and the answer to either one would negate the need for the other. Example:

· Condition 1: If the balance is greater than $100
· Condition 2: If the balance is less than $100

A Yes response to condition 1 would logically be a No answer for condition 2. If the balance is greater than $100, then it is clear that it cannot be less than $100. The Y response would confirm this. An example of a negative condition is illustrated in Figure 4-7.

EDP CONTRACTUAL SOFTWARE DEVELOPMENT COST		1	2	3
A	COST > $200,000	Y	N	N
B	COST ≤ $200,000 BUT > $100,000	N	Y	N
C	COST < $100,000	N	N	Y
D	OFFICE OF APPROVAL SAF/FM	X	-	-
E	OFFICE OF APPROVAL HQ USAF/ADC	-	X	-
F	OFFICE OF APPROVAL MAJCOM	-	-	X
G	APPROVAL AUTHORITY PARA 13a(5), AFM 300-2	X	-	-
H	APPROVAL AUTHORITY PARA 13b(6), AFM 300-2	-	X	-
I	APPROVAL AUTHORITY PARA 13d(4), AFM 300-2	-	-	X

FIGURE 4-7

Row B contains the negative condition. To answer Yes to COST EQUAL TO OR LESS THAN (≤) $200,000, but GREATER THAN (>) $100,000 (Rule 2), is the same as saying No to COST LESS THAN (<) $100,000. Figure 4-1 is the same as Figure 4-7 with the negative condition removed. In Figure 4-1, saying No to COST GREATER THAN $200,000, and No to COST LESS THAN $100,000 (Rule 3) is the same as saying Yes to

COST EQUAL TO OR LESS THAN $200,000 but GREATER THAN $100,000. The DLT in Figure 4-1 required the same actions as the DLT in Figure 4-7. Rule 3 in Figure 4-7 is Rule 2 in Figure 4-1, and vice versa.

INTUITIVE DLT CONSTRUCTION

What has been discussed thus far are the rules or steps to follow in finding a complete solution for a problem by using the bifurcated formula and 2^n factor. There is another method that is often used in the construction of DLT's. Some refer to this method as the intuitive DLT construction.

This intuitive method does not use the bifurcated formula and the 2^n factor. In preparing a DLT using the intuitive method, the analyst will set up the Y and N responses based on how well he understands the problem and his ability to identify the conditions that are present. The intuitive method has no set pattern; the Yes and No responses are based on the analyst's judgment.

When using the intuitive method, the analyst must rely on an arbitrary rule to insure that the DLT is complete. This rule is the ELSE rule. The ELSE rule will not insure the accuracy of a DLT. It only insures completeness of the table by providing a procedure or action to follow under all possible combinations of conditions. The ELSE rule is a catch-all entry to handle any omission of conditions or actions that may be overlooked in preparing a DLT.

After following the required action specified in the DLT and the problem is not solved or an action step is omitted, the ELSE rule serves as a sentinel to remind the analyst that his work is not complete. It forces the analyst to restudy the problem. It works this way:

- After the Yes and No entries (which are based upon the analyst's skills and knowledge) are intuitively and randomly written in the rule columns, one final rule—the ELSE rule—is added to the DLT.

- If none of the specified rules satisfies a particular condition (which may or may not be contained in the DLT), then follow the action specified by the ELSE rule.

- Should a condition entry response (Y or N) or a series of responses not be taken care of by some action (X) entry in the action entry quandrant, take the action specified by the ELSE rule.

The action to be taken is added at the end of the action stub, and the X is placed in the proper square of the ELSE rule column. The action that the ELSE rule may suggest may be to "rethink the problem through" or "check with supervisor," or some such comment. Figure 4-8 is an example of the intuitive method using the ELSE rule. However, this ELSE rule is redundant because all conditions are satisfied by action entries. The example shows only the placement of the ELSE rule.

	ORDER REQUEST	1	2	3	4	5	6
A	IS ORDER $\geq$ DISCOUNT QUANTITY	Y	Y	Y	N	N	E
B	IS CREDIT OK	Y	Y	N	Y	Y	L S
C	IS ORDER $\leq$ QUANTITY AVAILABLE	Y	N	Y	Y	N	E
D	PREPARE INVOICE AT DISCOUNT RATE	X	X	-	-	-	-
E	PREPARE INVOICE AT REGULAR RATE	-	-	-	X	X	-
F	SHIP QUANTITY ORDERED	X	-	-	X	-	-
G	SHIP QUANTITY AVAILABLE	-	X	-	-	X	-
H	BACKORDER BALANCE OF ORDER	-	X	-	-	X	-
I	SEND FORM LETTER DISAPPROVING ORDER	-	-	X	-	-	-
J	CHECK WITH SUPERVISOR	-	-	-	-	-	X

FIGURE 4-8

REDUNDANT RULES

In constructing a DLT, redundant rules will invariably be built in. However, the redundant rules are no problem to eliminate. DLT's offer the potential to eliminate inconsistencies and redundancies, while insuring the completeness of detail analysis.

Whether the bifurcated formula and the 2^n factor or the intuitive method of DLT construction is used, a certain amount of redundancy may be built into the DLT. Many rules may appear redundant and unnecessary, and no doubt many are. There is a method to eliminate these redundant rules, thereby making the table compact and more efficient to use. The method is this: When two rules result in the same actions, and the condition entry responses are the same except for one condition and the difference has no effect on the action, the two rules can be condensed into one.

Let's break this method down further:

· If two rules have the same condition entries (either Y or N responses) with the exception of *one condition,* which has a Y or N opposite the other, and if the one condition having the opposite response requires the same action for both rules, then the two rules can be merged into one rule. Figure 4-9, using the bifurcated formula and 2^n factor, demonstrates this principle.

Rules 3 and 4, and 7 and 8, are redundant and meet the above redundancy principle. Row C of these rules has responses that are opposite to each other but the action is the same. The redundancy is removed and the table is compressed to six rules including the ELSE rule, as shown in Figure 4-8.

Dashes may be substituted for the redundant Y or N response. This means it does not

ORDER REQUEST		1	2	3	4	5	6	7	8
A	IS ORDER ≥ DISCOUNT QUANTITY	Y	Y	Y	Y	N	N	N	N
B	IS CREDIT OK	Y	Y	N	N	Y	Y	N	N
C	IS ORDER ≤ QUANTITY AVAILABLE	Y	N	Y	N	Y	N	Y	N
D	PREPARE INVOICE AT DISCOUNT RATE	X	X	-	-	-	-	-	-
E	PREPARE INVOICE AT REGULAR RATE	-	-	-	-	X	X	-	-
F	SHIP QUANTITY ORDERED	X	-	-	-	X	-	-	-
G	SHIP QUANTITY AVAILABLE	-	X	-	-	-	X	-	-
H	BACKORDER BALANCE OF ORDER	-	X	-	-	-	X	-	-
I	SEND FORM LETTER DISAPPROVING ORDER	-	-	X	X	-	-	X	X

FIGURE 4-9

make any difference, or it does not matter what the response is, it will not affect the action required for that condition entry. This is demonstrated in Figure 4-10.

ORDER REQUEST		1	2	3	4	5
A	IS ORDER ≥ DISCOUNT QUANTITY	Y	Y	Y	N	N
B	IS CREDIT OK	Y	Y	N	Y	Y
C	IS ORDER ≤ QUANTITY AVAILABLE	Y	N	-	Y	N

FIGURE 4-10

The redundancy concept is independent of the actions and conditions that are related to the particular problem. It has no relationship to the problem logic. The ultimate test of a DLT is whether it will do the job for which it is intended. A little redundancy won't matter, but as experience is gained in the use of DLT's, redundancy is easily spotted and removed.

LIMITED-ENTRY AND EXTENDED-ENTRIES

DLT's are classified according to the type of entries contained in the table rules. A limited-entry table contains the whole condition in the condition stub and a Y or N in the appropriate rule in the condition entry quadrant. The action stub contains the complete action statement in the action row line and an X in the appropriate rule square of the action entry quadrant.

This type of table is written in such a manner that the condition must be answered with either a Y or N, and the action entry answered with an X or a dash (—). The "Order Request" DLT in Figure 4-8 is an example of a limited-entry table.

An extended-entry DLT contains part of the condition, or action, in the condition stub, or action stub, and the rest in the condition entry quadrant, or the action entry quadrant. Figures 4-11 and 4-12 are examples of extended-entry DLT's.

	PAY TABLE	1	2	3
A	SALARIED EMPLOYEE	N	N	Y
B	HOURS WORKED	> 40	≤ 40	≥ 40
C	PAY ACCORDING TO	Overtime Schedule	Regular Schedule	Regular Schedule

FIGURE 4-11

	MERIT PROMOTION				
R U L E	A	B	C	D	E
	If the analyst has completed all of Firm's EDP courses	and if he was recommended by supervisor	then promote to the next pay schedule	and assign more respon- sibility	then do not promote
1	Y	N	-	-	X
2	N	Y	-	-	X
3	Y	Y	X	X	-
4	N	N	-	-	X

FIGURE 4-12

It is permissible to have both limited-entry lines and extended-entry lines in the same DLT but the entries in the lines should not be mixed. They should be either limited-entry or extended-entry. Limited-entry lines can be converted to extended-entry lines and vice versa. Figure 4-13 is an example of a DLT containing extended-entries for the condition and action entries.

	CREDIT RATING				
A	RATING	Excellent	Excellent	Good	Good	Poor
B	AMOUNT OUTSTANDING	$<\$5,000$	$>\$5,000$	$<\$2,000$	$>\$2,000$	$\$100$
C	AMOUNT TO LEND	$<\$9,000$	$<\$6,000$	$<\$1,000$	$<\$500$	None

FIGURE 4-13

A NETWORK OF TABLES

As was discussed earlier, one way to expand a DLT is to add conditions and actions as the problem expands. But there is a limit to this. If the bifurcated formula and 2^n factor are being used, and if conditions are constantly being added, this presents a problem. The problem is this: Two to the 2nd power is four, two to the 3rd power is eight, two to the 4th power is 16, two to the 5th power is 32. This exponentiation factor will soon become too wieldy to work with.

This problem can be avoided by using a system or network of tables. A network of tables is linked together by a GO TO or EXIT TO statement. A network of tables should be used to solve a large problem. It will relieve the analyst from having to solve the problem on a large sheet of paper.

The EXIT TO statement is an extension of each particular rule, with lines leading from the rule. This is awkward because it may have lines criss-crossing from one page to another.

	ORDER REQUEST	1	2	3	4	5
A	IS ORDER ≥ DISCOUNT QUANTITY	Y	Y	Y	N	N
B	IS CREDIT OK	Y	Y	N	Y	Y
C	IS ORDER ≤ QUANTITY AVAILABLE	Y	N	Y	Y	N
D	PREPARE INVOICE AT DISCOUNT RATE	X	X	-	-	-
E	PREPARE INVOICE AT REGULAR RATE	-	-	-	X	X
F	SHIP QUANTITY ORDERED	X	-	-	X	-
G	SHIP QUANTITY AVAILABLE	-	X	-	-	X
H	BACKORDER BALANCE OF ORDER	-	X	-	-	X
I	SEND FORM LETTER DISAPPROVING ORDER	-	-	X	-	-
J	GO TO ORDER TABLE	-	X	-	-	X

FIGURE 4-14

	ORDER REQUEST	1	2	3	4	5
A	IS ORDER ≥ DISCOUNT QUANTITY	Y	Y	Y	N	N
B	IS CREDIT OK	Y	Y	N	Y	Y
C	IS ORDER ≤ QUANTITY AVAILABLE	Y	N	Y	Y	N
D	PREPARE INVOICE AT DISCOUNT RATE	X	X	-	-	-
E	PREPARE INVOICE AT REGULAR RATE	-	-	-	X	X

EXIT TO SHIPPING TABLE ←

EXIT TO CONTROL TABLE ←

FIGURE 4-15

The GO TO statement is a separate action statement contained within the action stub. In using the GO TO statement there are no lines leading from the DLT. The table is complete in itself and the criss-cross of lines is avoided. The GO TO action insures that there is at least one X in every rule of the DLT. Whatever method is used, stick to it. Do not combine both methods in a network of tables, because it will be confusing to people trying to interpret the tables. Figures 4-14 and 4-15 are examples of DLT's using the GO TO and EXIT TO statement.

ACTION TABLE

There is another feature of the network of tables that should be discussed. This feature, called the action table, reduces the size of the DLT. The EXIT TO or GO TO statement of a given DLT rule may direct the reader to a series of actions which are contained in a separate table. These actions are unconditional. They will be taken every time when directed by a given rule. For the action table, there is but one condition, and that is the condition entry rule that required the EXIT TO or GO TO statement in the original DLT. The action table itself does not have any condition entries. It is nothing but an action stub.

The action table will aid in developing clear, specific, easy-to-follow DLT's. An example of where an action table is useful in reducing the size of a DLT is when a series of actions are accessed by one rule. Reduce the DLT by extracting these actions, placing them in an action table, and using either the EXIT TO or GO TO statement to point to the action table.

DECISION LOGIC TABLES AS A SUBSTITUTE FOR PROGRAMMING FLOWCHARTS

The decision logic table will never make the flowchart obsolete. This is because flowcharts lend themselves to applications involving sequential steps, while DLT's provide for a simple procedure to handle interactions of complex variables. Another reason is that programmers are accustomed to and comfortable with flowcharts. Too much pressure for innovative ideas would be met with resistance.

DLT's can be used to eliminate some of the deficiencies of flowcharts. They show conditions and action more clearly, thus enforcing completeness of the problem analysis during the pre-programming documentation and the program development stages. Personal and symbolic comments which have meaning only to the programmer are not present in DLT's. DLT's aid training by permitting personnel to assume program maintenance without having to wallow through pages of flowcharts linked together with lines and symbols.

Flowcharts are difficult and laborious to draw and update because of the symbols, the spacing required, and the labyrinth of arrows and lines. There may not be a clear and obvious path from beginning to end through a flowchart, since actions and any particular condition depend on all prior conditions and actions. For instance: An

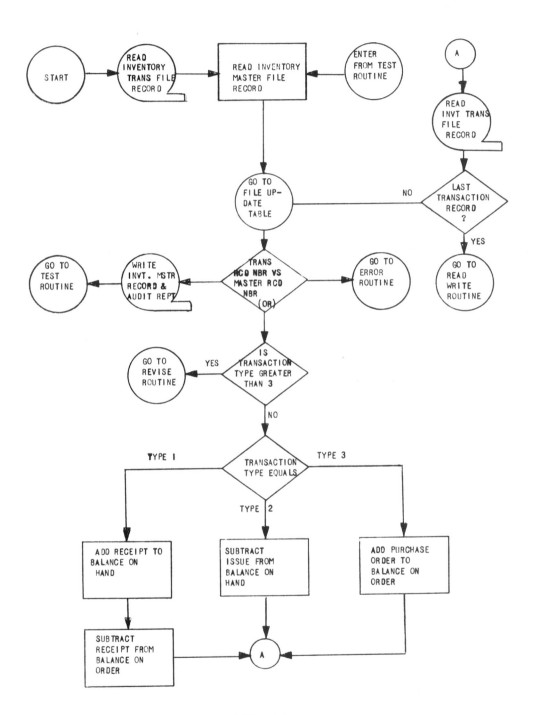

FIGURE 4-16

individual interpreting Figure 4-16 may ask if any master record is written before all the transactions affecting that particular record are handled. The answer is not obvious. The problem is nicely handled in Figure 4-17.

	INVENTORY CONTROL	1	2	3	4	5	6	7	8
A	START	Y	N	N	N	N	N	N	N
B	LAST TRANSACTION RECORD	–	N	N	N	N	N	N	Y
C	TRANSACTION NBR/MASTER RECORD NBR	–	>	=	=	=	=	<	–
D	TRANSACTION TYPE EQUALS	–	–	1	2	3	>3	–	–
E	ADD RECEIPT TO BALANCE ON HAND	–	–	X	–	–	–	–	–
F	SUBTRACT RECEIPT FROM BAL ON ORDER	–	–	X	–	–	–	–	–
G	SUBTRACT ISSUE FROM BAL ON HAND	–	–	–	X	–	–	–	–
H	ADD PURCHASE ORDER TO BAL ON ORDER	–	–	–	–	X	–	–	–
I	GO TO ERROR ROUTINE TABLE	–	–	–	–	–	–	X	–
J	PERFORM REVISE TABLE	–	–	–	–	–	X	–	–
K	READ INVENTORY TRANSACTION FILE RECORD	X	–	X	X	X	X	–	–
L	WRITE INVENTORY MASTER FILE RECORD	–	X	–	–	–	–	–	–
M	PERFORM TEST TABLE	–	X	–	–	–	–	–	–
N	READ INVENTORY MASTER FILE RECORD	X	X	–	–	–	–	–	–
O	GO TO INVENTORY FILE UPDATE TABLE	X	X	X	X	X	X	–	–
P	GO TO READ WRITE TABLE	–	–	–	–	–	–	–	X

FIGURE 4-17

In restructuring a procedure to DLT format, the following steps will aid in this process:

- Isolate the conditions of the narrative procedure by underlining each condition.
- Isolate the actions of the narrative procedure by underlining each action.
- List the conditions and actions separately on a sheet of paper.
- Standardize the language of the narrative by eliminating or combining the conditions or actions that talk about the same thing but in different ways. Example: (1) if the input/output device is magnetic tape; (2) if the peripheral is tape drive.

· Eliminate duplication by eliminating a condition that is a negative condition to another condition.
· Build the DLT, then
· Eliminate redundancy.

BIBLIOGRAPHY

Thomas R. Gildersleeve, *Decision Tables and Their Practical Application in Dataprocessing,* published by Prentice-Hall.

W. Hartman, H. Matthes, A. Proeme, *Management Information Systems Handbook,* published by McGraw-Hill.

Herman McDaniel (editor), *Applications of Decision Tables,* published by Brandon/System Press.

EDP ANALYZER, May 1966 issue, *How to Use Decision Tables,* published by Canning Publication, Inc., Anza Ave., Vesta, Calif. 92083.

U. S. Air Force Pamphlet 5-1-1, September 1965, for sale by the Superintendent of Documents, U. S. Government Printing Office, Wash. D.C. 20402.

5

Preparing EDP Management Policy Manuals

Knowledge is of two kinds: We know a subject ourselves or we know where we can find information upon it.

Samuel Johnson

In an EDP environment, there is a need for a manual containing the *why's* (policy) and *how's* (procedure) of the systems operations. This document should be the "Manual of Standards," designed to convey information to all echelons of EDP personnel. Time does not permit personal contact to find out what must be done, by whose authority, why, who must do it, and in what order. Manuals and other operating guidelines should answer these questions. They are the tools management has for disseminating EDP policies and procedures.

Where controlled documentation exists, analysts and programmers usually write and compile operating procedures to include user manuals, job setup instructions, and computer run procedures. In addition to this permanent or semi-permanent documentation, these same people write programming and operating guidelines to aid day-to-day operations and system maintenance.

Much information in an EDP environment concerning policy and operating procedures is written in notebook pads, or on pieces of paper and carried around in the supervisor's, programmer's, or operator's pocket.

Here is what Dick H. Brandon says about this subject.

It is common to see a "crackerjack" programmer spend hours in refining a subroutine to save a few microseconds. But the same programmer may be seen writing his operating instructions on a piece of scrap paper without any regard for the fantastic waste of machine time thereby created. . . . By not specifying the SE-

QUENCE in which the machine uses the input-output units at the beginning of the program . . . the operator may set up the alternate tape.[1]

Other information may be typed in memo notices and given blanket distribution. Memos may be placed on bulletin boards or taped to a wall or machine. The information is updated by pencil. Obsolete or outdated information may be scratched through and new information written in between the lines or in the margin. Obsolete notebook sheets are torn out and a new sheet written; "pocket" notes are discarded and new information "stuffed" in. Information that is given blanket distribution is updated by retyping the memo, whether one page or twenty, and reissued. Oftentimes, the old information is not cancelled; the new is filed with the old.

Such loose control on policy and procedures may have sufficed in the days when information was processed with electro-mechanical tab equipment, when policy and procedures, once established, changed infrequently. The tab operator and the person with the green visor perched upon a stool knew all that was required.

POLICY AND PROCEDURE STANDARDS MANUAL

Policy and procedure standards that are destined for long life for an EDP environment should be developed and placed in official binders. Procedures and controls for publishing and maintaining manuals should be established. It would be difficult to operate without defined policy and procedure standards. Each individual would tend to set his own rules. Much time would be spent in consultation trying to find *what* and *how* something is to be done.

Well-organized and well-written manuals containing company policy and operating procedures should be as much a part of an EDP operation as software documentation. In some of the better managed organizations, EDP managers insist on a Standards Manual that specifies the documentation requirement in detail. Well-established manuals of standards identify the various EDP forms, their use, and how the forms should be filled out. There are some EDP organizations that go to the extreme in establishing EDP guidelines, data processing aids, and operating rules. This author has seen the publishing of such rules result in a book as voluminous as a large metropolitan telephone directory. This documentation quickly becomes unmanageable.

In small EDP systems, one person may have the responsibility for determining policy and procedures, coordinating the information, and compiling and developing a manual of standards. In large systems, a team effort of experienced personnel, of which an EDP technical writer should be a member, is required. The EDP technical writer would be responsible for editing, organizing, presenting the contents, and publishing and disseminating the manual. (More about the technical writer's function appears in Part II of this book.)

---

[1] Dick H. Brandon, *Management Standards for Data Processing,* copyright 1963 by Litton Educational Publishing Inc., reprint by permission of Van Nostrand Company, Inc., 450 W. 33rd Street, New York, N.Y. 10001, p. 132.

It should be the responsibility of the team to determine and develop standards, operating procedures and guidelines for data processing. And until the initial manual draft has been completed, the members should be relieved of other duties.

Management at all echelons must enthusiastically support the standardization effort and provide positive enforcement of standards and procedures. Lack of support by management will destroy the team incentive and result in wasted effort in creating the manual.

PURPOSE OF GUIDELINES

Many connotations may be attached to the word "guidelines," but what has commonly been referred to as EDP guidelines are programming aids and day-to-day operating notices of a temporary nature. Guidelines are usually written on single sheets of paper and are either given blanket distribution or distributed to a limited number of individuals. In non-EDP environments, such notices may be referred to as memorandums or by some other name.

Guidelines may be used to disseminate changes to a more permanent document. Guidelines don't usually have the same significance as manuals or other bound documents and may be published more easily because of fewer controls over them.

The following information may be classified as guideline material:

- Subject matter that is advisory or directional in nature, with a temporary life span, e.g., 60 days.
- Procedure or policy guides that lead to a known or definite conclusion for a particular problem, and not intended as long-standing information.
- Other policy and procedure guides of general interest but not considered suitable for manual material.

For control purposes, this type of information should be issued with a number and an expiration or obsolescence date. A sequential numbering system will facilitate the recipient's control and filing of guidelines.

THE ROLE OF MANUALS

Manuals are preferred to guidelines and should contain well-defined EDP policies, standards and procedures of a permanent or semi-permanent nature. Manuals should be controlled by manual titles, volumes and reference numbers, and the contents may be labeled by subject, section, or work function. The manual should have chapters or volumes pertaining to the following major functions:

- System design standards
- Program design standards

- Documentation standards
- Operating functions and procedures, including job run instructions
- Performance (test and acceptance) standards

Other information that should be considered manual material:

- Information that is directional in nature, with an unknown or permanent life span concerning administrative EDP policies and procedures.
- Information (non-EDP in nature) that contains detailed procedures concerning the company's personnel policies.
- Information concerning policies on assigned EDP personnel responsibilities.

Some installations may use only guidelines to distribute company policies and operating procedures. It has been my experience that this method is ineffective because of the difficulty in controls and the lack of importance individuals attach to policies and procedures distributed on sheets of paper.

Within a company there may be several standards manuals, but the EDP manager will normally be concerned with those manuals involving EDP operations. These manuals concern EDP policy and operating procedures. In some EDP environments, one binder may be sufficient to contain both policies and procedures, while in others, several binders may be needed.

Manuals have many advantages over single sheet guidelines or word-of-mouth instructions. These advantages are:

- Policy and procedures are made official records, approved by management.
- Information is contained in uniform binders which serve as a handy compact reference.
- The manual is the focal point for information and serves as the bible for EDP operations.
- Procedures are in print and subject to tight controls, which improve continuity. People come and go; manuals stay.
- Manuals serve as training and on-the-job references.
- The use of manuals eliminates confusion; employees know "why, who, how, where, and when."
- EDP managers and analysts don't have to devote as much time to close supervision; decisions and instruction for each work function or problem are established.
- The use of manuals serves to reduce overlapping instructions and duplications and weed out obsolete and outdated information, through administrative controls and updating procedures.

CONTENTS OF MANUAL

The contents of manuals will vary from system to system. Manuals may serve any purpose that management desires. In addition to the main body as exhibited in Figure 5-1, the contents of the manual should include the following:

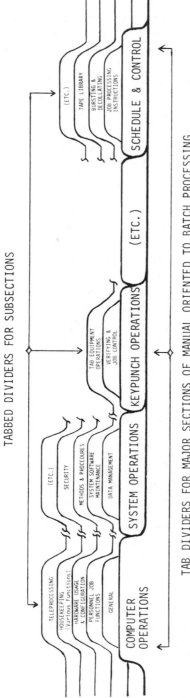

FIGURE 5-1

Tab Dividers for Manuals

The number of tab dividers and the subject on the tabs, and their arrangement, will vary from system to system depending on the EDP environment. For example: In some on-line message switching systems, keypunch and schedule and control may not exist as major sections or work functions. These two clerical functions, for the most part, are performed at the terminals. Tape Library would probably become a function of computer or system operations, while documentation on data management may not appear at all.

· Introduction letter: This is a letter of introduction giving the purpose of the manual, who authorized it, and its scope and application. This letter should be signed by a high official of the company or department.

· Table of contents: This is a listing of the information contained in the manual. The Table of Contents may be a composite listing by subject and page number, or it may be a listing by chapter, section, or work function with unique reference numbers instead of page numbers.

· Foreword or preface: This is a significant part of the manual. It may be one or several pages long. Its purpose is to tell how the manual is organized and how to use it, and to present instructions for making changes to the manual. The preface should also cover information on how to obtain extra copies, what to do with obsolete material, and where information may be obtained on questions that arise concerning the contents of the manual. Refer to Appendix A for an illustration of a preface.

· Main body: See Figure 5-1 for a topical listing of information that may be contained in the main body of an operations manual.

· Appendix: This section may contain exhibits, glossary of terms, illustrations, and flow-charts that are too bulky or that will interrupt the continuity if placed within the main body. However, sample forms and concise drawings and other illustrations should be placed with the policy or procedures to which they relate.

· Index: Most EDP policy and procedures manuals will not require an index if a subjective and comprehensive Table of Contents is developed. However, if the manual is voluminous with many policies and procedures for similar subjects but containing different information, an index should be created. An alphabetical index listing of key-words extracted from the document subject, topic and subtopic headings, and from the text of the policy or procedure, should be prepared and placed at the back of the manual. This index will aid day-to-day reference.

TABBED SECTION DIVIDERS

For convenience of information retrieval, manuals should be sectioned and tabbed according to content. Information relating to the individual tabs should be filed by subject behind that tab. For bulky manuals, such as user or operator instructions, program abstracts, subroutines or general purpose EDP information, tabs will facilitate the location of specific information and document maintenance. This information contained on the tabs may be arranged by subject title, alphanumeric headings, or numerically or alphabetically, or a combination of these, depending on the cataloging arrangements of the writer. There should be a tab for each major section, subsection, or work function.

Tabs can be arranged with several tabs to a bank for major sections. Behind the major tabs, smaller tabs may be placed to further the separation and identify the information contained in the major section. The most commonly used tab sizes are shown in Figure 5-2.

Figure 5-1 is an example of a typical batch processing operations manual, containing external documentation and general purpose information, with a bank of five tabs and smaller tabs placed behind the larger tabs.

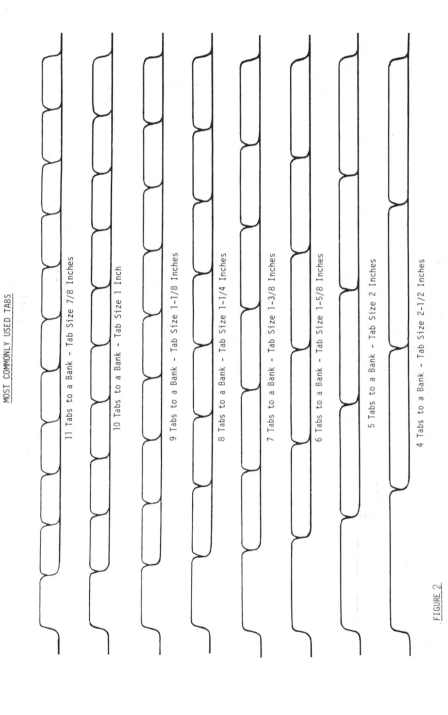

FIGURE 5-2

Most Commonly Used Tabs

UNIQUE REFERENCE NUMBERS

For ease of document maintenance and location of information, documentation (procedures) concerning the individual sections and work functions should be assigned a unique reference number. This will make it easier for individuals assigned to a particular section or work function to become familiar with those references that govern their work, without having to search through a bulky manual or a large table of contents for a particular subject.

Perhaps equally important, each section or work function supervisor would not be required to maintain a bulky manual in his section. The specific reference material pertaining to a particular section could be "lifted" from the large manual and retained in a smaller binder in that work area. The department manager or section manager who has several sections under his supervision may retain the complete manual in his office. The manual would serve as a comprehensive reference for the major department, while each section of that department could maintain only documentation pertinent to their environment. In effect, the "complete" manual would contain individual manuals of operations for the various sections.

As an example, refer to Figure 5-1. The department manager may wish to have all documentation contained in the manual in his office, while the Keypunch Operations Supervisor may retain instructions pertaining only to his section. The supervisor of Methods and Procedures may need only procedures pertaining to his work area.

Each reference number of the subsection or work function would be linked to the major section with an alpha prefix. The major section would be linked to the department by a unique alpha prefix. These alpha prefixes would reflect the "chain of command" for control and supervision.

Let's consider the reference number—EDP-CO-TP-XXX.
Where:
EDP = Electronic Data Processing (Document)
CO = Computer Operations (Major Section)
TP = Teleprocessing (Subsection or Work Function)
XXX = Reference number (assigned sequentially).

The reference number should be dictated by the EDP environment and the purpose and type of manual being created. Referring to Figure 5-1 again, a less involved number may be used by using a major and subsection alpha prefix and a numeric number.

Example: REF: SC-BD-XXX
   Where: SC = Schedule and Control
         BD = Bursting and Decollating
         XXX = Reference Number.

This last referencing system is preferred when the manual is developed and controlled within the EDP Department. The first example may be preferred when an individual section within a company is responsible for controlling and cataloging (not writing) all reference documents for that company.

Each reference within a section should have its own page numbering system.

Example: REF: SC-BD-001
              ISSUED: January 30, 19___
              Page 1 of 6

This will facilitate making changes to a document or manual. For example, assume that there are six procedures for the bursting and decollating section, under Schedule & Control, for a total of 21 pages. If all pages were sequentially numbered with numbers running across different subjects and references, when a change to a particular subject or procedure was made that required additional pages the entire section would have to be republished to change the page numbers, or the new pages would require an alpha or numeric suffix number, e.g., 5-1, 2, 3, etc., or 5-a, b, c, etc. When information is deleted that will cause gaps in the numbers, blank pages would have to be issued to retain the continuity of page numbers. However, depending on the size of the reference and number of pages deleted, it may be better to reissue the reference.

Appendices B, C, and D to this chapter are examples of typical operating procedures and the referencing method discussed above.

PUBLISHING AND PRESENTING THE MANUAL

The responsibility for the manual does not stop when the writing of the manual is complete. The manual must be printed and placed in binders. The writer or coordinator of the manual must familiarize himself with printing techniques to insure a good quality manual. He must determine the grade and weight and in some cases the color of paper to be used for ease of reading and maximum effect. Should the manual be multilithed, mimeographed, etc., or does it require some other printing process? If the manual is to contain photographs, camera and dark-room treatment with multilith offset process will be required.

If the writer is not familiar with these processes, a check with the reproduction shop will supply information on the best printing processes and type of paper best suited for a particular document.

Binders are another important element in the effectiveness and quality of a document. Binders that contain policy and procedures which are subject to frequent use should be durable. There are various types of binders on the market and vendors will be happy to supply samples for inspection. The three-ring binder is preferred for most EDP policy and procedures documents. Combed plastic binding may be preferred for some documents that do not require frequent updates. Due to the combing effect, it would be difficult for individuals to make page changes.

Vinyl covered binders are superior to plastic covered binders. The difficulty with plastic covered binders is that they crack when handled in cold weather, while vinyl covered "rolled edge" binders seldom crack when exposed to prolonged low temperatures and frequent use. Vinyl covered binders cost more but they are more durable and will withstand harsher treatment than plastic covered binders.

If inferior binders are used, the binders will crack and become "ragged." Individuals will be reluctant to use binders that are dilapidated, or they will shift the material to some other binder, or remove the contents and place them in a desk drawer. Such practices lead to lost documents or reliance on memory for policies and procedures guidance. Either method may be detrimental to EDP operations.

Binders should have the subject, volume number (if more than one binder is needed), and the department and company printed on them. The printing should be of good quality to withstand being worn or rubbed out through use.

APPENDIX A

PREFACE

COMPUTER CENTER OPERATIONS MANUAL (CCOM)

GENERAL

A. The purpose of this manual is to provide techniques and general operating procedures that are necessary to effectively operate and control the Computer Center and its related data processing functions. The manual is divided into various sections and subsections and provides procedural records of interrelated functions of Computer Operations.

B. For the purpose of this manual, *procedural information* refers to those procedures that have a direct impact on the operations of the computer center and related functions. Normally, such procedures have an indefinite life span and are subject to infrequent changes. Information which is non-procedural in nature will not be published in this manual.

CONTENTS OF MANUAL

A. Procedures concerning the various sections and/or their work functions are assigned unique reference numbers and filed behind index tab dividers labeled according to the following:

1. Computer Group

General (REF CG-GE-XXX): General information concerning functions of computer group, hours of operation, shift schedule, safety information, etc.

Equipment Usage (REF CG-EQ-XXX): Care and use of equipment, hardware configuration, etc.

Personnel Job Functions (REF CG-JF-XXX): Operator duties and responsibilities.

Housekeeping (REF CG-HK-XXX): Procedures concerning running and other processing functions involving the day-to-day operation of Computer Group.

Console Commands/Procedures (REF CG-CC-XXX): Information concerning console commands and operator procedures.

2. Support and Planning

General (REF SP-GE-XXX): Function of support and planning, supervisory span of control of the various sections, etc.

Data Management (REF SP-DM-XXX): Procedures concerning data management functions.

System Operations (REF SP-SO-XXX): Procedures concerning the systems software operations, maintenance, etc.

3. Schedule and Control

General (REF SC-GE-XXX): Non-procedural information similar to that listed for Computer Group and Support and Planning.

Job Processing (REF SC-JP-XXX): Procedures concerning the functions of job processing, scheduling and control.

Bursting Room (REF SC-BR-XXX): Procedures concerning the functions of the Bursting Room.

Microfilm Operations (REF SC-MF-XXX): Procedures concerning operations and processing of microfilm.

Tape Library (REF SC-TL-XXX): Procedures concerning the functions of the Tape Library.

4. Keypunch and Unit Records

General (REF KP-GE-XXX): Non-procedural information similar to that listed for computer group and support and planning.

Keypunch (REF KP-OP-XXX): Procedures concerning the functions of keypunch operations.

Unit Records (REF KP-UR-XXX): Procedures concerning the functions of unit records.

5. Data Control

General (REF DC-GE-XXX): Nonprocedural information similar to that listed for Computer Group and Support and Planning.

Reports & Procedures (REF DC-RP-XXX): Information and instructions concerning reports, analysis, and methods and procedures.

Security (REF DC-SE-XXX): Procedures concerning the safeguarding of computer data and security controls.

6. Miscellaneous

Miscellaneous (REF MISC-XXX): Information not falling into the above categories.

PREPARING PROCEDURAL INFORMATION

A. Procedures should be prepared by personnel responsible for a particular work function or section, but approval of appropriate supervisor is necessary prior to releasing for distribution.

   1. Persons originating procedures should prepare procedures according to format outlined in Figure 5-3.

   2. Do not assign reference numbers, issue date or page numbers.

REF:
ISSUED:
Page   of

COMPUTER CENTER OPERATIONS
WORK PROCEDURE

Work Section: (e.g., Computer Group)

Subject: (Meaningful title)

Purpose and Scope: (A brief statement of what the procedure is to accomplish and range of its application).

(Procedure Defined—A concise factual description of a work function as it should be performed.)

FIGURE 5-3

3. Be responsible for accuracy of contents.

4. Send draft to Data Control Group. Data Control will:

   a. Review procedures for standardization of format.

   b. Edit and coordinate procedures to eliminate duplication.

   c. Send final typed copy to the Documentation Management and Program Control Group.

B. The section's supervisor or custodian of procedural information is responsible for revising or canceling obsolete procedures.

1. Revisions should be handled as follows:

   a. For an entire revised procedure:

   Enter "Revised" under the reference number of each page (instead of "Issued") and the date of the revision.

   b. For revised portion (paragraph, sentence, or a few words):

   Enter a vertical line (|) in the right-hand margin opposite the revision on each page where revisions are made. In the lower left-hand corner, enter the same symbol and type "Revised" and the current date.

   c. Send the final typed *revised copy* or page(s) *with the original number* to the Documentation Management and Program Control Group.

   NOTE: Suffix number for revisions will not be used. In multipaged procedures, only the revised page(s) will be reproduced. The symbol (|) will indicate where the revisions were made.

   d. For obsolete or cancelled procedures, send memo identifying the procedure(s) by reference number and subject to the Documentation Management and Program Control Group.

ASSIGNING REFERENCE NUMBERS

A. Documentation Management and Program Control Group will:

1. Assign reference number according to the section and functional category set forth under CONTENTS OF MANUAL. Numbers will start with 001 and run consecutively for each category.

2. Prefix the numerical assignment with applicable section/functional alpha abbreviation.

3. Reference number may be reassigned to procedures with a different subject within the individual section.

DISTRIBUTION OF OPERATING PROCEDURES

A. Documentation Management and Program Control Group will:

1. Handle printing arrangements.

2. Arrange for distribution of operating procedures in accordance with approved list.

SECTIONAL CHANGES TO MANUAL

A. When changes (other than procedural revisions) are necessary due to the addition or deletion of a work function or transferring a work function to another section, changes should be handled as follows:

1. Send memorandum to the Documentation Management and Program Control Group giving details of the change, and TAB(s), if any, that should be deleted or added.

2. When an additional TAB is needed, give wording for the TAB, and identify the section under which the TAB is to be filed.

B. Other changes or suggestions to improve the validity and usefulness of the Manual should be sent to the office specified above.

APPENDIX B

REF: CG-HK-004
ISSUED:March 1,19___
Page 1 of 1

COMPUTER CENTER OPERATIONS
WORK PROCEDURE

Work Section: Computer Group

Subject: Tape Volume Labels

Purpose and Scope: These procedures explain and specify the information that should be contained on the Tape Volume Label.

A. Example of Tape Volume Label:

```
┌──────────────────────────────────────────────────────────┐
│ DS NAME      1           JOB     2                          │
│ VOL. 3  OF           USE CODE        4                      │
│ CREATION DATE   5     RETENTION PERIOD    6                 │
│ SYSTEM  7   UNIT 8    │   │ CPO  │ OPR INIT.│               │
│ OPERATOR     9        │   │ MICRO│          │               │
│ DESCRIPTION  10   11  │ C │ TP   │ P   } 12 │               │
│                       │ R │ PLOT │ R        │               │
│                       │ E │ LAB  │ O        │               │
└──────────────────────────────────────────────────────────┘
```

B. 1. DSNAME = ... Name of the volume
    2. Job = ... Job that created the volume
    3. Vol. __ of __ = ... Number of volumes for DSNAME
    4. Use Code = ... Master (M), Data (D), or Information Service Group code for test tapes
    5. Creation Date = ... Date the volume is created
    6. Ret. Period = ... Number of days volume is to be kept
                        May be coded with a scratch date
    7. System = ... The computer system that created the volume
    8. Unit = ... Tape unit the volume is created on
    9. Operator = ... Computer Operator's initials
  10. Description = ... As needed
  11. Created = ... Check appropriate box for type of volume created (if applicable)
  12. Processed = ... Check appropriate box when executed and Operator's initials

111

APPENDIX C

REF: SC-BR-001
ISSUED: December 1, 19___
Page 1 of 6

COMPUTER CENTER OPERATIONS
WORK PROCEDURE

Work Section: Bursting Room

Subject: Processing Mod 65 and 75 Computer Output

Purpose and Scope: These instructions define handling procedures for processing job outputs received from the computer room. Personnel involved in processing job outputs are responsible for compliance with these procedures.

A. Job cards received from the computer room will be clocked in on the time stamp. Each job deck is separated and placed on the work counter according to its priority. Jobs are arranged from left to right, with the highest priority (12) on the left-most position and the lowest priority (4) on the right-most position.

B. When the job input/output request, Form 299, is returned to the bursting room, it will be placed with the respective job cards. All jobs do not require a Form 299, just those requiring tape input or output.

C. Job printouts are received in large groups and are processed as follows:

   1. Separate printout groups into individual jobs by comparing the first page job name to the end of job name. This will eliminate errors in disposition by ensuring that individual jobs do not contain printouts of other jobs.

   2. The printout and cards for each job are placed together and processed as follows:

      a. Check the Job Request Form, Form 293, to ensure that all material and information is available to complete the job.

      b. Clock out time job is completed.

      c. Stamp job completed with rubber stamp.

      d. Check disposition and priority on job request form.

      e. If Priority 11 or 12, call the user for pickup.

      f. If other than Priority 11 or 12, and there is no delivery station assigned for the job, call the user for pickup.

REF: SC-BR-001
ISSUED: December 1, 19___
Page 2 of 6

D. Disposition of the Job Request Form is as follows:

1. The form consists of three copies and is initially received in the Control Room. The original remains in the Control Room for record purposes.

2. The first carbon copy is sent to the Bursting Room and maintained as a record for jobs in the Computer Room that are pending, and for filing once the job is completed and returned to the submitter.

3. The second carbon copy, released with the job cards to the Computer Room, remains with the card deck throughout the job processing. This copy is returned to the submitter with the job cards and printouts.

4. File trays divided into two divisions, Complete and Pending, are available for filing job request forms according to status and job priority while jobs are being processed in the Computer Room.

E. Hourly audit pending jobs to prevent loss of material or delays in turn-around time.

Job priority and turn-around times are:

Priority 11 and 12—2 hours plus estimated running time
Priority 9—4 hours plus estimated running time
Priority 7—8 hours plus estimated running time
Priority 4—24 hours plus estimated running time

1. Check each computer system to determine what jobs are active (running) or awaiting input into the system.

2. Compare active jobs in systems with jobs pending in bursting room.

3. From this audit it can be determined if:

a. A printout is lost.

b. A job was flushed through the system without (JCL) computer recognition.

APPENDIX D

REF: SC-JA-001
ISSUED: June 20, 19___
Page 1 of 2

COMPUTER CENTER OPERATIONS
WORK PROCEDURE

Work Section: Schedule and Control

Subject: Job Accounting

Purpose and Scope: These instructions contain information and procedures for preparing a job card layout worksheet form for job accounting and costing purposes. These instructions are applicable to application programmers.

1. The attached Job Card Layout Form (Form 20) gives the general format of a job card for all jobs to be run on the 360 MOD 65's or 75. (See Figure 5-4.)

2. Job Name is required on all job cards. It must be 7 or 8 characters in length.

3. At present, the three fields labeled "ACCOUNT NO.," "NATURE OF RUN," and "RUN TYPE" are the only required fields appearing between parentheses. However, all parameters which appear between the parentheses on the job card are considered as positional parameters and conform to the rules set forth in IBM/JCL Manual C28-6539 regarding positional parameters. The absence of one of these parameters is indicated by a comma coded in its place. Also, positional parameters may not have embedded blanks unless the parameter is enclosed by quote marks.

4. The information contained between the open and closed parentheses of the job card represents current accounting information. This information is described as follows:

   a. ACCOUNT NO. A twelve (12) character code reflecting the Company organization for which the work is being performed.

   b. PROJECT NO. A four (4) digit code showing the project for which the job is being run.

   c. SUB-PROJECT A four (4) digit code identifying the subproject for which the job is being run.

   d. PROGRAM NAME An eight (8) character field identifying a particular program being run.

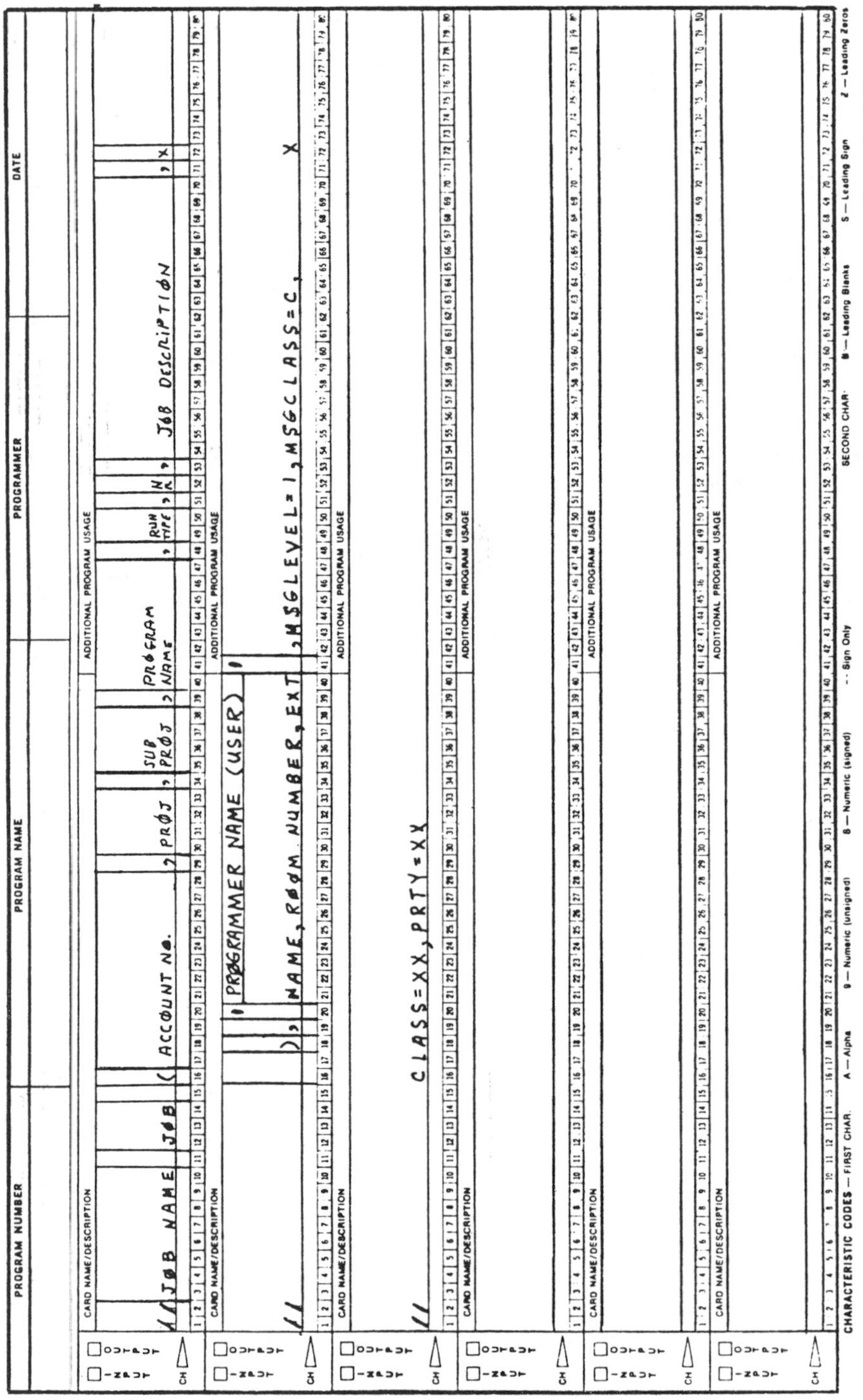

FIGURE 5-4

Job Card Layout Worksheet

e. RUN TYPE   A two (2) digit code identifying the type or run as to production, test and compile, or parallel. All other codes are considered as invalid and will require changing before the job will be accepted.

f. NATURE OF RUN   A one (1) character field which describes the job as being one of several categories.

g. JOB DESCRIPTION A twenty (20) character field identifying the job in a meaningful manner to the user. The completion of this field is to be controlled by the users. If a period (.) is used the field must be enclosed by quotes.

5. Requirements of the programmer name field are given as follows:

   a. The field is enclosed by quote marks.

   b. The total field should not exceed twenty (20) characters. The order of the information is programmer's name, room number, and extension if possible.

6. MSGCLASS is the sysout class.

7. CLASS is the job class.

6

EDP Forms Management and Design Considerations

Of what use are forms, seeing at times they are empty? Of the same use as barrels, which at times are empty too.

August W. Hare

An efficiently managed EDP organization will have an effective EDP forms management program. A paperwork simplification expert at Standard Register was quoted as saying:

> A meaningful form control program should include not only a sample of all the forms being used, notice of out-of-stock situations, purchase requisitions and inventory records, but also a filled-in sample of all forms, showing typical entries made, annual usage of the forms and number of locations at which they are used, a concise narrative or flowchart of the procedure showing who gets each part of a form and why they get them, and finally, a flowchart showing the interrelationship among various forms.[1]

The size of the EDP system and its nature of operation will dictate the type and quantity of EDP forms. It takes a variety of EDP forms to explain:

- The preparation of data.
- How the data should be entered into the computer.
- How jobs should be set up.
- How to process the computer output.
- How to report computer malfunctions.

---

[1] Albert L. C. Chu, "Forms Business Is Management's Business," *Business Automation,* December 1969, published by Hitchcock Publishing Co., Hitchcock Building, Wheaton, Ill. 60186.

· How to obtain computer service.
· How to record the use of equipment, the control and use of magnetic tapes, etc.

EDP forms are a valuable tool in the management and control of data processing organizations. A properly designed form can eliminate repetitive narrative correspondence and cut down on the administrative workload of EDP personnel.

A narrative report is time consuming, and, at best, it gives the reader the writer's point of view and manner of reporting. Too often EDP managers have difficulty deciphering the required data from the insignificant data.

FORMS ANALYSIS

One of the first things to be done in establishing a forms control program is to collect and evaluate existing forms, records, and other cards or paper sheets used for recording and transferring information from one individual or group to another. These items must be analyzed to determine the following:

· What is the form used for?
· How is the form filled in—by machine or man?
· What information is entered on the form?
· What EDP group or individual initiated the form?
· What authority authorized the form?
· What quantity of the form is used per week, month, or year?
· How is the form processed— its distribution and number of copies prepared?
· Where is the form filed and how long is it retained?
· What time frame is allowed for processing a form?
· Is the form a single or multipurpose form?
· Are criteria and standards established for the accuracy and control of forms?
· Can the form be eliminated, or consolidated with another form?

EDP forms analysis will provide EDP managers with a method for obtaining proper data on the proper form without having to sift through irrelevant information and time-consuming reports. The form must be designed to aid the operations staff in their job function and to provide accurate and needed information so that EDP managers, system analysts, and programmers may rely upon it for formulating EDP policy and making sound programming decisions.

One of the important functions of forms analysis is to guard against the recording of duplicated information. Before a new form is implemented, a careful review of existing forms should be undertaken to make sure that the information on the new form is not duplicated on some other form at some other point in the EDP organization.

Finding other ways to obtain the information will permit the elimination of unneeded or marginal forms. Automated methods (software) for compiling and retrieving the data may be more accurate and economical than the manual process of recording and retrieving information.

EDP forms are embedded in a work procedure. Because of this, forms analysis should scrutinize each form, each card or sheet of paper used as a form, and each item on the form. These forms, and items on the form, should be questioned as to their usefulness.

All the forms used in a procedure are interrelated and may overlap each other, even though the information recorded on the form may be used by different people at different times for different purposes. Because of the commonality of the forms, they invite scrutiny. If it is too time consuming and involved to scrutinize each form individually, apart from the procedure, then the work procedure and the form should be studied together.

The EDP Forms Analyst: EDP forms analysts are about as scarce in data processing as EDP technical writers. Normally, the majority of EDP forms used in an EDP organization are designed by the equipment vendor or some other business firm. To understand the role forms play in a procedure, the analyst must study the procedure firsthand to learn the reasoning behind them. By understanding the background reasoning behind each form, the analyst will be able to do an in-depth forms analysis. Appendix A at the end of this chapter is a guide to forms analysis.

In the analysis process, if the analyst relies upon what he is told and what he deduces from a sample form as the sole source for his knowledge, he may fail in his analysis efforts. He must go to where the work procedure is being performed, and observe its process. After discussing the forms with individuals who work with them and after studying the facts and observing the work procedure, the analyst is now ready for thinking about form revision. Here, the analyst is on his own. Individuals or directives cannot tell the analyst how to think. He either has this ability or he hasn't. The analyst should be careful in exercising his "cerebral" power until he knows every aspect of the procedure and the form under study.

Before an analyst presents a new form or forms, he should satisfy the following questions:

- Does the new form (or forms) improve the efficiency of the work procedure?
- Does it simplify, eliminate or consolidate any forms under study?
- Does the form save time in processing?
- Does the form eliminate error hazards in recording or extracting data?
- Does the form reduce the cost of forms?
- Does the form provide the proper information?

PREREQUISITE OF EDP FORMS

The EDP form represents a job to be done. It is an abbreviated narrative outline of a data processing function to be performed, or the condensed results about that function. The primary prerequisites of EDP forms are:

· Forms must be easy to understand and fill out.
· Forms must serve a useful purpose.
· Forms must provide sufficient captions and columns, and space for recording required data.
· Forms should be capable of being processed quickly.
· Forms should be economical to print.
· With few exceptions, forms should not exceed 8½ x 13 inches for convenience in processing and filing.

To determine if an EDP form is required, it must be viewed as to its contribution and the method of reporting the information that is needed for a given work function. The form's benefit and usefulness should go beyond a specific requirement for recording data on a form in a prescribed sequence or taking data from it in a similar manner. The benefit and usefulness of an EDP form can be measured by:

· *Current and Essential Data:* If the EDP form requires the recording of information that is not needed, but may be needed at a later date, the form becomes more than a management tool—it becomes a liability. This extra data requires processing and filing. If the data is to be used later, situations may have changed, thereby invalidating the data previously recorded. Form analysis should consider the need for a particular EDP form to record current and essential information about a particular function.
· *Ease of Obtaining the Data:* Study is required to determine the best way of obtaining the needed data and the simplest manner of recording the data on the form. Analysis in this area is also required to determine the most convenient and easiest method of correlating and sequencing the data for immediate use.
· *Speed of Processing the Data:* Analysis is needed to determine what personnel, equipment, and procedures will be required to handle and process the data. The speed of data flow from its source to the intended user can be affected by the way the EDP form is designed.
· *Simplicity of Recording and Extracting the Data:* The form should be functional in design so as to simplify the recording of data. Extracting this data and converting it to a useful purpose should be equally simple. This process should be done rapidly and economically.

DETERMINING THE NEED FOR EDP FORMS

If a form is to be a useful tool for all levels of an EDP organization, it must serve a required purpose. The information contained on an EDP form must be essential to the overall efficiency of the EDP organization.

As mentioned earlier in this chapter, EDP forms are one of the most neglected areas of data processing. One of the reasons for this is the obsolescence of a form or an item on a form due to changes in operations requirements. An EDP form or item should be eliminated if:

· It requires information which is no longer needed.
· The information can be combined with another form or item.
· It costs more to gather the information than it is worth.
· There is a better method of obtaining the information.

To challenge the need for a form or an item on a form requires just a little effort. Each EDP form should be scrutinized every six months, or oftener, to determine if the information is still required. If the information, or part of it, is no longer required or is obsolete, the form should be discarded or revised. Too often, outdated or unsuitable forms, or the need for a new form, causes many of the EDP manager's operating and documentation problems.

The EDP manager should not set himself up as a forms analyst, but he should be aware of the time he and his subordinates spend in correcting or explaining errors caused by unsuitable forms.

If forms are designed with simplicity in mind, their periodic review will aid in consolidation or the elimination of obsolete or unneeded forms. Simplicity should be a fundamental principle in form design. There are certain factors to use in judging the advantage of consolidating EDP forms. Some are:

· Standardization
· The necessity for the form
· The adequacy of the form

Standardization: Standardization of EDP forms, in the same way as program documentation standards discussed in Chapter Two, can contribute to EDP efficiency by eliminating duplication of data. Standardization of EDP forms can reduce form cost and aid EDP managers in controlling the data processing operations.

A form may be initiated to record certain data by various individuals in the performance of a particular work function when the data is already being recorded on a different or similar form by other individuals. One way to eliminate the introduction of a new form that would record duplicated data is to set up a control file to classify EDP forms by purpose or functional requirement. Request for a new form would be checked against the file to see if an existing form may serve the purpose. The function of this file is discussed later.on in this chapter.

The standardization of such factors as rulings, type sizes, type faces (gothic, italic, and roman), captions (on the line, under the line, or box design), and the form size will aid in:

· Reading the form
· Filling in the required data
· Distinguishing separate related vertical or horizontal lines or columns
· Association of the required data with the various captions on the form
· Extracting data from the form
· Filing and retrieval of the form

The form's rulings (lines), letter size and type should be acceptable in appearance and economical to reproduce. Appendix B at the end of this chapter contains form design standards.

The Necessity for the Form: A second way to consolidate and eliminate EDP forms is to determine the true need for a form: Does the form give the complete picture? Does it contain all the data required? Is a second or third form used to record information about a second or third processing sequence of steps of a given job function or work procedure? When different forms are used for successive processing steps, but the filling out of these forms is done at different times, an excessive number of forms may be filled out for later transcribing to a single form.

Perhaps all the information required can be contained on a single form left at the work position until all data is recorded about a particular job. This would permit getting the complete picture and all the required information on one form. The process of transcribing information from one form to another would be eliminated.

In cases where all transcribing is not eliminated, consolidation is still worthwhile. Perhaps several forms used in a particular job can be combined into a multipurpose form. A multipurpose form usually serves a community of interest. Information is entered on a common form, and as the form is processed, certain information is separated or extracted by different people for different purposes.

The Adequacy of the Form: The form should be designed to require the correct data, and the right amount of data. The form should contain sufficient captions with explanatory comments to simplify a work procedure. EDP forms that are difficult to understand will cause confusion when processed and may contain incorrect or inadequate data.

The purpose of a form is to simplify a work procedure and to obtain certain information about that work function or procedure. As mentioned under Forms Analysis, every EDP form is embedded in a procedure. It is the document which defines methods of accomplishing the procedure and recording of certain information about the procedure. The adequacy of the form is satisfied when:

- It makes easy the task of recording information on the form.
- The data can easily be extracted and put to use.
- The tendency to make errors in both entering and extracting the data is minimized.
- There is not a more efficient way of gathering the data.
- The form meets design standards.
- The sequence of items on the form is logically laid out.
- The layout achieves good visual effect.
- The form minimizes writing.
- The form provides management with the information sought.

DEVELOPING THE EDP FORMS CONTROL FILE

As mentioned earlier, samples of all authorized or "bootlegged" forms, temporary or permanent, should be collected. This collection should include numbered and un-numbered forms designed by the EDP organization or an outside firm. These forms should be categorized as to their purpose and procedural requirement. The title alone may be misleading. Several forms may have similar titles but be used for a different procedure. Therefore, a form should be classified by its purpose and procedural function.

After forms are classified, they should be filed in folders either by the form number or its procedural function, e.g., Job Processing, but according to the work section, e.g., Schedule and Control, to which the forms apply. Filing of forms by a numeric order within a work section may prove to be the simplest and most flexible procedure. Duplication of form numbers should be avoided. Forms should not be filed by title or subject.

When a new form is requested, a review of those already in the Control File will aid the analyst in eliminating unnecessary forms or items thereon, and will prevent the creation of new forms that duplicate any existing ones.

CONVENIENCE OF OBTAINING THE DATA

EDP forms design is the byproduct of forms analysis. Forms analysis determines the need for a form and what is to be contained on the form, while forms design is concerned with the layout and arrangement of a form for efficient processing.

Standards for form design should be flexible but not to the point where the standards are left to the whim of the form's initiator. As in programs documentation standards discussed in Chapter Two, when deviations from standards are required, they should be logically justified to explain the benefits to be gained by deviation. The objective of a standard is to attempt to define the best practice.

One of the main design criteria of an EDP form is to obtain correct information. To achieve this, the form must be easy to read and follow. If the user, in processing the form, is not sure of the meaning of the captions and statements, he may not respond favorably to the dictates of the form. Form layout and readability are key factors in EDP form design.

The wording of the form is no small matter. The title should be brief, but descriptive of the procedural function of the form. It should contain clear and concise captions. The form's title should not be vague or abstract, but should be clear and indicative of the purpose for which it was designed. A key word or words used in the title should indicate the form purpose. *Example:* Reporting Computer Job Run Problems, instead of Computer Operating Problems. The key words "Job Run Problems" indicate the purpose of the form. As a rule of thumb, titles should be relatively short for quick reference.

However, the title should not be so short that it misleads or confuses the purpose and function of the form.

In addition to a meaningful title, forms should be assigned a number, an edition date, and page number (for multi-page forms). A control code or office symbol of the form's originator (not designer) may be an option item to identify the office of origination.

The form's number can be used for quick reference, and as an aid in inventory and control of EDP forms. Many users of EDP forms use the form number as the only identification and reference factor. When making reference to an EDP form in documentation, both the form number and the title should be given.

The number, as well as the lettering of the title, should be of sufficient size for ready identification. The title and form number should not be placed within the same general area on the form. The title should be placed near the top, while the number should be placed at the bottom. The exact position and size of the title, captions, and number are left to the discretion of the designer; but readability, appearance, filing and referencing should be considered in the design effort.

There are certain advantages to placing the number in a conspicuous location at the bottom of the form. The lower right-hand corner would serve the following advantages:

· Prevent mutilating or obliterating the number when forms are stapled together.
· Prevent the number and title from being hidden, torn, or becoming "dog eared" when bound at the top.
· Aid in requisition, storage, and retrieval.

The form should contain clear and concise captions. The captions are usually abbreviated questions and may not contain sufficient information to aid the user in filling in and processing the form. The form designer should be mindful of ambiguous or misleading statements and captions.

Certain involved and complex EDP forms may require comprehensive instructions for their processing. If additional instructions or comments are required to clarify the purpose and function of the form, they should be contained at the bottom or on the reverse side of the form.

Some EDP forms may require separate instructions to explain their use and how to fill them in. Regardless of the complexity of the form, an example or specimen of a form filled in will be helpful to the user.

When it is necessary to issue separate or supplemental instructions to explain the use of a form, they should be contained in the Manual of Standards or the Operations Manual as discussed in Chapter Five. Chapter Seven contains various forms and instructions for their use, as applied to a typical Computer Center Operations.

RECORDING AND EXTRACTING DATA

The design of the form should aid these factors. To facilitate entering and extracting information, the sequencing or ordering of items on the form should correspond to the document from, or to, which the data is taken or posted. Another consideration for form design is that information should be entered from left to right. This is the visual habit of reading.

Related items should be arranged in logical order.

EXAMPLE:

Division	System	Application	Program Name	Programmer

NOT

Programmer	System	Program Name	Application	Division

Arranging the captions, items, boxes, etc., on a form in this manner follows the habitual and logical way of thinking, and the normal work flow.

Long-drawn-out questions or instructions should be avoided. A form that is difficult to understand may contain erroneous data when filled in. The form should be easy to read and fill in, and to extract data from. The following general rules will aid recording and extracting data.

- Make the writing flow from left to right.
- Make the writing flow from top to bottom.
- Provide for enough space for each entry.
- Make vertical and horizontal spacing fit the writing method.
- Word the printing on the form to minimize handwritten entries.
- Determine the best sequence or ordering of captions, items, and boxes to aid filling in and extracting information.
- If supplmental instructions are needed, place at bottom or on the reverse side of the form.
- Suit the form to its procedural purpose; consider the writing and handling method used for processing the form by man or machine.

If the form is used as a source document for transcribing information onto EAM cards which are prearranged to contain certain data in designated card fields, the form should be arranged to aid this process (Figure 6-1). The items and information contained in the items should be arranged on the form in proper keypunch sequence. If the keypunch operator must scan or turn the form over to find the next data item to be punched, the operator is handicappd and the keypunching speed and efficiency are hindered.

GUIDELINES FOR FORM CONSTRUCTION

A form that is properly thought out and designed can save much effort and clarify a work procedure or job function. Collectively, EDP forms can be labor savers and provide for a smooth and efficient operation. Individually, an ill-designed form can be

WRITING MADE EASIER BY ARRANGEMENT

1 Writing line flows from left to right and top to bottom

2 Related items grouped to follow work flow

3 Item sequence of source document and tab card identical

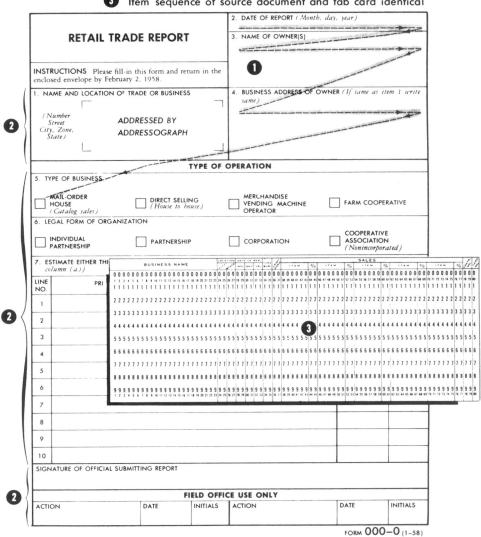

Courtesy of General Services Administration National Archives and Records Service Office of Records Management; Forms Analysis, Federal Stock Number 7610–655–8220; for sale by The Superintendent of Documents, U.S. Government Printing Office, Washington, D.C. 20402.

FIGURE 6-1

something less than efficient. It may be difficult to understand and confusing to comply with, resulting in costly errors.

A poorly designed form can usually be attributed to the following:

- It contains insufficient information.
- It contains unneeded information.
- It duplicates information required on other EDP forms.
- It contains unclear instructions on how to fill out the form.
- It contains incomplete information.
- It contains obsolete information.
- It is too difficult to fill out.
- It is the wrong form for the job or it is an obsolete form.

Certain parameters, guidelines and restraints are suggested for the forms analysis and design, including punched card design, as follows: [2]

FORMS

PARAMETER	GUIDELINES	CONSTRAINTS
Size of form	• Size forms to fit the amount of information to be contained. • Select sizes for convenience in preparation, for easy data collection and filing.	Cost-Standard
Code structure	• Delineate coded transaction records by suggesting format in each data field (i.e., for decimal points, commas in quantity fields, use tick-marks; to suggest layout of blocked long codes, use vertical dotted lines).	Some fields are unstructured
Form-writing aids	• Provide directions for training reinforcement printed on form. • Provide for shading to avoid line-skipping on wide forms or for table look-up tasks. • Reduce handwritten entries to a minimum by preprinting common coding on form set or by using computer prepared turn-around documents. • Locate complex handwritten fields with vertical proximity for "copy-down" tasks.	Cost, form Design time
Validation aids	• Use sequence numbers for unique identification or transactions. • Include redundant fields (i.e., description fields provide audit trail for ID codes).	Cost, form Design time
Aesthetics	• Neat, professional looking forms lead to more careful preparation.	Cost

[2] Timothy A. Davidson, "Design Guidelines to Minimize Human Transcription Errors in Information Systems Input," *The Office,* published by Office Publications, Inc., 1200 Summer Street, Stamford, Conn. 06904.

PARAMETER	GUIDELINES	CONSTRAINTS
	· Reduce clutter in layout. · Use consistent type styles, ink color. · Highlight key fields with half-tone shading.	

CARD DESIGN

PARAMETER	GUIDELINES	CONSTRAINTS
Order of fields of data	· Sequence of items should correspond to source document. · Layout transaction to maximize duplicating (via the "dup" key).	Standardized format
Keypunching	· Provide spaces between fields of data to reduce slipped field errors. · Indicate card column numbers on form for training/reinforcement. · Use drum card for field/character set restrictions.	Crowded card

Form Size: Another important factor to consider in forms design is the size of the form. In an EDP operation, a variety of sizes are required. Code sheets, flowchart sheets, console and maintenance records, and other types of forms on which to write or handprint information for transcribing to EAM cards are usually the largest types of forms required.

As mentioned earlier, a large percent of forms used in an EDP operation are purchased from an outside firm. When a company has a printing and reproduction facility, EDP forms expenditure can be minimized or eliminated if a forms program is instituted by EDP management and a forms analyst engaged to design forms and monitor the forms program. One source for the EDP forms analyst would be the EDP technical writer discussed in Part Two of this book.

Certain EDP forms could be sketched out on an 8 x 10½ or 8½ x 11 inch sheet of bond paper. A better method would be to use a sheet size 32 x 42 inches (see Figure 6-2). Various sizes of forms can be sketched out on this size sheet and cut to any dimension.

The need for standard EDP form size goes beyond ease of handling and elimination of waste paper. The use to which the form will be put should be considered before design is undertaken. This use should include the type of equipment used to process the form; filing, storage, and mailing should also be considered (see Figure 6-3). Standard sizes as contained in Appendix B at the end of this chapter should be used.

The amount of information printed on the form and the amount of information to be recorded on the form should be taken into account in determining size. The spacing of horizontal and vertical lines or columns can be determined by the amount of information to be recorded, and the printed matter, such as section headings, captions, items and boxes to be included.

Another key to the size of the form is the writing method used, i.e., hand, typewriter, printer, or other special office machines. If the information is to be recorded by a typing machine, the number of characters per inch of the type face, or font, used deter-

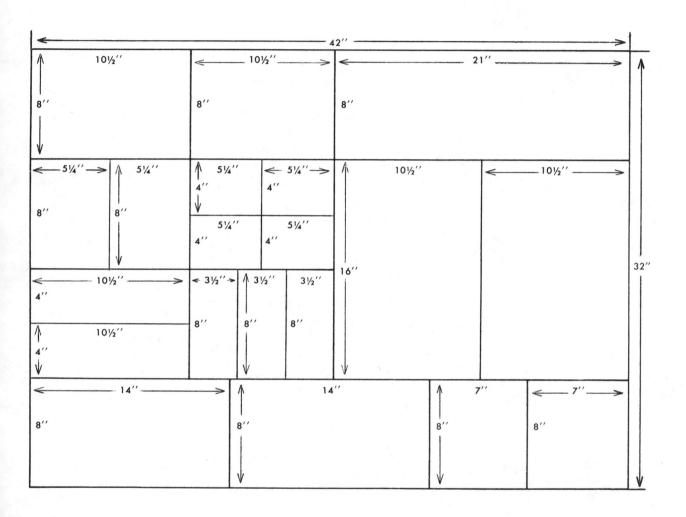

FIGURE 6-2

Paper Sizes That Can Be Cut from a Standard 42″ x 32″ Sheet

mines the amount of space to be allowed for printed matter. Horizontal spacing is determined by the characters that can be written per inch, while vertical spacing is based
on the number of lines that can be written per inch (see Figure 6-4).

Many EDP forms are designed for hand printing with columns or fields to match
that of an 80 column or field layout of an EAM card. The forms are used for punch
card layout arrangement. Information contained on these forms is usually transcribed to
EAM cards to be used as source input data or for card listing, or both. The overall
dimension and the horizontal and vertical spacing of these forms should be of sufficient

FORM DESIGN CONSIDERATIONS

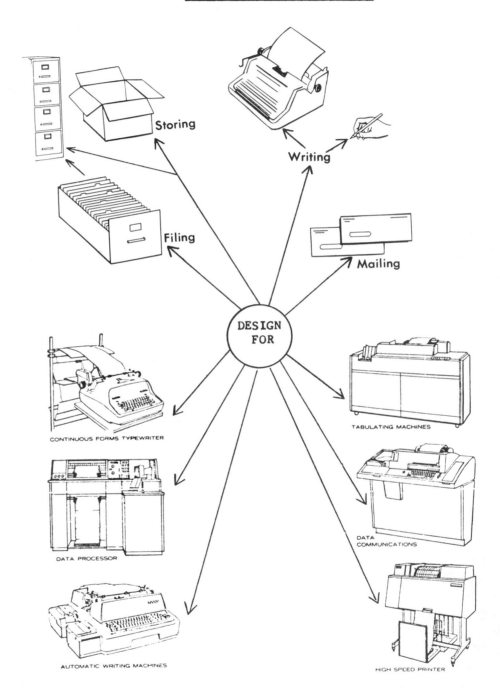

FIGURE 6-3

Form Design Considerations

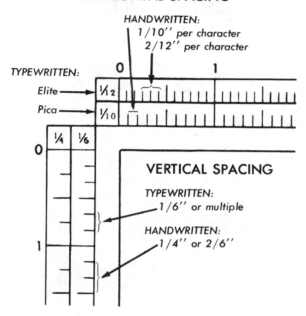

Courtesy of General Services Administration National Archives and Records Service Office of Records Management; Forms Design, Federal Stock Number 7610–753–4771; for sale by The Superintendent of Documents, U.S. Government Printing Office, Washington, D.C. 20402.

FIGURE 6-4

size to accommodate large hand printing and to aid keypunching. Figure 6-5 illustrates the recommended dimension for a punch card layout form.

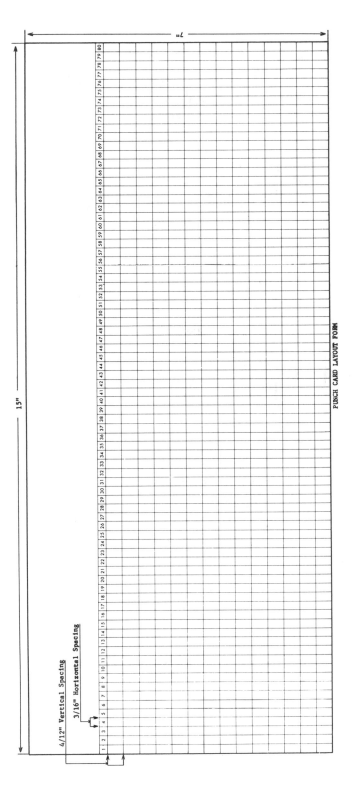

PUNCH CARD LAYOUT FORM

FIGURE 6-5

APPENDIX A

GUIDE FOR BASIC ANALYSIS

ASK—TO GET THE FACTS	ASK—WHY?	ASK—TO MAKE THE IMPROVEMENTS

NEED
 	
What do the forms in the procedure accomplish which justify their existence?
 	
What other forms are related, or duplicate in whole or in part the information requested?
 	
What inadequacies are there in the forms in the procedure?
	WHY this need?	**NEED**
		
		Is the information needed?
		
		Does the cost exceed the worth?
		
		Is there a better source or a better way?
		
		Can the forms or items on the forms be—
		    Combined?
		    Eliminated?
		    Simplified or resequenced?
		    Added?

PEOPLE Who requires the data? Who enters the information? Who extracts the information?	**WHY by these people?**	**PEOPLE** Can the work be assigned to other units or clerks to simplify the work or combine its handling? Can the forms in the procedure be resequenced to simplify the entering or extracting of the information?
PLACE Where are the forms in the procedure written and processed? Where are the forms sent? Where are the forms filed?	**WHY here?**	**PLACE** Can the writing of the forms and their processing be combined with similar work done in another unit? Can the forms be completed in the field without the need of feeder forms, or having to copy the information on another form in the office? Does the design of the forms aid in their filing, finding, storage and disposition?
TIME When are the forms in the procedure written? When are these forms processed? When are the forms filed?	**WHY at this time?**	**TIME** Are the various processing steps taken in their proper order? Can the peakloads be leveled off by better scheduling of the forms flow? Can information be requested so it can be processed during a slack period?
METHOD How are the forms in the procedure written? How is the information on these forms processed? How are these forms transmitted? How are forms filed?	**WHY this method?**	**METHOD** Can the writing method be changed for the better? Can the routing or mailing method be changed? Have the forms been geared to the most efficient office equipment?

FORMS ANALYSIS GUIDE FOR MULTIPLE COPY WRITING— SPECIALTY FORMS

UNIT SETS

Form can be written with—

    Pencil

    Ballpoint pen

    Typewriters

    Billing machines

    Addressing machines

    Accounting machines

    Fuel meters

    Printing scales

    Timeclocks

Consider if—

- Form is hand or machine written . . . .
- Different copies of form are routed to different places . . . .
- Two or more forms have common data which can be written in one writing . .
- Later entries are made . . . .
- Selective information is needed on some parts and not on others . . . . . .

Why —

Eliminates inserting and jogging of carbons.
Keeps forms in alignment.

Facilitates identification by permitting the assembling of various colors of paper into one unit.

Combines forms of varying widths and lengths.
Combines forms of varying paper weights.

Keeps set or part of a set as a unit for later entries and handling.

Permits the deleting of information on subsequent parts by spot or strip carbon, varying widths and lengths of carbon, or preprinted blockouts.

Remember—

- Not economical for low usage forms.

    For example—If the annual quantity is 50,000 sets and 1,000 sets are written annually at each of 50 points, this is a potential unit set application. However, if the annual quantity is 50,000 sets, written at one point, consider a continuous form.

PADDED ONE-PART UNIT SETS

Form can be written the same way as unit sets.

Why —

Consider if —

- Form is written in a number of copies—
  (1) beyond the unit set
  (2) which vary from time to time . . . .

Permits flexibility in the number of copies written.

Remember—

- Does not permit combining different forms for one writing.
- All copies must be the same paper weight as each sheet might serve as the original.

CONTINUOUS FORMS—MARGINALLY PUNCHED
(Have same general features as unit sets)

Consider if—	Why—
• Machine on which form is written uses an aligning or feeding device	Permits accurate registration from part-to-part and from set-to-set across and down the form.
	Permits a continuous flow of sets through writing machine.
• Size can be reduced through the close registration of copies which permits single instead of double typewriter spacing	Reduces printing and processing costs.

Forms can be written with—

    Typewriters
    Billing machines
    Addressing machines
    Teletype machines
    Integrated data
        processors
    Electronic data
        processors

Remember —

• Usually impractical unless the forms are used in large quantities in a continuous writing operation.

• *Marginal punched continuous strip forms are used to advantage when various parts must be different weights, grades or colors of paper.*

• *Marginal punched fanfold forms are used when the same weight and grade of paper is specified for all parts, or when parts and carbons must remain together for later entries. Side-tie perforations hold forms together without staples, clips or pins.*

CONTINUOUS FORMS—NOT MARGINALLY PUNCHED
(Have same general features as unit sets)

Consider if —	Why —
• Machine on which form is written does not have forms aligning or feeding device, but a large quantity of form is written	Permits continuous flow of sets of forms through the writing machine.
	Permits easy movement of form from one typewriter to the other or from one place to the other.

Form can be written with—

    Typewriters
    Billing machines

Remember—

• Forms can slip during typing and realignment will be necessary.

• There are continuous forms available without carbon, but the writing machine must be equipped with a carbon shifter device.

SALESBOOKS

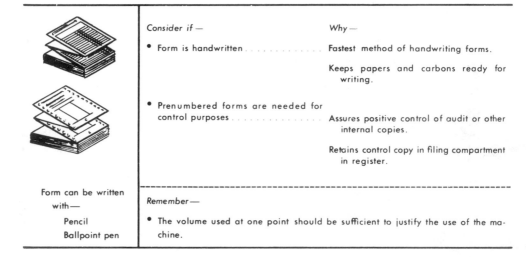

	Consider if —	Why —
	• Form is handwritten	Simplifies inserting carbons.
		Keeps forms in alignment.
		Eliminates inserting and jogging carbons.
	• Form is carried from place to place . .	Prevents the loss and wrinkling of forms.
	• Form will receive rough handling. . . .	Keeps top form clean.
		Prevents dog-eared sheets.
	• Later entries are made	Keeps set as a unit for later entries and handling.
	• Portion of form is retained	Keeps receipt stubs or file copies in book until all sets are written.

Form can be written
with—

   Pencil
   Ballpoint pen

Remember—

• Book cover must be inserted to prevent the writing from coming through on more
  copies than intended, or

• Last copy of each set must be on sufficient heavy stock to prevent writing from
  coming through on more copies than intended.

AUTOGRAPHIC REGISTER FORMS

(Have same general features as continuous forms)

	Consider if —	Why —
	• Form is handwritten	Fastest method of handwriting forms.
		Keeps papers and carbons ready for writing.
	• Prenumbered forms are needed for control purposes	Assures positive control of audit or other internal copies.
		Retains control copy in filing compartment in register.

Form can be written
with—

   Pencil
   Ballpoint pen

Remember—

• The volume used at one point should be sufficient to justify the use of the machine.

*Courtesy of General Services Administration National Archives and Records Service Office of
Records Management; Forms Analysis, Federal Stock Number 7610–655–8220; for sale by
The Superintendent of Documents, U.S. Government Printing Office, Washington, D.C. 20402.*

APPENDIX B

FORMS DESIGN STANDARDS

1. Cut Form Sizes

Various form sizes can be designed on and cut from a standard sheet of paper 32 x 42 inches without waste, particularly 3½ x 8, 4 x 5¼, 8 x 10½, and 16 x 10½. (Note Figure 6-2.) Other sizes (8½ x 11, 8½ x 13, etc.) may also be designed on and cut from the 32 x 42 inch sheet.

Normal file card sizes: 3 x 5, 4 x 6, 5 x 8.

Post card sizes: 3¼ x 5½. *obsolete*

Considerations:

(a) Avoid crowding content;

(b) Conform to dimensions of storage and filing facilities (i.e., legal size, letter size, etc.);

(c) Fit to standard office machines for fill-in (i.e., typewriter, bookkeeping machines, etc.);

(d) Fit to standard-size envelopes.

2. Paper Weight and Grade

Operating unit ordinarily should specify one of the following four:

Mimeograph	36 lb. (basis 17 x 22)
Card	180 lb. (basis 25½ x 30½)
Sulphite	32 lb. (basis 17 x 22)
Bond (25% rag)	32 lb. (basis 17 x 22)

Selection should be based upon:

a. Handling requirements;

b. Writing method;

c. Number of copies to be made at one writing;

d. Length of time the form will be retained;

e. Printing requirements (i.e., printing on two sides, by a given process, etc.);

f. Filing and storage space requirements (affected by thickness of paper).

3. Color of Paper

Specify color only when needed for emphasis or for more efficient filing, routing or sorting. Reduce the need for colored paper by use of sorting symbols, bold headings, heavy rules lines or other devices when possible. Exceptions permissible for specific organization or operating requirements.

4. Color of Ink

Specify other than black ink only when fully justified by volume and increased efficiency in use of the form and when the more economical possibilities of colored paper are inadequate. The use of two colors should be avoided except under extreme justification.

5. Identification and Heading

Heading may be centered across entire top of form or centered in space to the left of any entry boxes placed in upper right. (Upper right should be designed for file or other ready-reference entries if needed.) Within space decided upon, arrange generally as follows:

Form number and issuance or revision date—upper left corner.

Agency name and location (if needed)—upper left (under form number) or top center (depending on item's importance in use of form).

Form title—center of top (under agency name and location, if that item is centered). Use conspicuous type.

Exception: Run identification across bottom of vertical-file-card forms unless needed for file-reference purposes.

6. Instructions

Well-designed forms require few instructions other than captions and item headings. When required, instructions usually should:

a. Be set in two or more narrow columns rather than full-width lines.

b. Be listed as numbered items rather than in paragraph style.

c. Be placed as near items to which they apply as possible (unless length would detract from effective layout).

When instructions are segregated on form, they should be placed:

a. At top right or top center, if concise and applicable to the whole form.

b. At bottom, if that will make possible more economical use of space.

c. On reverse, if no space available on face.

7. Address

If name and address are inserted on form by agency prior to mailing, position of name and address should be suitable for window-envelope use. Forms requiring return to an agency should be properly identified, as provided under Standard No. 5.

Forms intended for use in window envelopes must conform to postal regulations, which in general provide that nothing other than name and address, and possibly mailing symbol, shall appear in the window. The form must fit the envelope to avoid shifting of the address. Standard-size envelopes only should be used. Post Office Department Schedule of Award of Contracts for Envelopes is the guide to standard envelope sizes.

8. Preprinted Names or Facsimile Signatures

If form is to be stocked for continuing use, personal name or signature of official may be preprinted only on special justification or by legal requirement (to avoid having large numbers of forms made obsolete by change of officials). Pre-printing of titles only or the use of rubber stamps or automatic signature inscribers are alternatives to be considered.

9. Form Arrangement

a. Align beginning of each writing space on form vertically for minimum number of tabular stops.

b. If box design is used:

(1) Serially number each box in its upper left-hand corner;

(2) Start caption in upper left-hand corner, to right of number, leaving fill-in space below caption;

(3) Draw box size to provide sufficient space for fill-in.

c. Place essential information where it will not be obscured by stamps, punches, or staples, or be torn off with detachable stubs.

d. Group related items.

e. Include "to" and "from" spaces for any necessary routing.

f. Provide for use of window envelopes, when appropriate, to save additional addressing.

g. To the extent practicable, provide same sequence of items as on other forms from which or to which information is to be transferred.

h. Arrange information for ease in tabulating or transferring to machine punch cards, if those are involved.

10. Check Boxes

Use check boxes when practicable.

a. Place check boxes either before or after items, but all in the corresponding positions within any line series.

b. Avoid columnar grouping of check boxes if possible, because of poor registration when carbon copies are required. Place check boxes before first column and after second column when there are two adjacent columns of questions.

11. Margins

Printing Margin. Printed all-around borders usually should not be used since they tend to increase production problems and costs. In any event an extra margin of ⅜ inch or not less than 3/10 inch from edge of paper should be allowed on all 4 sides for gripping requirements in printing and as a safety margin for cutting. No printing—neither border nor text—should be permitted in that space.

Binding Margin. For press-type fastener, side or top, 1 inch; for ring binder, 1 inch (printing permitted but no fill-in within these margins).

Fill-in Margin. Top typewriting line, at least 1⅓ inch from top of paper if possible. Bottom typewriting line, not less than ¾ inch from bottom. Hand fill-in permissible above or below these lines.

12. Space Requirements for Fill-in

Typewritten:

10 characters to the horizontal inch to accommodate both elite and pica typewriters;

3 fill-in spaces to the vertical inch, each space being double typewriter space.

Handwritten:

⅓ more space horizontally than for typewritten fill-in;

3 spaces to the vertical inch, each space double that of typewriter space.

13. Rulings

a. Use heavy 1½-point or parallel ½-point rulings as first and last horizontal lines, between major divisions, and across column headings.

b. Use ¾-point rulings across bottom of column headings, and above a total or balance at the foot of a column.

c. Use hairline rulings for regular lines and box lines when no emphasis is required.

d. Use ¾-point rulings for vertical subdivision of major sections or columns.

e. Use leaders as needed to guide eye in tabular or semi-tabular items.

14. Signature and Approval Date

Single handwriten signatures usually go at bottom right of last page. Allow ½ inch (three single typewriter spaces) vertically and three inches horizontally.

Two handwritten signatures, normally left and right at bottom of last page.

Space below the ¾-inch bottom typewriter margin generally reserved for handwritten signatures and dates.

15. Two-Sided Forms

a. Two-sided forms ordinarily should be printed head to foot (top of front to bottom of back), especially if top-punched for binder use.

b. If punched in left margin for binder use, 2-sided forms should be head to head.

c. Three- or 4-page forms (one sheet folded once) should be head to head throughout if open-side style, and head to foot if open-end (so that, when opened for use, head of third page follows foot of second page).

d. Head-to-foot open-end forms are preferable for machine fill-in.

e. For multi-page forms, separate sheets of proper page size should be used instead of larger sheets folded to page size, unless the larger sheets can be cut economically from standard paper sizes and run on standard printing or duplicating equipment.

16. Prenumbering

Use prenumbered forms only if accounting or control is required for each form or document. Place number in extreme upper right corner.

17. Punching

For standard press-type and 3-hole ring binders, distance from edge of paper to center of hole should measure ⅜ inch;

If 2 holes are punched, for press-type fastener, the distance between centers should be 2¾ inches;

If 3 holes are punched, distance from center to center of adjacent holes should be 4¼ inches.

18. Guide Sheet

A design guide sheet aids in designing a form speedily and accurately. It provides a preprinted scale of measurement in nonreproducible blue ink which corresponds to the measurements of the writing methods. The layout of the form on the guide sheet should be done in pencil so that changes can be made easily. Figures 6-6, 6-7, and 6-8 illustrate the use of a guide sheet.

OUTLINE

FORMS DESIGN GUIDE SHEET (8″ X 10½″)

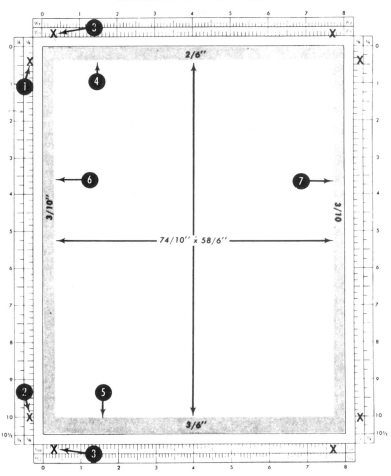

On the *Forms Design Guide Sheet* place an "X" on the

① 2/6″ mark from the top on the side scales.

② 3/6″ mark from the bottom on the side scales.

③ 3/10″ mark from each side on the top and bottom scales.

The area framed by the gray tone is the image size.

74/10″ across, 58/6″ down.

The gray tone area indicates the margins.

2/6″ top, 3/6″ bottom, and 3/10″ on each side.

	Line up triangle or ruler—	Draw a light line from—
④	At top with "X" mark on left scale with "X" mark on right scale.	Left to right
⑤	At bottom with "X" mark on left scale with "X" mark on right scale.	Left to right
⑥	At left with "X" mark on bottom scale with "X" mark on top scale.	Bottom to top
⑦	At right with "X" mark on bottom scale with "X" mark on top scale.	Bottom to top

FIGURE 6-6

PLOT DOWN

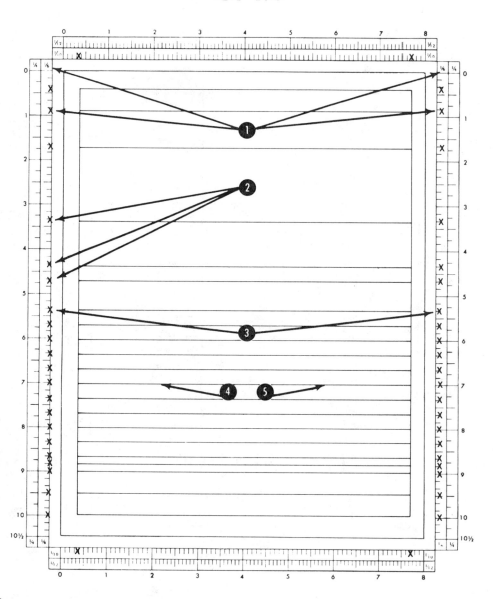

1. Use scale at left and right of guide sheet.

2. Count off space down in accordance with final measurements on rough draft (i.e., Step 3).

3. Place an "X" on sixth mark on left and right scale where lines are to be drawn.

4. Line up triangle or ruler with matching "X" marks.

5. Draw lines from left to right.

FIGURE 6-7

PLOT ACROSS

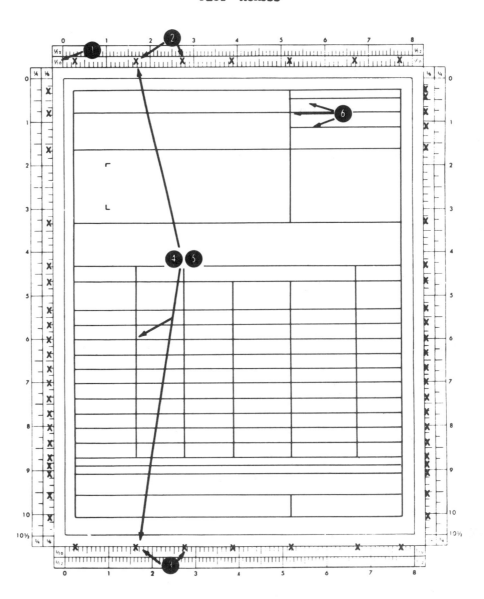

1 Use scale at top of guide sheet.

2 Count off space across in accordance with final measurements on rough draft (i.e., Step 3).

3 Place an "X" on tenth mark on top and bottom scale where lines are to be drawn.

4 Line up triangle or ruler with "X" marks.

5 Draw line to separate spaces into boxes or columns.

6 Draw horizontal lines which start from a vertical "line" and not left margin.

Courtesy of General Services Administration National Archives and Records Service Office of Records Management; Forms Design, Federal Stock Number 7610–753–4771; for sale by The Superintendent of Documents, U.S. Government Printing Office, Washington, D.C. 20402.

FIGURE 6-8

7

Forms as a Management Tool in Computer Center Operations

Forms are but symbols; we should never rest in them, but make them the stepping stones to the good to which they point.

Nathaniel Emmons

For efficient management and control of computer center operations a variety of forms are required. This chapter identifies certain work functions of a typical computer center and provides a sampling of forms associated with the work functions. In some cases, a narrative is given to explain the work function and the purpose of the forms.

EDP forms perform a vital role. They provide the means for coordinating the EDP and the computer center operations. Forms are used by analysts and programmers to get information to keypunch operations, job setup clerks, and computer operators for processing and running jobs. EDP forms are used by computer operators, clerks, and keypunch operators to get needed information and problem items to programmers, analysts, and EDP managers.

EDP forms are an indispensable item in an EDP operation. They collect and transmit important information. They provide a compact and clear record of various aspects of EDP operation. It would be impossible to manage an EDP organization efficiently without forms; but yet, there are some EDP operations where the only EDP forms that can be found are the code forms (sheets) and keypunch cards.

Because of the lack of emphasis placed on forms, many EDP managers find themselves devoured by an ever increasing number of reports explaining certain actions, or the results of no action by man, program or machine.

An EDP form is usually designed to ask questions, give instructions, and obtain information about a particular procedure or work function. Many factors of an EDP organization and the computer center operations will influence the need, the quantity, and design criteria for EDP forms.

MACHINE RUN RECORD

The console operator is usually responsible for running all jobs, obtaining and conditioning material and equipment for a run. He is normally responsible for input tapes, cards, and restarting the program after system failure.

An experienced operator is familiar with the various utility and application programs used in the system. To aid him in the understanding and recording of various job runs and conditions that may occur during a run, forms for console record keeping should be made available. The console record should be designed to provide, as a minimum, the following information:

- Which programs are run
- Job classification
- The programmer or custodian for the program
- The time when program started
- The time when program finished
- The elapsed time
- The equipment used—tape drive, disc drive, etc.
- Errors that occurred during runs, and reflected as program, equipment, or operator error.

A variety of forms may be devised to record information. The type of EDP operations and the type of information required by EDP management will dictate the form layout and the information needed. Two or more console record forms may be required to record this information. Figures 7-1, 7-2(a), and 7-2(b) are examples of console forms for record keeping. Information that is recorded on the console records is needed to audit previous runs and to determine:

- Lease charges
- Utilization of equipment
- Cost factors for user departments
- Type of errors that occur
- The frequency of an application program run
- The frequency of the use of a utility program to aid an application program
- Debug consideration
- Training requirements for operators
- Accuracy of job setup instructions and run manuals

In addition to the automatically printed error conditions and the console operator keyboard entries, and operator responses by the system, console records provide a continuous history of the activities of the system.

CATEGORI-ZATION CODE	JOB NO.	DEPARTMENT	SYSTEM	START TIME	FINISHED TIME	ELAPSED TIME	OPERATOR INITIALS	REMARKS

MACHINE RUN RECORD

DATE: PAGE OF PAGES

CATEGORIZATION CODES:

A PRODUCTION
B SCHEDULED MAINTENANCE
C NON-SCHEDULED MAINTENANCE
D MACHINE SET UP TIME

E OPERATOR TRAINING
F PROGRAMMER TRAINING
G DEMONSTRATION RUNS
H MAINTENANCE TESTING (HARDWARE)

I PROGRAM TESTING
J RERUN - MACHINE ERROR
K RERUN - OPERATOR ERROR
L RERUN - PROGRAMMER ERROR

FIGURE 7-1

Machine Run Record

SYSTEM LOG

MONTH _____ DAY _____ YEAR _____
      (1-2)   (3-4)   (5-6)

SYSTEM _____
         (7)

PAGE _____ OF _____

PROCESS TIME		CHG	TEST CØDE	JOB NAME	TAPE UNITS						9-TRK.	REMARKS
ON	OFF	CØDE			1	2	3	4	5	6	186	
8 9 10 11	14 15 16 17	20 21	24 25 26 27 28 29 30 31	34 35 36 37 38 39 40 41								

– RERUN CODES –
RO = RERUN OPERATOR   RI = RERUN INFORMATION
RK = RERUN KEYPUNCH/TAB   RS = RERUN SUPPORT/PLANNING
RC = RERUN CONTROL   RP = RERUN PROGRAM

– TEST CODE –
TAKEN FROM FORM 29

– LOST TIME CODES –
LO = LOST OTHER
LS = LOST SOFTWARE
LH = LOST HARDWARE

Figure 2

FIGURE 7-2(a)
System Log

FIGURE 7-2(b)

System Incident Log

MAGNETIC TAPE CONTROL FORMS

One of the problems of magnetic tape control is keeping track of tapes. Maintaining a tape library can be made easy and efficient if proper procedures and forms are used to catalog tapes and keep records of their use. In establishing control procedures and forms that will be compatible with the data processing system, certain judgments must be made as to the use of tapes and the number of tapes that will be required. The following information will aid in making those judgments.

· The amount of information to be contained in each input and output file
· The number of characters for each record
· The number of blocks for each file
· The number of tracks in a tape
· The number of bits per inch (BPI) in a tape
· The number of master history tape files required
· For each master history file, two extra reels of tapes are usually required for updating purposes; one reel would be written to as the update (new) master history file, the other reel is used as backup. The old master can then be used as a scratch tape.
· A few extra reels should be on hand for utility tapes for testing and for other program generation purposes.

As magnetic reels are received they should be assigned a serial number. Tapes should be assigned to the various programming sections and recycled through the library by the serial number. A schedule can then be worked out and forms designed to control the use and recycling of magnetic tapes.

Master history files may require several tape reels to contain the information pertaining to a given file. A separate form should be used to control each master file, as illustrated in Figure 7-3. This form contains a complete record of each master file beginning with the date of its creation. When a master file is updated a new form is filled out and the old file's reels may be returned to scratch condition for reissue.

A separate form should also be maintained for each reel, as illustrated in Figure 7-4. This form gives the historical use of each reel and the different files that each reel has been used with.

Another useful form for the control of magnetic tape is illustrated in Figure 7-5. This form can be used to keep track of scratch tapes. When a master file is updated, the old tape reels can be logged in on this form for release for other jobs.

Certain information recorded on magnetic tapes may be classified for confidential or restricted use. The use of such information can be accounted for and controlled by such forms as those illustrated in Figures 7-6(a), 7-6(b), and 7-6(c).

Another useful form that may be used in the control of magnetic tapes is illustrated in Figure 7-7. After a list is distributed periodically by the librarian to the various programming sections, identifying the tapes that each section is responsible for, the section supervisor selects the tapes he would like to have scratched and enters them on this form and returns it to the tape library.

Figure 7-8 is an illustration of a card layout for updating the tape index master.

FILE HISTORY	Page _____ of _____
Tape Library	File Name _____
	File Number _____

Date Written _____	Jobs Used On
Effective Date _____		
Retention Cycle _____		
Scratch Date _____		
Release Date _____		

Serial Number of Reels					Issued and Returned		
					To	Out	In
1							
5							
9							
13							
17							
21							
25							
29							
33							
37							
41							
45							
49							
53							

Reprint by permission from "Planning for an IBM Data Processing System," by International Business Machines Corporation (F20–6088–2).

FIGURE 7-3

File History Form

MICROFILM PROCESSING FORMS

Microfilming is becoming an effective peripheral support function of many data processing organizations. Some microfilming functions are under the control of a central

REEL HISTORY			REEL SERIAL NO. _____	
TAPE LIBRARY			Date Received: _____ Present Length: _____	
FILE	Reel, Of	Length of Reel	Remarks	

Reprint of Figure 7-4 and 7-5 by permission from "Planning for an IBM Data Processing System," by International Business Machines Corporation.

FIGURE 7-4

Reel History Form

TAPE LIBRARY Tapes Available as of This Date _____			
Reel Serial No.	Reissued To	Date	For Job

FIGURE 7-5

Tape Library Form

```
┌─────────────────────────────────────────────────────────────────────┐
│                  RESTRICTED COMPUTER OUTPUT CONTROL                   │
│                                                                       │
│ Computer Program Identification: _____   │
│                                                                       │
│ Data Set Identification: _____   │
│                                                                       │
│ Output To Be Used For: _____   │
│                                                                       │
│ _____    │
│                                                                       │
│ _____    │
│                                                                       │
│ No. of Copies Required: _____   Expected Retention Period: _____   │
│                                                                       │
│      Requested By: _____   Date: _____    │
│      Approved By:  _____   Date: _____    │
│                                                           Form 60-3/71│
└─────────────────────────────────────────────────────────────────────┘
```

FIGURE 7-6(a)

Restricted Computer Output Control

```
┌─────────────────────────────────────────────────────────────────────┐
│                  OUTPUT DISTRIBUTION AND DESTRUCTION                  │
│                 Distribution            │       Destruction           │
│ Copy  Signature of Recipient    Date    Signature of Recipient   Date │
│ ────  ─────────────────────    ────    ─────────────────────    ──── │
│ ────  ─────────────────────    ────    ─────────────────────    ──── │
│ ────  ─────────────────────    ────    ─────────────────────    ──── │
│ ────  ─────────────────────    ────    ─────────────────────    ──── │
│ ────  ─────────────────────    ────    ─────────────────────    ──── │
│ ────  ─────────────────────    ────    ─────────────────────    ──── │
│                                                           Form 61-3/71│
└─────────────────────────────────────────────────────────────────────┘
```

FIGURE 7-6(b)

Output Distribution and Destruction

```
┌─────────────────────────────────────────────────────────────────────┐
│                    STATUS OF OUTPUT NOT DESTROYED                     │
│ Date   Name of Contract              Status                          │
│ ────   ─────────────────    ──────────────────────────────────────  │
│ ────   ─────────────────    ──────────────────────────────────────  │
│ ────   ─────────────────    ──────────────────────────────────────  │
│ ────   ─────────────────    ──────────────────────────────────────  │
│ ────   ─────────────────    ──────────────────────────────────────  │
│ ────   ─────────────────    ──────────────────────────────────────  │
│ ────   ─────────────────    ──────────────────────────────────────  │
│                                                           Form 62-3/71│
└─────────────────────────────────────────────────────────────────────┘
```

FIGURE 7-6(c)

Status of Output Not Destroyed

TAPES TO BE SCRATCHED		
Serial Number	Data Set/Job Name	Creation Date
Programming Group Supvr.		Date

FIGURE 7-7

Tapes to Be Scratched

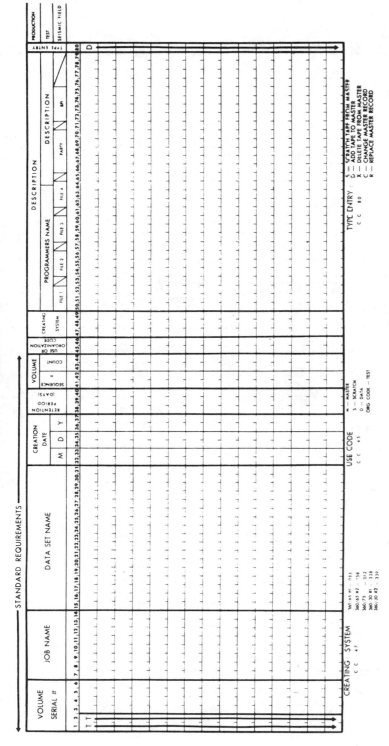

FIGURE 7-8

Update Card for Volume Index Master

computer, e.g., Computer Output Microfilm(COM). Others are manual processing functions using off-line devices for filming, developing, copying, and installing film in cartridge assemblies. As in other EDP support functions, certain forms are required. Figures 7-9 and 7-10 are useful forms for microfilming.

MICROFILM REQUEST						
JOB NAME		JOB ACCT NO.			DATE	
PRIORITY		PREPARED BY			GROUP CODE	
DESCRIPTION:						
TAPE IDENTIFICATION	Serial Number	BPI	Serial Number	BPI	Serial Number	BPI
CAMERA SETTING	NORMAL ☐		LIGHT ☐		DARK ☐	
FORM INTENSITY	NORMAL ☐		LIGHT ☐		DARK ☐	
TUBE ROTATION	DEGREES			EXPAND IMAGE		
	-90	0	+90	Yes	No	
OUTPUT DISPOSITION	NAME			LOCATION		
USER COMMENTS						
OPERATOR COMMENTS						

FIGURE 7-9

Microfilm Request

MICROFILM LOG

PAGE _____ OF _____

MONTH ___ (CC 1-2)   DAY ___ (CC 3-4)   YEAR ___ (CC 5-6)

SYSTEM ___ (CC 31)

PROCESS TIME		RE RUN		PROJECT	SUB PROJECT	JOB NAME	JOB ACCTG. NUMBER	FRAMES				REEL NUMBERS - REMARKS
ON	OFF	PGM	H/W OPR.					16MM	35 MM	HARD COPY	TOTAL	
10,11,12,13		17,18	17,18	17,18	19,20	21	22,23,24,25,26	27,28,29	30,31,32,33,34,35,36,37,38,39	40,41,42,43,44,45,46,47,48,49,50,51	52,53,54,55,56,57,58,59,60,61	62,63,64,65,66,67,68,69,70,71	

INSTRUCTIONS: OBTAIN JOB ACCOUNTING NUMBER FROM SET-UP INSTRUCTIONS OR T.P. MESSAGES.

FIGURE 7-10

Microfilm Log

SYSTEM DATA MODIFICATION FORMS

Certain forms are needed for requesting and recording modifications to data bases, such as data files, data sets and program libraries. System data modifications normally involve additions, replacements or changes to data bases. The person seeking modification should document the problem and give reasons for the change. He should also provide test procedures and other special instructions, if required, for testing and implementing the modification. Figures 7-11, 7-12, and 7-13 are useful forms of this process.

REQUEST FOR SYSTEM MODIFICATION					
REQUEST BY	DIVISION OR GROUP	SYSTEM	APPLICATION		DATE
DATE MODIFICATION REQ'D		OS RELEASE OR VERSION NO.	NAME OF DATA SET MODIFIED		
MO	DAY	TIME			
MEMBER ADDED ☐ REPLACED ☐ CHANGED ☐ OTHER ☐ (Specify)					
NAME(S) OF MEMBER AFFECTED:					
REASON FOR MODIFICATION:					
CAN MODIFICATION BE PROCESSED UNDER CONTROL OF OS?: yes ☐ no ☐ OTHER ☐ (Specify):					
JCL FOR MODIFICATION PREPARED BY:					
METHOD OF TESTING: NORMAL ☐ SPECIAL TEST ☐ OTHER ☐ (Specify)					
REMARKS:					

FIGURE 7-11

Request for System Modification

JOB-PROCESSING FORMS

Processing jobs requires a variety of forms. For the control of a job from the time computer services are requested to the time it passes through Keypunch, Schedule and Job Control, etc., and to the disposition of the job output, an array of forms are needed.

SYSTEM MODIFICATION
-Request and Results-

DATE: ____________

MODIFICATION REQUESTED BY: ____________

DATE REQ'D FOR IMPLEMENTATION: ____________

FIX CODES: VERSION (V)
E = EMFT
C = SHR CATALOG
S = SOCO, INCL RJE
V = VAR ISAM
M = MVT

TYPE (T)
1 = LINK EDIT
2 = SUPERZAP
3 = ASSEMBLY & LINK
4 = UTILITY PROGRAM
5 = PRE-SYSGEN

MOD. CAN BE PROCESSED UNDER CT'L OF OP. SYS.: __ ☐
HANDLING OF MODIFICATION: ROUTINE __ ☐ SPECIAL __ ☐
IF SPECIAL, SEE REVERSE SIDE ____________ ☐

CARD SEQ NO		Pre-Fix LTR	MODIFICATION NO.		DATE APPLIED YY MM DD		DATA SET NAME		MEMBER OR CSECT		FIX CODES VERSION	FIX CODES TYPE		COMP SYS NO		SUPERCEDING MOD NO		PRECEEDING MOD NO	COMMENTS (GENERAL AREA OF FIX)
1 2 3	4	5	6 7 8 9 10	11	12 13 14 15 16 17	18	19 20 21 22 23 24 25 26	27	28 29 30 31 32 33 34 35	36	37	38	39	40 41 42	43	44 45 46 47 48	49	50 51 52 53 54	55 56 57 58 59 60 61 62 63 64 65 66 67 68 69 70 71 72 73 74 75 76 77 78 79 80

MODIFICATION APPLIED BY: ____________ MODIFICATION CHECKED BY: ____________ DATE: ____________ TIME: ____________

MODIFICATION SUCESSFUL ? YES ☐ NO ☐ IF NOT, WHY? ____________

FIGURE 7-12

System Modification—Requests and Results

SYSTEM MODIFICATION LOG

JULIAN DATE	START TIME	SYSTEM (NUMERIC CODE)	TYPE CODE	JOB NAME	MODIFICATION NUMBER	VOLUME SERIAL BUFFED	BUFFED TO TAPE VOLUME SERIAL NO.	VOLUME SERIAL RESTORE	RESTORE TAPE VOLUME SERIAL NUMBER	PERSON RESPONSIBLE FOR MODIFICATION ENTRY	OPERATOR RESPONSIBILE FOR SYSTEM WHEN MODIFICATION MADE	ENTRY NUMBER	ENTRY REF.	R E P L
1 2 3 4	5 6 7 8	9 10 11 12	13 14 15	16 17 18 19 20 21 22 23	24 25 26 27 28	29 30 31 32	33 34 35 36 37 38	39 40 41 42	43 44 45 46 47	48 49 50 51 52 53 54 55 56 57 58	59 60 61 62 63 64 65 66 67 68 69 70 71 72	73 74 75 76	77 78 79	80

FIGURE 7-13

System Modification Lob

These forms are required to give instructions and obtain information concerning the handling and processing efforts associated with a job. Figures 7-14 through 7-22 are sample forms for this process.

PROGRAMMING CODE FORMS

A variety of forms are required to aid coding, card and record layout and flow-charting. The forms will vary depending on the language and the record and card layout arrangement of the user. Figures 7-23 through 7-29(b) illustrate certain forms to aid programming.

REQUEST FOR COMPUTING SERVICES

JOB INFORMATION:

(Include Job Name (if known), Job Description and reference to User Instructions, Instruction Letters, Statement, and other information as necessary to insure services requested.)

DATE:

☐ Keypunch

☐ Verify

☐ Reproduce

☐ Sort

☐ List

☐ Validity Check

☐ Decollate

☐ Burst

☐ Trim

☐ Other _____

USER IDENTIFICATION CODE

USER	CODE
Division or GO	
Department	
Section	
Operating Area	
Resp. District	

COPIES REQUIRED	ESTIMATED PROCESSING TIME	TIME		RETAIN WORK FILES	REQUESTED BY:
	COMPUTER: Minutes	DESIRED	REQUIRED	☐ YES ☐ NO	CO: _____ LOC: _____
		Hr ___ Date	Hr ___ Date	LENGTH OF TIME _____ DAYS	PHONE NO. _____

FIGURE 7-14

Request for Computing Services

KEYPUNCH AND VERIFICATION INSTRUCTIONS			
PREPARED BY	FORM NAME AND NO.		
DEPARTMENT	SECTION OR GROUP		
CARD FORM	DISPOSITION OF CARDS		
DATE	PAGE OF		
NAME OF FIELD	COLUMNS FM	TO	REMARKS

FIGURE 7-15

Keypunch and Verification Instructions

KEYPUNCH TIME CARD									
Keypunch	Start	Stop	Acct No.	Job No.	Cards	Date Month Day		Operator Initials or No.	
Verify	Start	Stop	Cards	Errors	Date Month Day		Operator Initials or No.	Supervisor Initials	
Remarks:									

FIGURE 7-16

Keypunch Time Card

JOB REQUEST							
SUBMITTER	PHONE NO	GROUP		DISPOSITION	MONTH DAY YEAR		EST. TIME
JOB PRIORITY		JOB NAME	DEPARTMENT		JOB CLASS		
SPECIAL INSTRUCTIONS YES NO			JOB TYPE		SYSTEM REQUIRED		DEVICE TYPE REQUIRED
FORM 99 ATTACHED?			NON SET-UP		M-30		7 TRACK TAPE
RESTART ALLOWED?			SEP-UP		M-55		9 TRACK TAPE
FORM 87 ATTACHED?			SYSTEM MAINTENANCE		M-65		2321 DATA CELL
PUNCHOUT EXPECTED?			PRODUCTION		M-75		2314 DISC PACK
AUTO CODER COMPILE?							
SYSOUT CLASSES				AUTHORITY			

FIGURE 7-17

Job Request

JOB INPUT REQUIREMENT					
SUBMITTER	LOCATION		DATE		PAGE OF
STEP NAME	DATA SET NAME	DEVICE TYPE OR UNIT	VOLUME/TAPE SERIAL NO.	DISPOSITION/DESCRIPTION INSTRUCTION	
CONSOLE REPLY:					
SUBMITTER'S COMMENTS:					

FIGURE 7-18

Job Input Requirement

OUTPUT JOB REQUIREMENT									
JOB NAME		GROUP/DIVISION CODE					ESTIMATED TIME		
PRIORITY		RESTART ALLOWED					DATE	PAGE OF	
DATA SET NAME	OUTPUT FUNCTION	FORM		COPIES	CARRIAGE LOOP	ALIGNMENT INSTRUCTIONS		TAPE	
		STD.	SPECI- AL NO.					DISPOSI- TION	DENSITY
DISPOSITION OF OUTPUT									
DISPOSITION OF OUTPUT									
DISPOSITION OF OUTPUT									
DISPOSITION OF OUTPUT									
DISPOSITION OF OUTPUT									
DISPOSITION OF OUTPUT									
DISPOSITION OF OUTPUT									
SYSOUT CLASSES									
OPERATOR's COMMENTS:									

FIGURE 7-19

Output Job Requirement

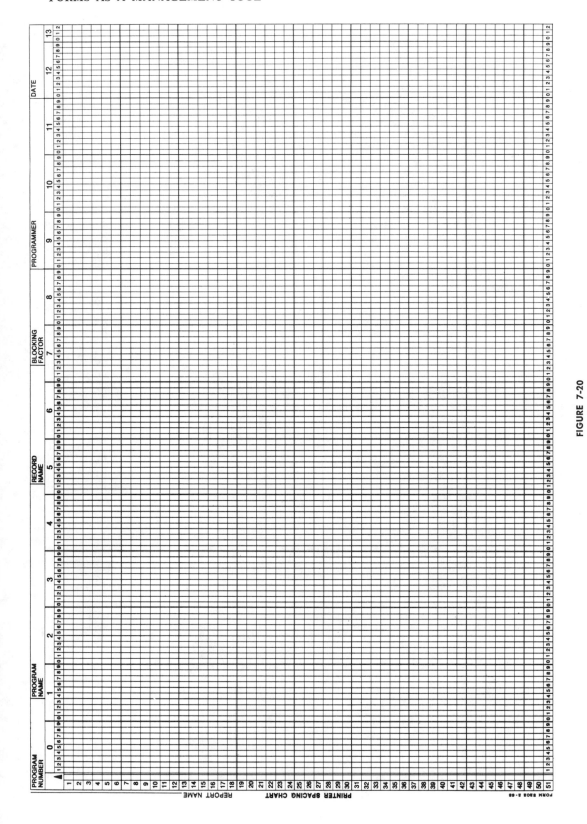

FIGURE 7-20

Printer Spacing Chart

COMPUTER OUTPUT DATA SHEET

Effective Date _____   Computer Job No. _____

COMPUTER JOB NAME _____
FREQUENCY _____ RELEASE DATE _____
REFERENCES: (1) _____ (2) _____ (3) _____
CONTACT _____
PRINTED ON FORM NO. _____ NUMBER OF COPIES _____
PROCESSING: DECOLLATE ☐; BURST ☐; TRIM ☐ R ☐ L; OTHER (SPECIFY) _____
SPECIAL INSTRUCTIONS: _____

DISTRIBUTION DATA — COMPUTER SECTION								RELEASED (Date)
					Recipient			
Div.	Dist.	Area	(Other)	Copy	Title		Location	

	19 ___
J	
F	
M	
A	
M	
J	
J	
A	
S	
O	
N	
D	
	19 ___
J	
F	
M	
A	
M	
J	
J	
A	
S	
O	
N	
D	
	19 ___
J	
F	
M	
A	
M	
J	
J	
A	
S	
O	
N	
D	

Remarks _____
Authorized By _____ Date _____
Issued by Bulletin No. _____

FIGURE 7-21

Computer Output Data Sheet

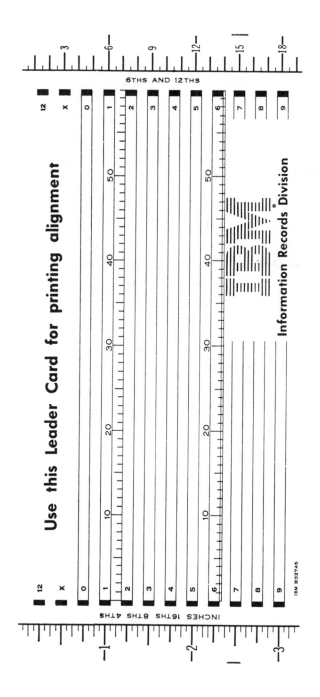

Reprint by permission from International Business Machines Corporation.

FIGURE 7-22

FIGURE 7-23

Card Layout Worksheet

RECORD NAME

PROGRAM NAME

PROGRAM NUMBER

FILE DESCRIPTION LIBRARY NO.

PAGE OF

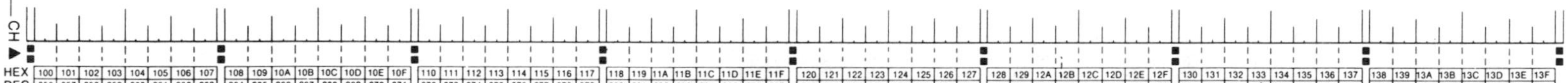

DATE

BYTES	HEX	DEC	HEX	DEC	HEX	DEC
8 — double word	00	0	400	1024	800	2048
4 — word	100	256	500	1280	900	2304
2 — halfword	200	512	600	1536	A00	2560
1 — 2 packed-decimal digits	300	768	700	1792	B00	2816
			C00	3072		
			D00	3328		
			E00	3584		
			F00	3840		

CHARACTERISTIC CODES ▶

C — character, 8-bit code
X — hexadecimal, 4-bit code
B — binary
F — fixed-point, full word
H — fixed-point, halfword
E — floating-point, full word
D — floating-point, double word
P — packed decimal
Z — zoned decimal
A — address value, full word
Y — address value, halfword
V — address, external symbol
S — address, base displacement

FIGURE 7-24

Record Layout Worksheet

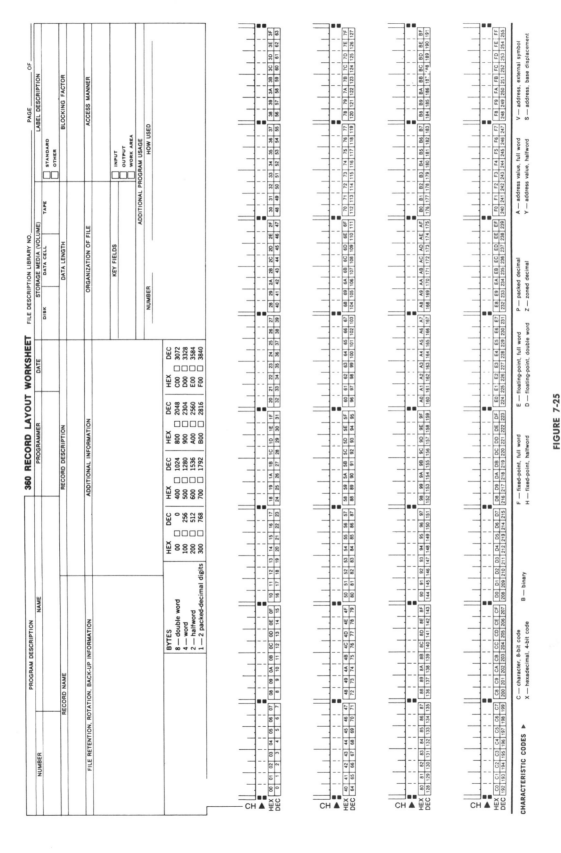

FIGURE 7-25

360 Record Layout Worksheet

		A	B	C	D	E	F	G	H	J	K	L	M	N	P	R	S	T	V	W

FLOWCHART LOGIC LAYOUT

PROGRAM NAME (TITLE)   PROGRAM INTERNAL NAME (MNEMONIC)   PAGE   OF

SYSTEM   APPLICATION   PROGRAMMER   DATE   REVISION DATE

A

B

C

D

E

F

G

H

I

J

K

L

M

N

O

P

Q

R

S

T

U

V

W

X

Y

(An illustration of a flowchart logic layout form with alpha coordinates to identify each symbol as discussed in Chapter Two)

FIGURE 7-26

Flowchart Logic Layout

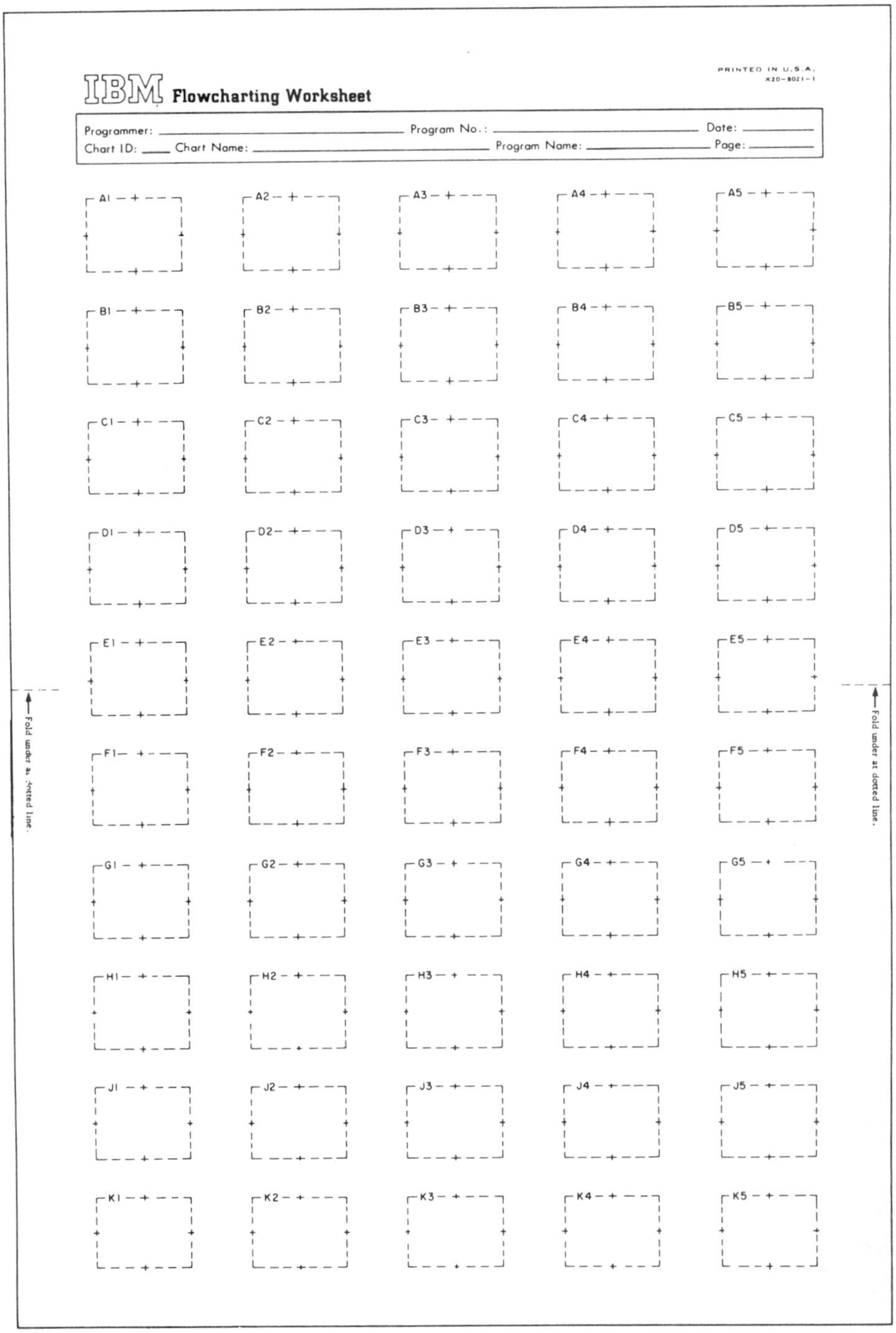
IBM Flowcharting Worksheet

PRINTED IN U.S.A.
X20-8021-1

Programmer: ____ Program No.: ____ Date: ____
Chart ID: ____ Chart Name: ____ Program Name: ____ Page: ____

A1 A2 A3 A4 A5
B1 B2 B3 B4 B5
C1 C2 C3 C4 C5
D1 D2 D3 D4 D5
E1 E2 E3 E4 E5
F1 F2 F3 F4 F5
G1 G2 G3 G4 G5
H1 H2 H3 H4 H5
J1 J2 J3 J4 J5
K1 K2 K3 K4 K5

Fold under at dotted line.
Fold under at dotted line.

Reprint by permission from Flowcharting Techniques (Form C20–8152), by International Business Machines Corporation.

FIGURE 7-27

Flowcharting Worksheet

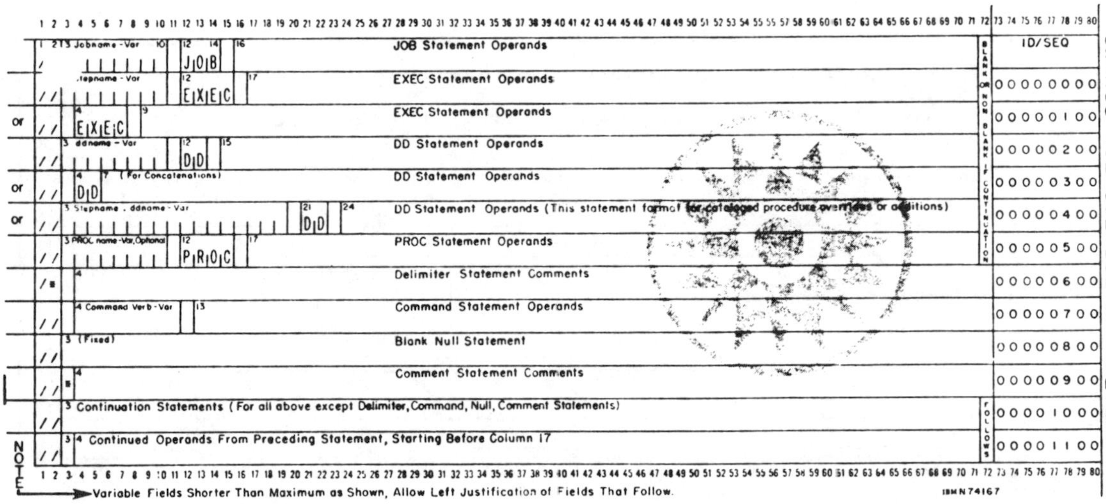

Reprint by permission from Standard Stock Card Formats by International Business Machines Corporation.

FIGURE 7-28(a)

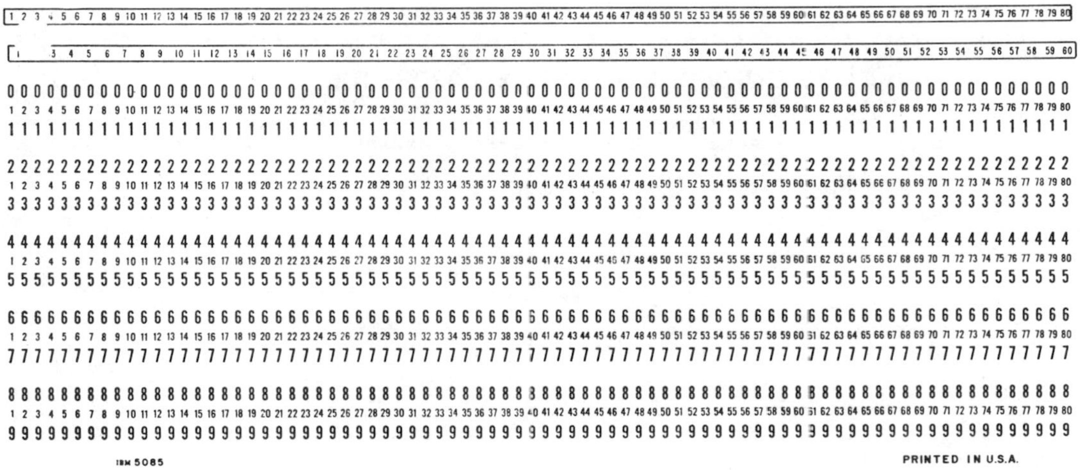

Reprint by permission from Standard Stock Card Formats by International Business Machines Corporation.

FIGURE 7-28(b)

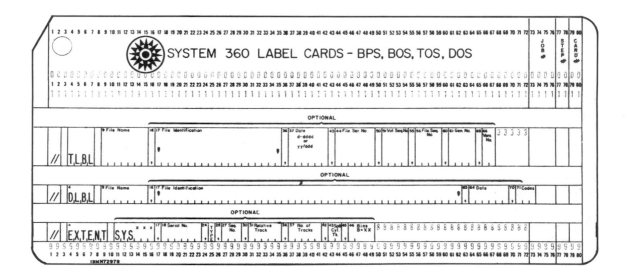

FIGURE 7-29(a)

FIGURE 7-29(b)

8

Organizing and Maintaining Data Processing Documentation Libraries

The great consulting room of a wise man is a library.

G. Dawson

Much duplication of programming efforts can be reduced when methods are used for conveniently saving past and current programs for instant recall and use. For documentation to be useful, an efficient means of making it known to EDP personnel must be established.

Techniques and experiences in public library cataloging and retrieval methods that have been developed over the years can be adapted to data processing libraries. These techniques have passed the test of time—they work.

Documentation libraries should be an essential function of a data processing organization. To be a successful depository for information, they must provide customers with needed data processing information in a form that can be immediately converted to a meaningful purpose. Documentation libraries must do this at reasonable speed and at minimal cost in equipment and personnel. The documentation library should be the focal point and the only source for recorded professional experience on which data processing personnel may rely for knowledge of previously developed systems and programming techniques.

The combination of narrative descriptions, program abstracts, flowcharts, manuals and other forms of documentation, if properly cataloged, can do more to further data processing techniques than any other single function of an electronic data processing system.

The filing system normally used, where a documentation library exists, is shelves or bookcases containing manuals, documents and computer listings, and file cabinets containing punched cards and other general documentation. The cataloging and retrieval of this material is a makeshift system. Manuals and bound documents are usually assigned a number and placed on a shelf or in a bookcase. The subject of the document and the number are usually recorded in a ledger book or on a card. Retrieval of these documents is by the number assigned to it. The system works; therefore one cannot argue against this method of filing and retrieving documents. But that is not the main purpose of a documentation library.

INDEX INFORMATION—NOT DOCUMENTS

The main purpose of the library should not be the depository of bound documents, punched cards, and program listings. The primary function should be the indexing and filing of pertinent documentation (information) generated in the pre-programming and program development of a system of programs. Usually, this information consists of programming analyses, flowcharts, program abstracts, and manuals. This documentation should be furnished to the library in a format that will aid cataloging, filing, and retrieval of this material to be used as off-the-shelf programs.

The trend in public libraries is to mechanize and automate the storage and retrieval of information and to make the library a place for study and research. To enhance the efficiency of data processing documentation libraries, and to make the library a specialized center for data processing information, the functions should be automated where economically possible. The method of updating documentation could be relegated to machines. Here is what Vannevar Bush said as far back as 1945 on the potential use of machines in library work.

> The repetitive processes of thought are not confined, however, to matters of arithmetic and statistics. In fact, every time one combines and records facts in accordance with established logical processes, the creative aspect of thinking is concerned only with the process to be employed and the manipulation thereafter is repetitive in nature and hence a fit matter to be relegated to the machine.[1]

Program Magnetic Library:

As programs are developed and documented, a method of cataloging and condensing the large bulk of external narrative as well as certain internal documentation into a more convenient method of storage for subsequent recall and use should be established to minimize program duplication.

This could be achieved by archiving current documentation on magnetic tape or disc packs or by microfilming.

Programs subject to frequent recall are best stored on magnetic tape or disc packs for four reasons:

---

[1] Joseph A. Becker and Robert M. Hayes, *Information Storage and Retrieval,* published by John Wiley and Sons, Inc., New York, N.Y., p. 40. Reprinted with permission, copyright © 1945, by the Atlantic Monthly Company, Boston, Mass.

1. The entire application program can be written out to tape or disc from main storage or from an external storage device.
2. As each program or routine is developed, the documentation material is available either on punched cards or in narrative form which can be keypunched or input via an optical character reader.
3. Tape or disc equipment would be readily available.
4. Approximately 40,000,000 bytes (alphanumeric characters) or 480,000 punched cards (240 boxes) can be stored on a 2,400 foot magnetic tape. (This does allow for record or tape gaps.) Disc packs can contain up to 30 million bytes per pack. Thus, one magnetic tape or disc pack can contain a large volume of documentation.

This library of programs would serve as both a historical record and a useful tool in developing subsequent programs. When a request for a new program is received, a catalog search could reveal a routine or program with similar operational features. Magnetic tapes or discs could be searched off-line, and the desired features of programs printed for review and comparison.

Various features, system concepts, and programming logic could be extracted, or an entire program modified to fit the user's request. This would save much programming time in system design and developing program logic for new programming requirements.

In its original form, EDP documentation would soon require too much time for a manual search for desired programming features, and would become too bulky to retain "on-the-shelf." The method of cataloging and indexing would be the key to the program library.

Perhaps the most convenient and fastest method of retrieving and updating programs could be accomplished by using visual display devices. Selected portions of the catalog, stored programs, and associated narrative documentation could be randomly retrieved, reviewed and modified. OCR equipment and CRT visual display units can be highly effective means of automating documentation updating, and are becoming increasingly popular as data input and visual inspection devices for EDP systems. If a program is to accomplish one function and then be discarded, documentation is not too important. But if the program is long lived, documentation and methods of updating must be considered as important as the software and hardware.

Documentation Reference Library:

This should be a must for any EDP organization. The Documentation Reference Library should be where all programming documentation (flowcharts and narrative), vendor's documents, and user-developed reference manuals are deposited. System feasibility studies, technical summaries, reports, and other bulky documents applicable to the hardware and the system's operations should be on file in the library. For many EDP systems, it may be more practical to combine the Program Library and the Documentation Reference Library into one Central Documentation Reference Library.

As a program or application system is developed, all documentation associated with the design, development and implementation of the program or system, including the test and acceptance documents, should be on file in the Central Documentation Reference Library. Individual programming sections may establish separate reference files for their own programs or those they are responsible for. These files may include the vendor's manuals for the equipment that the programs are run on.

If a Program Library is not established, and the Documentation Reference Library is to be the focal point for all documentation material, then a catalog system similar to the one discussed for the Program Library should be established for indexing and cross referencing.

An external numbering system should be devised to identify each programming feature, routine, or stand-alone program. This numbering system would be for library administrative and control purposes and could take several forms. For example: A program could be assigned a series of numbers to represent the Gregorian calendar, the date that a program was implemented, e.g., 092870; 09 is the month, 28 is the day, and 70 is the year. The Julian date could also be used to accomplish the same purpose, e.g., 31070; 310 is the day of the year and 70 is the year. (In both examples, the two digits to represent the century have been omitted.)

The identification number could also include the equipment configuration which is required to run the program. Example: U1108/31070—where U1108 is the nomenclature or trade name of the CPU, and 31070 is the Julian date.

Of course, the number would vary depending on the equipment and other naming convention the user may elect to use to externally identify programs. These are just two examples of a numbering system which would aid administrative library control of programs. The number, along with the subject of the program, could be assigned by the librarian after the program is developed and ready for implementation.

SETTING UP PROCEDURES FOR THE DOCUMENTATION LIBRARY

Thus far in this chapter, the discussion has been concerned only with the aspects of establishing a reference library, archiving and cataloging programs, as well as the general condition of certain EDP documentation libraries. In-house procedures for libraries will vary with EDP systems. However, procedures and methods discussed here, with some modifications, may be adapted to a given EDP organization in setting up documentation library procedures.

The function of the EDP library is to provide specialized information. This contrasts with a general public library in that the public library makes books available. The layout, cataloging, and indexing of EDP information to satisfy the demand for specialized information should be the primary concern of the EDP librarian.

As documentation is received in the library, certain administrative procedures are required to control and keep track of the documentation. These procedures should provide for recording, identifying, and filing the documentation in a simple and convenient manner. The filing method should aid retrieval of documentation for off-the-shelf program review.

As discussed in Chapter One, certain types of documentation are prepared during pre-programming and program development, and identified on the Documentation Checklist. In the case of user-developed programs, the subject or name of the program should be recorded and the program abstract, including the MACRO flowcharts and listing, should be assigned the same identifying code or number.

The program abstract, MACRO flowcharts and listing should be filed together. These three items would become a "program package" for off-the-shelf review. At this time a catalog listing containing a brief abstract, as discussed in Chapter One under "program abstracts," should be prepared, stating the purpose of the program. This catalog listing should contain the file number for the program. A copy of the catalog should be circulated in the EDP organization for programmer familiarization with existing programs.

As mentioned earlier in this chapter, the Documentation Reference Library should be the focal point for all documentation, including vendor manuals applicable to a given system. Usually, when a system is installed, the vendor will furnish sufficient manuals to cover the hardware and software characteristics of the system. The vendor will also provide a subscription service to provide new and updated manuals to the user.

As manuals are received from the vendor, they should be cataloged, placed in binders (or their equivalent) and arranged on shelves in a manner that will aid research and referencing. Manuals should be arranged in such a manner that the various subjective contents of a manual can be visibly identified.

To inform the user of new and revised manuals, some vendors provide a monthly library service in the form of a newsletter containing an accumulative index of current manuals. In addition to the accumulative index, printed updates to these documents are released periodically. Other vendors notify the user of current or updated manuals by reissuing revised manuals and attaching a listing of current manuals associated with a given system.

Vendor manuals may comprise most of the bound documentation contained in an EDP library. However, books, trade journals, and other publications relative to computer sciences should be available in the library. This type of literature is discussed later on in this chapter.

Arrangement and Display of Bound Documents:

Manuals received from the vendor are identified by a number and title. Manuals should be arranged by subjective contents and displayed as illustrated in Figures 8-1(a), 8-1(b), and 8-1(c). In large EDP libraries containing a large quantity of manuals, a color code system is helpful in readily identifying the manual and its subjective contents. For example: As manuals are displayed, each manual is separated with a divider card with a designated colored tab. The tab contains the manual number and subject title, identifying the contents of the manual.

Each color is associated with a series of manuals containing information on a particular subject category. Example: A green label may identify general information on a particular computer system; red may identify information on input/output devices;

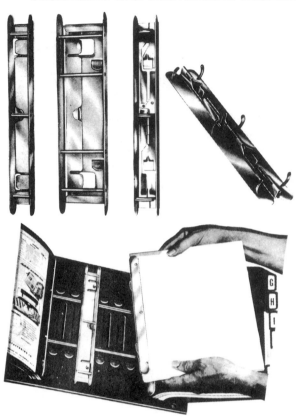

Figure 8-1(a) illustrates three- and four-ring sections suitable for containing EDP manuals. The ring sections are easily inserted and removed from the cabinet base. Figure 8-1(b) illustrates a cabinet base that can hold 20 one-inch ring sections (or manuals). The cabinet base comes in add-on sections, permitting the librarian to display a large number of manuals. Figure 8-1(c) illustrates a display of manuals. Courtesy of Master Products, 3181 14th Street, Los Angeles, Calif. 90023.

FIGURE 8-1(a)

FIGURE 8-1(b)

FIGURE 8-1(c)

amber may identify information on teleprocessing and physical planning specifications; yellow may identify information on a particular language, e.g., COBOL.

Users of the library usually know the general subject area of their interest. Without some type of visual indexing method to point them to a specific subject area, much time is spent searching through manuals.

A chart depicting the color code system can be prominently displayed, explaining the various color code combinations and how to locate a particular subject or document. By making the library a self-help system, the librarian can direct the user to his area of interest. The color code system will permit the individual to readily locate the information sought, with minimum assistance from the librarian.

The color code method also serves another vital purpose. It frees the EDP librarian from having to remember where the various categories of a given subject are filed. And too, it eliminates the need for the librarian to search for manuals for the user. Many people prefer to do their own searching, but appreciate a well-arranged library with guidelines pointing them to certain information. In large computer systems where the system is a 24-hour operation and the library is available during this period, programmers and operating personnel can use the library without the aid of the librarian.

An EDP library that is efficiently arranged, with the "information" indexed instead of documents, can save valuable time in locating and researching a particular subject. The physical arrangement of manuals should be conducive for research.

Library and office equipment vendors will provide catalogs and brochures identifying library equipment and suggesting certain types of equipment best suited for a given library for the display of books, manuals, or magazines. The figures in 8-1(a), (b), and (c) depict one type of equipment that this author has had experience with. It is ideal for displaying EDP manuals.

For best utilization, this equipment should be arranged on two levels. The first level should be at the "sit-down" level. The top or base of the sit-down level should be wide enough to allow for working space when researching a subject. Regular office tables are suitable for this level.

The second level should be arranged on the "stand-up" level. Again, the top or base of the second level should be wide enough to allow placing a scratch pad for writing. For the second (top) level, shelves affixed to the walls are recommended. To avoid blocking the light from the manuals on the first level, and to prevent bumping, the shelf should not protrude as far as the first level.

Inventory and Control of Documentation:

Two sets of manuals should be maintained in the library. One set should be displayed as discussed under the previous topic. This set should be the master set. The other set should be identified and indexed in the same manner as the "displayed set." The second set is for circulation and may be checked out on request.

The reason for the duplicated set of manuals is to provide a check-out service for office or home study, and to provide a permanent library reference of any manual available with a given EDP system. The circulation set should not be on display but may be filed in regular five-drawer file cabinets. The patrons of the library should not have direct access to these documents, but should obtain them through a check-out service provided by the librarian. A check-out card identifying the document should be contained with each document. When the document is checked out, sufficient information should be recorded on the card to identify the person, his room number and phone number.

Some computer vendor's subscription services permit the user to update their entire stock of manuals by submitting new manual requirements semi-annually. Through the subscription service, the vendor furnishes the user with any new manuals applicable to a particular system.

When new manuals are received, a memorandum containing a list of the manuals with a form "Request for Manuals" may be sent to the various programming sections identifying the new manuals. See Figure 8-2. Individuals wishing to obtain copies of the manuals may fill out the form and return it to the librarian. The subscription service provided by many vendors notifies the librarian of obsolete or superseded manuals through a monthly library newsletter. The librarian may notify the individual holders of obsolete manuals by a memo form (illustrated in Figure 8-3).

The Request for Manuals form may also be used for requesting manuals not available in the library but listed in the monthly service of the accumulative index for current manuals mentioned earlier.

One of the problems of a library is keeping track of who has what manual and the number of copies issued to an individual. Another problem is keeping track of manual orders.

One method of keeping track of who holds what manuals is to maintain a file on EAM cards of each individual and the number of manuals issued to that individual. This card file can be easily updated when a manual is added or removed from the individual's list (see Figure 8-4). Another method to identify holders of manuals is by an EAM card file identifying each manual by number and title, and the number of individuals holding that manual (see Figure 8-5).

In large systems where several hundred manuals are issued to a number of library subscribers, and an equal number of manuals are on file in the library, manually updating a card file for a printer listing can be a time-consuming task. In modern and efficiently managed EDP documentation libraries, software programs are written to handle this task. The manual subscriber file is maintained on magnetic tape or disc pack. Updates and listings are made by card input and job run instructions.

The software to handle the update and obtain printer listings for the manual subscriber file works similarly to the following: The updating is done by deleting selected names or manual numbers and making name and address changes. The name of each manual subscriber and the manual number are written on a workfile which can be sorted by name or manual number later in the job run. List of changes is produced as well as a new subscriber file. Depending on control cards used, the program may produce two listings: (1) a listing by subscriber name, giving manual number and title issued to an individual; and (2) a listing by the manual number and title, giving the name of each subscriber to that manual. Refer to Figure 8-4 and 8-5.

REQUEST FOR MANUALS					
Vendor	Manual Number	Quantity	Title/Subject of Manual	Requestor's	
				Name	Ext No

Manual Status
To be ☐ not to be ☐ placed on automatic update service
Signature of supervisor:　　　　　Date:　　　Ext No:
Remarks:

FIGURE 8-2

Request for Manuals

Keeping track of subscription orders for manuals, who requested them, and updating back orders for manuals can be efficiently maintained on an EAM card file. Transcribing information received on the Request for Manuals, as illustrated in Figure 8-2, onto punched cards, obtaining a listing and mailing a copy to the vendor will insure that current manuals are available to library users.

OBSOLETE REFERENCE MANUALS		
TO:	SECTION:	ROOM No:
The following manuals have become obsolete as announced in:		
Obsolete Manuals (list No.)	Superseded by manual (list No.)	
Librarian Signature:	Ext No:	Date:
Remarks:		

FIGURE 8-3

Obsolete Reference Manuals

Two card decks on manuals to be ordered should be punched. The initial punching of cards should contain the name of the requester. A listing of this deck should be made and retained in the librarian's files for distribution of manuals when the order arrives. The name of the requester should not be sent to the vendor.

```
TO:  OLSON J
     E 220


RE:  MANUAL SUBSCRIPTION

     BASE              TITLE

     A22-6810    SYSTEM SUMMARY                                              C000800
     A22-6821    PRINCIPLES OF OPERATION                                     0001100
     A22-7000    SYSTEM 370 PRINCIPLES OF OPERATION                          C005200
     C26-3756    ASSEMBLER (F) PROGRAMMERS GUIDE                             0026200
     C28-6514    ASSEMBLER LANGUAGE                                          0029900
     C28-6534    OS/360 INTRODUCTION                                         C030300
     C28-6535    CONCEPTS AND FACILITIES                                     C030400
     C28-6538    LINKAGE EDITOR                                              C030500
     C28-6539    JOB CONTROL LANGUAGE                                        0030600
     C28-6550    SYSTEM PROGRAMMERS GUIDE                                    0030900
     C28-6586    UTILITIES                                                   0031600
     C28-6628    SYSTEM CONTROL BLOCKS                                       C032300
     C28-6644    MASTER INDEX                                                0032700
     C28-6646    SUPERVISOR & DATA MANAGEMENT SERVICES                       0032800
     C28-6647    SUPERVISOR & DATA MANAGEMENT MACRO INSTRUCTIONS             0032900
     Y28-6658    MVT CONTROL PROG LOGIC PLM                                  0055300




TO:  REF LIBRARY
     E 209


RE:  MANUAL SUBSCRIPTION

     BASE              TITLE

     A21-9025    1442 N-1 & N-2 COMPONENT DESC                               0000100
     A21-9026    2501 MODEL B-1 & B-2                                        0000200
     A21-9027    2520 B1 B2 & B3 COMPONENT DESC                             0000300
     A21-9031    1231-N1 COMPONENT DESC & OPERATING PROCEDURES               0000400
     A21-9033    2540 COMP DESC & OPER PROCEDURES                            0000500
     A21-9081    1288 OPTICAL PAGE READER MODEL 1                            0000600
     A22-6810    SYSTEM SUMMARY                                              0000800
     A22-6813    MODEL 40 CONFIGURATOR                                       C000900
     A22-6814    MODEL 50 CONFIGURATOR                                       0001000
     A22-6821    PRINCIPLES OF OPERATION                                     0001100
     A22-6822    SYSTEM/360 BIBLIOGRAPHY                                     0001200
     A22-6823    INPUT/OUTPUT CONFIGURATIONS                                 0001300
     A22-6824    DATA COMMUNICATIONS & ACQUISITION CONFIGURATOR              0001400
     A22-6828    7340 HYPERTAPE DRIVE MOD 3                                  0001500
     A22-6843    INPUT/OUTPUT INTERFACE OEM                                  0001600
     A22-6844    2701 DATA ADAPTER UNIT OEM                                  0001700
     A22-6845    DIRECT CONTROL & EXTERNAL INTERRUPT FEATURES                0001800
     A22-6846    2702 TRANSMISSION CONTROL                                   0001900
     A22-6861    7340 MODEL 3 HYPERTAPE DRIVE                                0002000
     A22-6862    2400 MAGNETIC TAPE UNIT                                     0002100
     A22-6864    2701 DATA ADAPTER UNIT COMPONENT DESC                       0002200
     A22-6866    2400 SERIES MAG TAPE UNITS & 2816 SWITCHING UNIT            0002300
     A22-6868    1827 DATA CONTROL UNIT                                      0002400
     A22-6869    2361 CORE STORAGE ORIGINAL EQPT                             0002500
     A22-6872    1827 DATA CONTROL UNIT CONFIGURATOR                         0002600
     A22-6874    MODEL 44 CONFIGURATOR                                       0002700
     A22-6875    MODEL 44 FUNCTIONAL CHARACTERISTICS                         0002800
     A22-6877    1052 COMPONENT DESC & OPERATION GUIDE                       0002900
     A22-6881    MODEL 40 FUNCTIONAL CHARACTERISTICS                         0003000
     A22-6884    MODEL 65 FUNCTIONAL CHARACTERISTICS                         0003100
     A22-6887    MODEL 65 CONFIGURATOR                                       0003200
     A22-6888    MODEL 75 CONFIGURATOR                                       0003300
     A22-6889    MODEL 75 FUNCTIONAL CHARACTERISTICS                         0003400
     A22-6892    SPECIAL FEATURE - CHANNEL TO CHANNEL ADAPTER                0003500
     A22-6895    2301 DRUM STORAGE & 2820 STORAGE CONTROL                    0003600
     A22-6898    MODEL 50 FUNCTIONAL CHARACTERISTICS                         0003700
     A22-6906    POWER CONTROL INTERFACE                                     0003800
     A22-6907    MODEL 91 FUNCTIONAL CHARACTERISTICS                         0003900
     A22-6908    MODEL 50 OPERATING PROCEDURES                               0004000
     A22-6909    MODEL 75 OPERATING PROCEDURES                               0004100
     A22-6910    MODEL 44 OPERATING PROCEDURES                               0004200
     A22-6911    MODEL 40 OPERATING PROCEDURES                               0004300
     A22-6916    MODEL 85 FUNCTIONAL CHARACTERISTICS                         0004400
     A22-6920    MODEL 85 CONFIGURATOR                                       0004500
     A22-6927    MODEL 85 OPERATING PROCEDURES                               0004600
     A22-6935    SYS/370 MODEL 165 FUNCTIONAL CHAR                           0004700
     A22-6942    SYS/370 MODEL 155 CHANNEL CHAR                              0004800
     A22-6943    MODEL 195 FUNCTIONAL CHARACTERISTICS                        0004900
```

Figure 5

FIGURE 8-4

PRINTED IN U.S.A.   E-Z-READ ®   UARCO BUSINESS FORMS PARIS, TEN.

```
C26-3709   1130 DISK MONITOR SYSTEM INTRODUCTION          0024700

REF LIBRARY        E 209

C26-3715   BASIC FORTRAN IV LANGUAGE                      0024800

COX J              S 381
FINGERLE B         S 318
HARALSON H         N 656
LEWIS C (09)       E 413
LOONEY B           N 656
REF LIBRARY        E 209
WYATT B            N 201

C26-3717   1130 DMS VERSION 1 PROGRAMMING & OPERATORS GUIDE   0024900

LEWIS C            E 413

C26-3718   MULTIPROGRAMMING EXECUTIVE SYSTEM INTRO        0025000

GORDON J           N 656
LEWIS C (05)       E 413
LOONEY B           N 656
REF LIBRARY        E 209
WYATT B            N 201

C26-3720   1800 MULTIPROGRAMMING EXECUTIVE OPERATING SYS PROG GUIDE   0025100

DIVITTORIO N       S 318
FINGERLE B         S 318
GORDON J           N 656
HARALSON H         S 318
HOBBS V            E 413
LEWIS C (07)       N 656
LOONEY B           S 318
MAHON B            E 209
REF LIBRARY        S 381
TERHUNE B          N 201
WYATT B

C26-3723   TIME-SHARING EXECUTIVE SYS SUBROUTINE LIBRARY   0025200

GORDON J           N 656
LEWIS C            E 413
REF LIBRARY        E 209

C26-3724   1800 MULTIPROGRAMMING EXECUTIVE OPERATING SYS SUBROUTINE   0025300

DIVITTORIO N       S 318
```

FIGURE 8-5

Figure 6

A second deck, the order deck, should be made by duping the first deck but omitting the name field (Figure 8-6). A listing of this duped deck is sent to the vendor according to an agreed-upon procedure and schedule.

THE ROLE OF THE EDP LIBRARIAN

The librarian must have many qualities, one of the foremost of which is his or her ability to work with others. The users of the library usually develop a feeling about the librarian; one is friendly and the other is hostile. The librarian must demonstrate an aura of friendliness toward the library patrons.

The EDP librarian is supposed not only to educate users on how to locate information but also to let them know what is available in the library and to provide it as quickly as possible upon request. The librarian is in a position to know the titles and subjective contents of program documentation and manual contents. This is possible because the EDP library is relatively small in comparison to a public or company library.

The librarian establishes a close working relationship with library users, and soon gets to know the projects and area of programming responsibility of many individuals. Such close familiarity with the user and his work permits the librarian to direct him to the source material immediately. In some cases the librarian may be able to do the research and provide the information to the user.

Oftentimes the two may work together in researching the information. A close communication relationship between the librarian and the user permits them to augment their friendship through the joint research effort. When a friendly relationship exists between the librarian and the user "the problem of communication is thus eased considerably by making the communication [and research] process less formal and by allowing for more accurate and meaningful feedback from the library patron." [2]

In addition to the vendor-provided bound documents, the librarian may obtain certain literature for the EDP library from a wide range of sources. Catalogs listing the documents of federally financed research relating to computer science may be obtained from various national documentation centers. Such facilities as the Department of Defense (Defense Documentation Center, Arlington, Va.), the Atomic Energy Commission (Division of Technical Information Extension, Oak Ridge, Tenn.), the National Aeronautical and Space Administration (Scientific and Technical Information Division, Wash., D. C.), the Department of Commerce—Clearinghouse for Federal Scientific and Technical Information—Springfield, Va.), may have information relative to computer science that may be obtained free or for a nominal fee.

EDP trade journals, books, research and technical papers and reports relative to the EDP field should be obtained and displayed in the library. These items should be cataloged and controlled just as the other documentation that is contained in the

---

[2] William A. Katz, *Introduction to Reference Work,* Vol. II, Reference Services, copyright © 1969, by McGraw-Hill Book Company, New York, N.Y., p. 167.

00A06 0001	MANUAL & TNL	
00A00 0002	ORDER IS	
00A00 0003	UP-TO-DATE	
01A22-6846		08-03-71
01A22-6846		08-03-71
01A22-7000		08-03-71
01A26-1592		08-03-71
01A26-1592		08-03-71
01A27-3005		08-03-71
01A27-3005		08-03-71
01C26 3751	BACKORDERED	03-24-71
01C28-6380		07-13-71
01C28-6396		07-13-71
01C28-6396		07-13-71
01C28-6396		07-13-71
04C28-6396	1ACKORDERED	06-24-71
01C28-6396	BACKORDERED	06-24-71
01C28-6514		08-03-71
01C28-6535		08-03-71
01C28-6550		08-03-71
02C28-6550		07-21-71
01C28-6550		08-03-71
03C28-6551		07-21-71
01C28-6586		07-21-71
07C28-6628		07-21-71
C6C28-6631		07-21-71
C28-6631		07-21-71
01C28-6631		07-21-71
06C28-6631		07-21-71
01C28-6631		08-03-71
15C28-6646		07-21-71
15C28-6647		08-03-71
01C28-6647		08-03-71
01C28-6670		08-03-71
01C28-6691		08-03-71
01C28-6692		08-03-71
01C28-6698		07-21-71
C1C28-6698		07-21-71
01C28-6698		07-21-71
67C28-6703		07-21-71
01C28-6703		08-03-71
20C28-6703		08-03-71
20C28-6704		08-03-71
01C28-6704		08-03-71
01C28-6704		08-03-71

FIGURE 8-6

library. To inform the library users of these items, a list should be circulated periodically identifying these documents.

In the case of reports, book, and other related items, the librarian or another interested person should read the documents and prepare an abstract briefly stating what the documents are about and circulate the abstract to programming sections. Over a period of time, a catalog of abstracts can be compiled concerning this type of information. The catalog should identify the documents and where they are filed.

DOCUMENTATION MANAGEMENT AND PROGRAM CONTROL

To provide effective control and management for documentation applications, it is essential that a control group be established to supervise documentation development and maintenance. This group would also evaluate and act as the clearing house for all programming requirements, and monitor program implementation. The concepts discussed thus far cannot be effectively implemented without such a group to direct library activities and all aspects of program documentation management.

The control group should be the focal point where all documentation from the various programming sections is routed for review to insure that documentation standards and policy are complied with. All programming requests should also be routed to the control group for comparison with the program abstract and other documentation previously developed on programs. When a "match" is found, a task sheet (Figure 8-7) referencing the library documentation is attached to the programming request and sent to the programming section designated to do the programming.

The programming section could then check out the reference material, or print that portion of the documentation or program desired from the Program Library tape or disc. The programming section would then use this documentation, plus the originator's programming request, to prepare programming analysis studies and other software objectives for program development.

The control group would also serve as liaison between the departments or customers requesting computer services and the programming sections. Before a programming task is released to a programming section, the control group would insure that adequate user requirement documentation is available. Any question arising concerning the user's programming requirements would be referred to the control group rather than to the originator of the requirements.

The control group could also keep track of available resources (core, processor schedule time for debug testing, and job runs) and coordinate test acceptance and program implementation. When a program is modified, the responsible programming group would provide updated documentation to the control group. The control group would be responsible for updating the documentation stored on the program's machine records of the Program Library, or on file in the Document Reference Library. The control group would be responsible for communicating these changes to all other appropriate programming sections. It would remain the responsibility of each affected programming section to update any documentation on file in its office.

PROGRAM TASK SHEET		
Control Number:	Logged in Task Book No:	Date:
Program Name/Number:	System:	
Division:	Lead Analyst:	
Requesting Authority:	Completed Date:	
Estimated Completion Date:	Test and Acceptance Date:	

DOCUMENTATION AVAILABLE ON SIMILAR PROGRAM/SYSTEM		
Program Name/Number:	System:	Library File Number:

CHRONOLOGICAL STATUS
(Update Weekly/Monthly)   Page   of   Pages

FIGURE 8-7

Program Task Sheet

One centralized control group intimately familiar with systems and documentation principles would be in a better position to monitor the overall system and guard against duplication than several decentralized control groups located in each major programming section. In large systems, several individuals could make up the Central Control Group. The group would supervise the EDP technical writers (discussed in Part II of this book), and the Library functions. (An EDP technical writer working with the various programming sections would serve as the link between the control group and the programming sections.)

Finally, to insure that the control group does not become a bottleneck and delay programming projects, its function should be clearly defined. This group should evaluate programming requirements, establish standards and guidelines, and control procedures for documentation and program development. The control group should supervise and manage Library functions, and coordinate documentation between the various sections involved in the design, development, and maintenance of programs for an EDP system.

Program Modification:

Changes to on-going programs, or programs in the final stages of design, should be done in an orderly and coordinated manner. Procedures should be established to control the initiating, evaluating, and monitoring of program changes. Until a program is installed or in its final stages of design, few control measures are needed, other than debugging procedures which are established by the lead analyst.

Changes are inevitable and must be regarded as necessary. Changes to on-going programs must be controlled systematically and implemented on a regulated and supervised basis. Close control in this area is vital to avoid confusion and duplication of effort. But more importantly, it will guard against making arbitrary and uncoordinated changes to a program or system parameters. After changes are made, the affected internal and external (user) documentation must be updated.

When the program enters the final stage of design, changes should be frozen until the program is implemented. If the program requirements and design efforts are well thought out, only minor "convenient" changes that do not appreciably affect the functioning of the program may be desired. These changes should be postponed until a reassembly or recompiling is necessary.

A change request may be initiated by the EDP manager, analyst, programmer, or user. The need for a change may be caused by a number of factors. A change request as illustrated in Figure 8-8, or its equivalent, should be submitted to the Documentation Management and Control Group, giving reasons for the change.

The Control Group will review and coordinate the change with the EDP manager. Members of the Control Group, jointly with the EDP manager, lead analyst, and programmers of the affected program or system will consider the change. This committee will determine if the change should be made. If the change is not made, the initiator of the request should be notified as to the reason why the change was disapproved, e.g., unnecessary, undesirable, deferred for later discussion, etc. The reason should be brief —only one or two paragraphs long.

The committee, before approving or disallowing a program change, should consider the cost effectiveness of the change. Consideration should be given to the following questions:

- Will manpower be available for making the change?
- Can the change be installed within the allotted time frame?
- Can the change be effected without a prolonged down-time?
- Will the change affect the schedule completion date for the total project (for a program of system under final development)?
- What effect will the change have on the total system and the user?

REQUEST FOR PROGRAM MODIFICATION		
SYSTEM:		CHANGE REQUEST NO:
PROGRAM/ ROUTINE:		DATE CHANGE NEEDED:
SECTION/ DEPARTMENT:	SUBMITTED BY:	DATE REQUEST ISSUED:

REASON FOR CHANGE:

JUSTIFICATION FOR CHANGE:

MAN-MACHINE INTERFACE IMPLICATION:

GENERAL REMARKS:

FIGURE 8-8

Request for Program Modification

RECORD OF PROGRAM/SYSTEM CHANGES				
SYSTEM:				
PROGRAM/ROUTINE:				
USER:				
CHANGE NUMBER	TITLE OF PROGRAM/ROUTINE	DATE OF REQUEST	ACTION STATUS	DATE OF ACTION

ACTION STATUS LEGEND:

O = Open, pending disposition   I = Implemented
D = Deferred for later review   R = Rejected
A = Approved but not installed

FIGURE 8-9

Record of Program/System Changes

When a change is approved, a schedule for its implementation should be prepared and sent to the affected parties (including the initiator). The change should not be considered implemented until all associated documentation, particularly user documentation, is updated.

A summary of program changes to a particular system, identifying the program, should be recorded and maintained as part of the system documentation. Figure 8-9 suggests a log for recording program changes.[3]

---

[3] Portions of this chapter were extracted from an article "Documentation for Application Programming," written by William L. Harper, published in the September 1969 issue of *Modern Data,* Delta Publications, Inc., 3 Lockland Avenue, Framingham, Mass. 01701.

Documentation for Vendor-Provided Application Systems

If you want to converse with me, define your terms.

Voltaire

When a system is designed and installed by a contractor and turned over to the user for maintenance, the quality and type of documentation furnished by the contractor is critical. EDP managers must identify and specify the type and quantity of documentation for application programs that will be provided by the contractor.

Standards for the preparation of this documentation should be identified in the contract. Detailed specifications for each application program to include its function, structure, operating environment, constraints, data base organization, flowcharts, narrative description, and input and output data source should be specified.

Acceptance of this documentation by the user should depend upon the quality and completeness with which it describes, narratively and graphically, the general and detail technical structure and operational functions of the system. The description should be given in sufficient detail to define the design and development of each application program in order to permit easy modification by maintenance programmers.

A description of the program logic and data flow should be stated in narrative, figures, and equations, or a combination of all three. It should state the equation to be solved, the algorithm used, and other conditions required of each application program. This description should make reference to the appropriate flowcharts.

QUALITY OF VENDOR-PROVIDED DOCUMENTATION

The quality of documentation provided by contractors is more critical than documentation developed by the user. This is so because after the system is installed, its maintenance is left up to the user. And unless explicit documentation is available on the various application programs, maintenance programmers would have difficulty in tracing and isolating problems. It might require the recording of certain contractor-supplied programs. This could be very costly and disruptive for the EDP operations.

Training and familiarization with the various application programs would be awkward and in some cases impossible without redesigning and reprogramming. Computer operators, job set-up clerks, and other EDP personnel would have difficulty in understanding and running jobs and operating the equipment without clearly defined documentation.

Many of the documentation standards discussed in Chapter Two for user-developed application programs should be required of the vendor. However, standards and details for vendor-supplied documentation should be more explicit. The types of documentation, as appropriate, discussed in Chapter One should also be required of the contractor. The contractor should be required to supply to the user's satisfaction the following three areas of detailed documentation:

Program Technical Description:

This documentation should contain the technical description, including the structure and functional aspects and the organization of the data base, for each application program. The procedure for establishing and assigning symbolic names and the register assignment conventions used in each program should be identified. This information should be presented in a narrative and graphic form, as appropriate, to describe the mathematical description, timing requirements, and data manipulation required for operations and maintenance of the system.

Each application program should be narratively and graphically defined at a level of detail that will explain the design configuration and operational functions of the program. The program abstract as discussed in Chapter One could be modified to serve this purpose.

Operation Allocation of Functions:

The relationship of each application program should be specified. The sequencing of control, display of error message (console or video), and recovery procedures should be stated. Any options or other functional relationships, as appropriate, should be identified. Source and type of inputs and outputs associated with each application program should be given in quantitative terms, and the frequency of input or output should be stated.

Organization of Data Base:

The data base requirements should include quantitative description of the data, constants and parameters, and, when required, specify techniques necessary to convert constants and parameters into data that can be used by various programs of the system. Depending upon the design criteria of the system, the data base may be designed collectively or singularly for the application programs.

The data base should contain detailed definition of the contents and storage location of each file and table, and items contained in the data base. Each item within a file or table, and its storage location, should be identified. The contractor should provide a precise description of the layout of the file, table, and items of the data base. The following information on each factor should be given:

- *File Description:* A list of files that are contained in the data base should be provided, including the length of the file and its makeup, and a descriptive name for each file. The file address in storage and the number of tables contained in the file should be specified.
- *Table Description:* A list of tables that are contained in the data base should be furnished, including techniques for accessing the tables. The length of each table, its makeup, and a descriptive name should be required. The table address within the file and the number of words in the table should be given.
- *Item Description:* A list of all items contained in the data base should be required. For each item, the bit configuration (to include the most significant bit and number of bits), a descriptive name, and other appropriate information, as required, should be given. The location of the item within the table and the scaling factor, etc., if required, should be stated.

To aid training and familiarization with the data base configuration, a graphic presentation depicting the relationship of files, tables, and items should be required. The graphic portrayal of the file organization should be sufficiently detailed to identify the words in a block, records per block, items, bit allocation, etc., and type of table construction.

Interface Requirements:

A narrative and graphic presentation showing the functional interface areas and relationship between the equipment and the application programs should be provided. The documentation should specify the input and output requirements to include console communications and program-to-program interface boundaries and other requirements imposed upon the system.

Interface characteristics of the equipment should be given. This documentation should define core size, word size, access and interrupt methods, etc. The human and computer interactions that are required for system performance, including a time period for operator decision making and system response, should be stated.

The interface documentation should also identify other types of documentation, as applicable, that are external to the data base but required for system performance. This information may include, but is not limited to, the following:

· The source, format and content of all input data
· The destination, format and content of all output data
· A list of subroutines and other utility programs called by an application program
· A list of tables, records, constants and parameters, etc., external to the data base, but subject to access by an application program.

Flowcharts:

The user should demand from the contractor a certain series of various levels of flowcharts. The three levels of system flowcharts discussed earlier in Chapter Two should be required. The second and third level flowcharts are a vital area of contractor-supplied documentation.

This documentation should graphically portray the operations performed by the applications programs to the level of detail necessary to identify the functional entities and the processing steps, and sequence and relationship necessary to accept, process, and protect data while it is under the control of application programs.

The flowcharts should depict the following graphic, narrative, and symbolic information:

· A first-level flowchart or series of flowcharts, to diagram the overall data flow and identify the various applications programs and the hardware configuration associated with this data flow.
· A series of second-level flowcharts to identify the functions of each application program, including the source of input, general processing areas, the decision points, entrance and exit points for subroutines.
· A series of third-level flowcharts of each application program to depict the detail processing steps and procedures, and to identify the decision points and logic symbology required to satisfy each application.

Some EDP systems have relatively small data bases. For example, in a store and forward message switching system, they are usually referred to as tables. These tables contain the constants and parameters upon which certain predetermined "switching" arrangements are made. Other than the statistical and historical requirements, the "data" in a digital switching system are dynamic. That is, the data are the interchanges (switching) of messages among users of the system.

Contractor-provided documentation should be comprehensive and accurate, and referencing made easy. When documentation requirements for a large EDP system are too complex and bulky to be published and distributed in one bound volume, the documentation should be separated in individual binders. The material should be arranged by functional work elements. In discussing the material layout of documentation presentation, Chapter Five will give the user some idea as to how the documentation should be arranged and presented.

Operating Instructions:

The type of vendor documentation discussed thus far is concerned with *internal* documentation. Internal documentation is defined as that documentation which is system and programmer oriented, i.e., programming techniques, flowcharts, data description, data structure and organization, etc. This type of documentation concerns the action and interaction of programmer, software, and hardware.

Another important area of vendor documentation is *external* documentation. External documentation is defined as that documentation which is operations and operator, or clerical, oriented. This documentation is primarily narrative and is concerned with the day-to-day EDP operations—not programming.

The nature of the EDP system will dictate the type and quantity of external documentation provided by the vendor. The following is a representation of certain work functions of an EDP system for which the vendor should furnish operating procedures.

- Input data preparation (keypunch, TAB operation, job scheduling)
- Setting up and running of jobs
- Output data preparation (bursting and decollating)
- Input/output device assignment and scheduling
- Handling of tapes and disc packs
- Calling in and use of utility programs
- Internal and external labeling of tapes and disc packs
- Updating program tapes
- Identification and updating of data files
- Job accounting and run error correction
- Restart/recovery
- Console messages and codes, and operator responses

The manner and media in which external documentation is made available are of importance to the user. Much of the operating instructions and procedures mentioned in the twelve points above may be contained in an operations manual, as discussed in Chapter Five.

In addition to narrative procedures and instructions that are contained in manuals, certain EDP forms are needed to simplify and aid operating procedures, and to obtain information about certain work functions. The operation of an EDP organization is made cumbersome and inefficient without EDP forms. In some cases, a form which can be made self-explanatory may preclude the need for lengthy narrative procedures, or narrative reports about particular work functions. EDP forms are discussed in Chapters Six and Seven.

ACCEPTANCE OF VENDOR-PROVIDED PROGRAMS

Before acceptance of a system of programs from the vendor, the user should require the vendor to validate the performance of the system by a test and evaluation demonstration. The purpose of the test is to verify the operational requirements as specified by the user. The test should be conducted on the user's operationally configured equipment. Programs turned over to the user without comprehensive testing and validation of the operational specifications may cause complete chaos for maintenance programmers and operating personnel when trying to implement and operate the system.

Some EDP systems require a more involved testing procedure than others. For example: The measurement of a successful test and evaluation of an on-line message switching system depends on many variables that are not present in a batch system. Errors in a batch system can be more easily detected and corrected than in an on-line system because of the nature of the two systems. In on-line systems, there are fewer stand-alone programs and subroutines. The majority of the programs must interface, process, and "pass on," and in some cases alter data, and perhaps do this at different core locations. This makes interfacing numerous interrelated programs extremely difficult, making in-depth testing a logical follow-through in vendor-supplied systems.

The vendor should be required to test the system on the user's in-house equipment. However, some systems may require, in addition to local equipment, remote equipment to simulate actual "live" conditions (Figure 9-1). This would be an ideal arrangement when local as well as remote input and output are required. In the case of a major modification, and when remote testing is required, unless part or all of the existing terminals can be made available for testing, additional communication lines and equipment will have to be installed to parallel the existing system.

When the vendor provides the programs, the user's personnel (programmers and operations analysts) should write the test criteria that will validate the operational aspects of the system. This does not include the following programmed test procedures:

- Program/Routine Test: This is a machine test of a completed program to discover errors in the program or malfunctions in hardware. These tests are usually built-in programmed checks and the results of these tests are compared with known results, or a test deck of sample data may be run to check certain software features of the program.
- Diagnostic Test: This is a programmed testing technique to detect malfunctions in a program or system. These diagnostic tests are designed to isolate malfunctions either ·as an operator, programmer, or hardware error. These progam-testing techniques are methods used by program designers to incorporate built-in software checks for trouble-shooting and debugging.

It is imperative that the vendor-supplied programs be tested against the actual conditions as specified in the user's specification requirements.

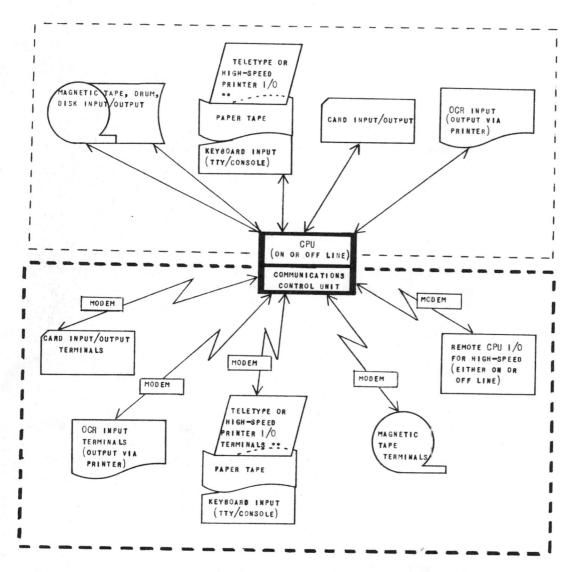

The hardware configuration will depend on the type of system and the type of I/O devices being used for data processing. Sufficient data should be entered on each I/O channel, having different characteristics, i.e., transmission codes, hardware, etc., to satisfy code conversion and validate data controls and other processing requirements.

Legend: Local testing using existing in-house equipment for Input/Output.

Remote testing using existing terminal lines or parallel lines and hardware made available for testing.

These hardcopy positions may be used for visual comparison of Input/Output test data.

Telecommunications lines, i.e., telegraph, voice, Broadband, etc.

FIGURE 9-1

Equipment Configuration for Testing

Saturation Testing: [1]

During testing, every condition should be simulated with specially prepared data to specifically test each programming feature. Some features, such as statistical requirements, throughput, and format and control will be fairly simple to validate. But restart/recovery, data accountability during system failure, and data storage and retrieval during system overload and channel outage will require more involved test procedures. To adequately test these features, the system should be saturated with sample data of all categories and the system purposely stalled and restarted to test all aspects of these features.

It is vital that the overload conditions be tested in an on-line system. This should be done by data saturation. The system should be designed so that overload occurs before the system becomes actually filled to capacity. Given a system of different data priorities and data classifications, and with perishable data, overload should be "triggered" when the storage capacity has reached 80 to 90%. This 20 to 10% leeway should leave sufficient space to process high priority and other urgent types of data.

To create an overload condition, more data will have to enter the system than the system is capable of handling. This can be accomplished by writing test data to magnetic tape, disc, or drum, and then reentering the data into the system simultaneously. If this is not practical, output channels and devices could be "shut down," which would create the same effect. When the system reaches this predetermined figure, the overload feature will activate and low priority data will be written to a "save" area (external storage device). When the system falls below this figure, data should automatically reenter the system and be queued for output processing.

Some errors may occur only once during testing but when repeating the process that seemed to have caused the error, the same error condition may not repeat. Many errors will have to work themselves out over a period of time. Some errors may be caused by hardware or line conditions; such errors may be infrequent due to random and low volume input.

The validity of the system may not be proven until it has been run on-line in a dynamic data processing environment. After the system has been tested and implemented, it should be under close scrutiny for a period of time by the vendor or vendor-trained user programmers, and an operations analyst. These individuals should be readily available to correct any software or operational problems that may arise. A system may test out successfully when dummy data are used in an off-line environment, but when run on-line under "live" conditions may experience difficulty. There are certain variables inherent in off-line testing that are not present in an on-line situation. In off-line testing, the input is calculated and controlled, and for the most part, testing is done at favorable times when the processing of live data is low and when the off-line

---

[1] William L. Harper, "The Remote World of Digital Switching," published in the March 15, 1971, issue of *Datamation;* reprinted with permission of *Datamation* ®, copyright, Technical Publishing Co., Barrington, Ill. 60010.

equipment is less likely to be seized for on-line use due to equipment problems with the primary system.

Problems encountered during test and evaluation, which necessitate software and operational changes, should be documented by the vendor and all affected software and operational documentation updated accordingly. Changes made in the system software specifications during testing and not adequately documented can cause frustrating problems long after the system is operational.

Cutover: Before the system is accepted from the vendor, operator training, if required, should be conducted by the vendor. This is necessary to familiarize operators with the peculiarities of the system. After acceptance of the system, it may be necessary to run the old system in parallel with the new system until sufficient confidence is built up with the new system. At this time, the old system may be disbanded.

To make for a smoother cutover, and to aid transition of system responsibility from vendor to user, a few user programmers should work with the vendor in the program design and coding efforts; otherwise, the services of the vendor's programmers may be required long after the system has been implemented. This is necessary for the user's maintenance programmers to "get on board" with the vendor- provided systems documentation.

TRANSITION OF PROGRAM MAINTENANCE FROM VENDOR TO USER

Good vendor-provided documentation of application programs eases the transitional task considerably. Adequate flowcharts, narrative descriptions, operator manuals, and maximum comments in the program listing aid maintenance programmers and operating personnel in the understanding of systems applications.

The user should require that the vendor-furnished documentation provide maintenance programmers with the necessary information needed to determine what and how application programs perform their intended function. If the quality of the documentation is not up to desired standards, it becomes difficult to determine the intent of a program.

A system of programs turned over to user programmers is not static. It will require periodic changes. Even though a system may have been installed and successfully operated for a period of time, certain changes will be required. The need for changes may occur immediately after assuming system responsibility from the vendor. Some of the reasons for immediate changes may be:

- Management's need for additional output of information
- Operational requirement to change input and output requirements or report formats, etc.
- Normal business changes brought about because of a new company policy, i.e., changes in inventory or product line, or discount and commission rate changes, etc.
- Changes due to additions or deletion of equipment.

· The need to increase, or enhance, the function and scope of an application program because of its marginal efficiency.

Such changes are usually not the fault of the vendor. Some stem primarily from unrealistic or unclear programming requirements as initially specified by the user. Others are required because of normal fluctuations in business conditions. When a system is installed and the documentation turned over and accepted by the user, the vendor is usually not concerned with or required to make modification to an on-going system. Documentation describing the program design, coding and operating instructions at each functional step of each application program should be an indispensable requirement levied on the vendor.

It is vital that EDP managers insist on quality documentation from the vendor. Clear and complete documentation will aid the EDP manager in:

· Providing training aids to serve as the communications media between the vendor and user programmers
· Establishing maintenance procedures and assigning responsibility for program maintenance
· Establishing good relations with other company departments requiring computer services, enabling these users to benefit from the vendor-provided system immediately without undue delay or difficulty due to program maintenance problems after installation of the system.

PART II

Documentation Preparation

10

The Role of the EDP Documentation Writer

Elegance of language may not be in the power of all of us, but simplicity and straightforwardness are.

William Cullen Bryant

Too many EDP managers require that programmers be as proficient in writing documentation as they are in systems design or coding. A programmer receives continuing schooling in the techniques of programming and systems work, but little if any training in EDP documentation writing. The programmer must follow certain rigid standards laid down by restraints of the manufacturer's hardware and syntax of the computer language to develop a program. There are no deviations from these restraints. They have been predetermined for him. However, there is no "perfect" or exact method that dictates how the logic will be developed for a program. The programmer is free to "think" as he chooses in creating the logic for a program, providing he stays within the restraints mentioned above.

An experienced programmer can trace and follow the internal documentation prepared by another programmer for a given program. But he may have difficulty interpreting the external documentation, or get a different meaning of what was written and how it may be used.

Without established rules and guidelines for writing documentation, most programmers will revert to their high school or college training on expository and creative writing. This simply is not good enough for EDP documentation writing.

The writer must describe accurately what has happened or will happen in a given process without personal feelings. This is not to imply that EDP technical writing should be dull. The facts, presentation, and content of the document should be clearly stated so the reader will be convinced by logical process instead of emotions.

The writer must be able to write on different levels and for different people. At times, he may write for managers with masters and doctors degrees, and at other times, he is required to write for computer operators, clerks, and even messengers, some of whom may be high school dropouts. The writer will be required to switch from "general announcement" type expository writing to a technical level on the capabilities and characteristics of the software and hardware of a given system.

The writer may be required to write two documents on the same subject at the same time, one in non-technical language (i.e., announcements or educational material for general employee consumption), the other in technical language (i.e., internal and external documentation for programmer and operator consumption). As an example, consider the automation of a company's payroll. A system is designed to convert from a manual to a computerized system. Software is developed and documentation written. This information is technical and for EDP personnel, but to inform company employees of the benefits of the new system and "how" it works, nontechnical information is needed.

The writer must understand the experience, position, and objective of the reader for whom a particular document is intended. Understanding of these factors is vital in determining the scope of presentation and the degree of detail that each document, memo or report, must contain.

The programmer should not be asked to fill both roles as programmer and documentation writer. He is ably trained for one but often ill equipped for the other. Documentation writing should be the function of EDP technical writers, who, by training or experience, are proficient at writing. The role of the EDP technical writer is to ease the documentation strain by making the unreadable readable and the unfamiliar familiar.

EDP INFORMATION EXPLOSION

The computer gave impetus to the technical information explosion that erupted in the decade of the 60's. Man now spends more time than ever before generating and interpreting this information. He also feeds more and more information to the computer, hoping to solve all our business problems.

Too often the printed (computer and man generated) solutions to these problems are bulky and full of irrelevant information that requires more time to be spent interpreting this data than is devoted to solving problems. If only relevant and essential information is entered, much of the information that is fed to the computer can be reduced and the printed output made more meaningful. EDP documentation quality controls are needed to guard against entering "polluted" information. Part of this control would be served by the use of EDP documentation writers.

The computer and other communication devices are only tools to facilitate and speed the flow of information for human consumption. The marshalling of this data so that only relevant information may be documented, entered and retrieved should be a prime concern for EDP managers. Unless the information is carefully planned, documented and edited before being published or computer processed, EDP personnel at all levels may be so inundated with information that they will have to spend considerable time sifting through irrelevant data to find the significant facts on which to base decisions.

IDENTIFYING AND SELECTING DOCUMENTATION WRITERS

Electronic Data Processing has its own terminology, scores of job titles, and a mystique unique to the computer field. Most people engaged in EDP work have the title of computer analyst, systems analyst, programmer, coder, operator, or supervisor/manager. Few people have the title of EDP Documentation Writer. There is a need for them. The logical source for recruitment of qualified individuals for this work is the EDP field.

There may be programmers who would prefer EDP technical writing rather than coding. They should be sought out and placed in writing positions. These individuals would require no EDP training other than brushing up on good technical writing habits. Their background in systems and programming techniques would make such individuals invaluable as EDP technical writers.

Unless the technical writer has a background in EDP systems, his services may be limited initially until he has obtained sufficient knowledge of EDP operations and understanding of programming techniques and concepts. However, he could easily train himself to write about the EDP operations in a clear and accurate manner because of his technical writing ability.

A technical writer obtained from another field may be adept at writing in his specialty but may find it difficult to write concisely and clearly without programmer training and considerable experience in computer operations. He could be trained to acquire the terminology and jargon sophistication of the programmer and communicate this in written documents because he is a writer.

With the continuing increase in EDP technology, coupled with a wider range of job specialization and computer applications, the EDP community is confronted with a documentation problem. Owing to the increasing complexity of computer science, a larger amount of EDP information is shared among more people with unrelated EDP experience. The flow of this information must be rationally controlled if managers hope to optimize EDP efficiency.

The flow could be rationalized and the quality of documentation improved by the effective use of EDP technical writers. The technical writer should work as a team member with programmers in developing documentation.

Much of the task of preparing documentation should be the responsibility of EDP technical writers. It is not necssary that EDP technical writers possess a degree or extensive programming experience, although college training and some programming experience are recommended. The technical writer should have an extensive background in EDP operations and demonstrate good English usage and ability to write logically and functionally.

The Function of the Documentation Writer: An EDP technical writer should be assigned to a programming section or project as a team member at its inception. The programmers would be responsible for developing the flowcharts, logic, input/output formulas, record layouts, data files, etc., to be used as internal documentation. The technical writers could assist in this documentation, but they would be primarily responsible for compiling, formatting, and organizing material for external documentation, e.g., reference manuals, reports and narrative summaries, and program abstracts needed by management and operations personnel to operate and maintain an EDP system.

By the nature of his training and experience, the EDP technical writer would be able to comprehend technical information presented to him, or observed by him. He would develop this information in easy-to-read documents. He is able to do this because he is a writer, adept in the technique of technical writing. Oftentimes, the programmer is not. By being part of the EDP environment, the technical writer could clearly and logically write about a subject he understands well. He would remove this administrative burden from the programmer.

The technical writer working with the programming staff would act as liaison and coordinator for the documentation development. He would be responsible for compiling, editing, and formatting external documentation at its source. He would provide the guidelines and controls necessary for quality documentation.

The technical writer's job is not to tell the programmer what he already knows. He is to record in straightforward and simple English what the programmer has accomplished and communicate this information accurately to others for immediate or historical use. The writer should let the facts and not his preconceptions guide him. In his research and fact gathering, he may start off in one direction and discover that he is on the wrong trail.

A technical writer's function is a difficult one. As he develops material, he must consult with analysts and programmers. Oftentimes, he will be required to reconstruct a large portion of his documentation. This is not easy. It takes time to write contradictory analysis and concepts in a document that has been developed carefully for its total effect. Like altering an old building, it may take more time than building a new one.

One of the most involved jobs about an EDP environment is planning, organizing and writing documentation for it. While in programming, the rules are laid out which must be followed. There are few EDP writing and documentation guidelines available to aid the technical writer.

Dick H. Brandon has this to say about the importance of documentation. "By far the most important long-range development function is the accurate documentation of all aspects of the job. Good documentation provides complete operating instructions to meet all possible conditions and complete program instructions, so that changes can be made independent of the person who created the program. Documentation takes place throughout all phases of the project. It is especially important during logical design, coding, and testing phases, where it is most often neglected." [1]

In EDP, the documentation writer is primarily concerned with writing about the

---

[1] Dick H. Brandon, *Management Standards for Data Processing,* copyright 1963 by Litton Educational Publishing Inc., reprint by permission of Van Nostrand Company, Inc., 450 W. 33rd Street, New York, N.Y. 10001, p. 12.

inner workings of computer language, which is comprised of alphanumeric and symbolic characters, and documentation on the use and control of the computer and its support functions. The support function includes keypunch, data management, job schedule and control, and computer terminal operations, etc. Instructions dealing with man-machine communications and preparation of input to the computer must be accurate and presented in concise and clear writing.

The EDP documentation writer will find himself involved in defining, compiling, and organizing the documentation for an EDP system. He may be completely responsible for this task. The documentation writer may require the assistance of other writers in preparing the documentation. The amount of time and staff required to create and maintain accurate documentation is justified when compared with the problems that can occur if proper attention is not given to system and program documentation.

The EDP documentation writer will be required to develop or to assist in developing documentation guidelines and standards for an EDP system. The writer may be asked to determine the amount and type of documentation that is needed for a given system. Insufficient documentation may require complete reprogramming when modification is required. On the other hand, too much documentation may prove to be burdensome and time consuming to maintain. With experience, the documentation writer will be able to judge just what and how much information should be documented to provide sufficient documentation to:

- accurately identify methods used and the function of the program or system;
- serve as the narrative and graphical communication link between programmers and operation personnel (users);
- aid program modification.

IDEA BROKERS FOR DOCUMENTATION REQUIREMENTS

An EDP documentation writer will lend stability and continuity to a programming project. Technical writers would become knowledgeable about programming and system developments in related areas. They could serve as "idea-brokers" for documentation requirements in the analysis and development of new programming projects. The technical writer would prove invaluable in establishing documentation standards or lending documentation continuity to programming projects. Max Gray and Keith R. London in their book *Documentation Standards,* published by Brandon/System Press, touched upon the turnover problem with programmers.

It is true that economic conditions and the "supply and demand" factor will affect the turnover problem, but it is unlikely that technical writers would be as nomadic as programmers. Although they may be working in the same EDP environment, their specialty is different. The tools (computer and language syntax) the programmer works with are manipulated the same way with the same EDP environment. If a programmer is proficient in one language and machine, e.g., COBOL/IBM 360, he would be equally proficient in the same system of another company, and could be productive immediately.

The technical writer would not. He would have to acquaint himself with the external documentation concepts and methods. External documentation requirements differ from system to system, while internal documentation, records and file layout for payroll data and the manipulation of the language to create this documentation are essentially the same, providing the same language and machine configuration are used.

The technical writer should not be apart from the activities he is to write about, and have information given to him in bits and pieces. He needs to be included in the discussions and meetings, and to be where the analysis and coding are being done. The technical writer must accurately describe the exact definitions, comparisons, and symbolic details as they relate to the internal and external documentation and the man-machine interrelations. He would be unable to do this if he were removed from the day-to-day details of the subject he is to write about.

Without an in-depth knowledge of the system in which he is to work, the EDP technical writer would be handicapped. He would fail to recognize some essential details and require more of the programmers' time in consultation. When technical information is obtained second or third hand, some essential facts will be lost in translation.

He should be a team member physically located where the action is taking place. He must be privy to all information and discussions concerning the subject so that he will understand the history and background in order to accurately and completely describe what he has observed.

Several benefits can be realized from having the EDP technical writers and programmers working together as a team:

- It would free the programmer from writing manuals, program abstracts, and narrative summaries and reports.
- Programmers could devote the greater part of their time to the logical aspects of programming.
- EDP technical writers require less formal and technical training and normally are less expensive to employ than experienced programmers.
- It would lend documentation stability and continuity to a programming project.
- External documentation would be available concurrently with the software and internal documentation.

All of these advantages are readily apparent except, perhaps, the last.

When the software and internal reference documentation are available before the external reference material, implementation will be precluded until manuals and operating instructions are available to enable the operator to run the various jobs and communicate with the computer.

POORLY PREPARED AND INADEQUATE DOCUMENTATION CAUSES MANY PROBLEMS

Too much EDP writing is replete with nonessential preliminaries and verbose writing which adds nothing to the meaning of what is being conveyed. Poor or inadequate documentation, ambigious statements, and incorrect facts that other people rely on to make their machines run cause a greater number of machine halts and disruption in data processing than management may realize.

Not only has new computer technology forced EDP personnel to write more, but the same personnel must spend more time than ever before reading in order to stay competent in the data processing profession. Too much of this time is spent reading and sifting through poorly written and loosely organized documentation.

James Martin stated in his book *Telecommunications and the Computer,* published by Prentice-Hall, "The number of documents an employee in the computer industry would like to read is going up by leaps and bounds. The first computer programmed by this author [Martin] had one manual of operations which contained all that had to be known about the machine. Then came the 'second generation' of computers, and before long there were the manuals that described parts of the software of the machine. Now we have the 'third generation.' The rack next to a typical test center computer has six feet of tightly packed manuals, and yet they are not complete." Using IBM's 360 System as an example, there are several hundred manuals involving the operations, software and hardware characteristics. In addition to the ever increasing documents published by vendors, the user generates an ever increasing number of documents.

There are numerous books written concerning technical writing, but for the most part, they do not serve the needs of the EDP documentation writer. They do not address the problem of writing, organizing and presenting EDP documentation.

The quality of the EDP technical writer's work can be improved and the quantity reduced by using good writing concepts. To aid the writer in this effort, management must specify and enforce documentation standards and good writing techniques.

Quality of Documentation: The concern for quality documentation is beginning to emerge in industry as well as in government. Quality documentation lends itself to off-the-shelf programs and a reduction in the programming staff. (How this can be done is discussed in Chapter One.)

The quality of documentation has not kept pace with that of the software and hardware furnished by vendors. The poor quality of documentation is attributed to:

- Bad writing habits.
- Lack of documentation standards and guidelines.
- Absence of qualified EDP technical writers.
- Programmers not having the time to devote to the administrative side of documentation.
- Programmers not "debugging" their logic prior to releasing to keypunch, or proofreading secretary's copy that others must interpret and keypunch. This is more prevalent in small interface programs, "patches," and Job Control Language (JCL).
- Lack of control over the use of EDP forms.
- Programmers' dislike for documentation.
- Programmers not having proper office environment conducive for writing or programming.

Much of the time that programmers spend developing external documentation can be cut down. Improvement in the quality, with a corresponding decrease in quantity, can be obtained if EDP documentation writers are employed to assume responsibility for external documentation, including the design and control of EDP forms.

It is not sufficient just to train technicians how to program. It is equally important to know *what* to program—and how to prevent this information from being lost in a maze of uncoordinated, irrelevant records and insignificant information.

Some of the potential for using computers to manage information is wasted because management gets too much information. Unless there are policies to censor and edit the information that enters the EDP system, management will be increasingly overloaded with "polluted" information that increases its workload without increasing efficiency. Too often we get too much of "other people's" information which clutters our mind. We don't have the time to think through or research the validity of our own logic.

AN EDP DOCUMENTATION/TECHNICAL WRITING STAFF

With the proliferation of data processing systems and the complexity of the equipment, coupled with the manufacturer's documents on the use of these systems, the user in turn generates more programming, operations, and management documentation. In the beginning one person may have been sufficient to cope with the documentation writing. This is not possible now. The trend is toward EDP technical writers.

Many individuals may be involved in writing documentation, internal and external, for large EDP systems. This writing is being done primarily by programmers. In a survey of documentation practices at several Federal Government agencies,[2] it was reported that in some EDP organizations program documentation other than actual "run books" was generally completed by system analysts designing the program. Run books were produced by the programmer implementing the program. Technical writers were not employed for purposes of program documentation, editing or review. EDP managers provided sufficient time to permit programmers and analysts to complete documentation to the level required by procedures.

Some programmers spent as much as 50% of their time writing and processing external documentation. Skilled programmers should not be required to spend this much time developing documentation. To do so is a misuse of their talents and becomes costly.

Mr. Arnold E. Keller, Editor-Publisher of BUSINESS AUTOMATION, revealed some interesting facts about the programmer's work habits in the December 1969 issue. Mr. Keller was reporting on information discovered in recent research studies conducted by Mr. Bob Propst [3] and his research associate Mike Wodka.

Mr. Propst reasoned that since the computer had generated new work tools, and a new breed of performers, such as programmers, the computer-related office offered

---

[2] Bernard E. Scott, et al, *Computer-Program Documentation Practices at Seven Federal Government Agencies,* prepared under contract to Computing Technology Inc., 26 Park Place, Paramus, N.J., for sale by the U.S. Department of Commerce, the Clearinghouse for Federal Scientific and Technical Information, Springfield, Va., 22151.

[3] Mr. Propst is Director of the Herman Miller Research Corp., a division of Herman Miller, Inc. Mr. Propst is an artist, sculptor, teacher and inventor. He has spent ten years in a study of office environment. His recent book is titled *The Office, A Facility Based on Change.*

a super model for investigating new environmental problems. He went on to say that a "saturation study" was needed to develop a total information spectrum about a programmer. Because the information had to be stable and unclouded by a major intrusion into the programmer's environment, the traditional time-motion study was ruled out.

By mounting a small camera in the corner of a programmer's office, Mr. Propst was able to do time lapse movie analysis plus post-analysis interview to clarify various situations and to ensure the accuracy of the information gathered by film. The chart in Figure 10-1 shows the amount of time the programmer spends doing various things during the time he spends in his office. (Note the amount of time that the programmer spends reading and writing.)

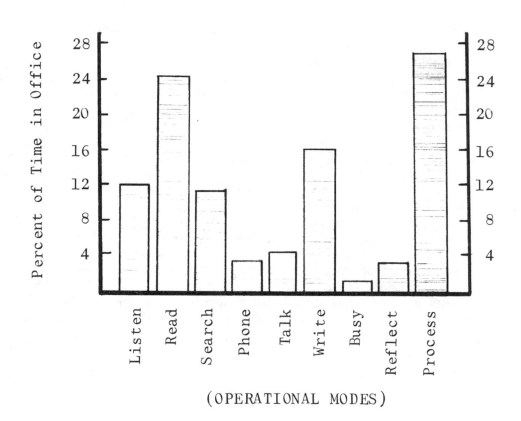

PROGRAMMER'S TIME/TASK DISTRIBUTION

(OPERATIONAL MODES)

Source: Business Automation, December 1969, Vol. 16, No. 12, published by Business Press International, Inc., 288 Park Avenue, West, Elmhurst, Ill. 60126.

FIGURE 10-1

Programmer's Time/Task Distribution

Due to the extraordinary growth in data processing systems, a large percent of EDP personnel are directly involved in the EDP support functions rather than the design, programming and maintenance of a system. These include administrators, EDP managers, computer operators, and other personnel removed from the details of programming. These personnel possess varying degrees of EDP knowledge and require EDP information written in a manner which they can understand.

In medium to large EDP systems, a staff of EDP technical writers should be employed for this task. In small systems, the documentation problems are small and a technical writer may not be needed. The monitoring of documentation practices may be handled by the lead programmer or the EDP supervisor. Appendix A is an example of a technical writer's job description.

A Case Study Supporting EDP Technical Writers:

In a documentation survey of several EDP organizations, the following observations were made: [4]

- The weakness in program documentation most frequently cited is the lack of good narrative description relating in clear English what the program functions are. . . . The generation of a clear prose statement of what a program does, how it relates to other programs in the system, etc., is something programmers as a group seem unable to provide; it is something that a technical writer could generate without having to be overly familiar with the details of program logic.
- If programmers as a group may be said to lack anything in the way of writing ability, it is the writer's special ability to empathize with the reader. . . .
- Programmers in general lack an essential ingredient necessary for high quality documentation—namely, the ability to write for the needs of others. The ability to empathize with the mind of the reader is what makes a good writer, and programmers are generally not good writers. There is, therefore, a built-in reason why program documentation, no matter what the documentation policy, will not be above a certain level of quality. This is particularly the case when it comes to descriptive, narrative materials. There are going to be ambiguities, inconsistencies, information gaps and the like in any documentation prepared by someone who lacks the writer's sense.

One of the questions that was asked in the above mentioned survey was: "Would the services of a technical writer be useful to programmers?" The table in Figure 10-2 reflects the response to this question. The organizational makeup, integrated vs. non-integrated, nature of applications, and documentation practices, to some degree, determined the type of response that was given.

---

[4] Scott, *loc cit.*

EDP ORGANIZATIONS

RESPONSE	AVERAGE	A	B	C	D1	D2	D3	E1	E2	F1	F2	F3	G1	G2
VERY MUCH	20%	0	12	44	0	0	14	10	40	0	0	53	50	17
SOMETIMES	37%	12	63	33	44	60	28	50	40	30	37	23	10	17
RARELY	37%	75	25	23	44	40	29	30	20	70	50	24	30	66
DON'T KNOW	5%	13	0	0	12	0	29	0	0	0	13	0	0	0
BLANK	1%	0	0	0	0	0	0	10	0	0	0	0	10	0

FIGURE 10-2

Programmer Responses to Question Concerning Usefulness of a Technical Writer

Source: Survey of Computer-Program Documentation Practices at Seven * Federal Government Agencies, by Bernard E. Scott, et al., Computing Technology Inc., 26 Park Place, Puramus, N.J.; for sale by the U.S. Department of Commerce, the Clearinghouse for Federal Scientific and Technical Information, Springfield, Va. 22151.

* Some of the agencies had more than one EDP organization. A total of thirteen EDP organizations were surveyed.

APPENDIX A

POSITION TITLE: EDP Technical Writer or EDP Documentation Writer

Summary:

- Collect, organize, format and write EDP documentation.
- Edit, review and approve the presentation of documentation.
- Establish criteria for documentation development, publishing and disseminating.
- Provide documentation guidance.
- Analyze and design EDP forms.
- Consult and liaison with the EDP manager, analysts and programmers to provide the necessary external documentation requirements.

Duties and Responsibilities:

The incumbent does the following: Compiles, edits, and formats external documentation. Writes (not determines) system design criteria, operational concepts and procedures. Establishes program control procedures and prepares implementation schedules. Assists the analyst and programmer in writing the test and acceptance (quality control) criteria and computer run procedures. Provides narrative update service for existing documentation. Performs analysis and writes feasibility studies, technical summaries, and reports concerning the progress and performance of system design, development, implementation, and operations.

Analyzes and interprets technical data contained in system specifications and user requirements and writes descriptions that can be clearly understood by the EDP manager, analysts, programmers, clerks, and computer operators. Establishes procedures for cataloging, filing, and retrieving documentation.

Participates in the company's engineering and system application design planning, including equipment requirement specifications. Prepares system specification documents for system development and the acquisition of EDP equipment.

Recommends documentation policy and standards to optimize programming efforts and minimize program duplication; standardizes terminology, record-keeping and documentation functions. Establishes documentation quality controls at various processing and preparation points to insure good documentation.

11

Planning and Organizing for Documentation Writing

The writer does the most who gives his reader the most knowledge, and takes from him the least time.

Sidney Smith

The hard part about writing is getting started. To start, the EDP technical writer must think about what he is going to write. The writer must be conditioned for writing. The conditioning plan is easier if a written plan is prepared.

If the writing assignment is small—just a few pages—then planning is not much of a problem. This type of writing would not require a detailed written plan. But, regardless of the length of the document, the writer can write a more meaningful document if he plans for the writing assignment. In short writing assignments, a mental plan may suffice. But in writing long documents, it would be difficult and time consuming to write without a plan.

Some writing assignments may be the revision and updating of existing manuals, documents, and technical papers. Planning in this case is just a matter of following the present format and topic outline of the documents. This type of writing is not too difficult as it does not demand much research or creative writing. When a technical writer is asked to write on a subject and no previous documentation is available, the writing assignment would be difficult without a detailed plan.

Planning is the key to clear writing, just as problem definition is the key factor preparatory to programming. The first ingredient for good planning is clear thinking. In order to think clearly, the technical writer must organize his thinking. The writer must dwell on what he is going to write. Thinking is an important process to clear writing.

The technical writer may find it necessary to think upon a subject for hours, or even days. He should get his ideas formulated in his mind before he attempts to put anything on paper. The writer should be mentally organized before he starts writing.

THE WRITING OBJECTIVE—THE OUTLINE

The best way to organize your thinking is to prepare a step-by-step topic outline designed to guide you systematically through the writing assignment. The technical writer should gather as much material as possible relating to the writing assignment and research the subject thoroughly. An outline will help to limit a subject and serve as a writing plan, just as the carpenter's blueprint serves as the building plan. The limits that are placed on the subject should depend on the purpose for writing the document and the needs of the reader. After the technical writer has pinpointed and limited his subject, he should ask himself the following questions:

- Is the document to direct others in performing a task?
- Is the document to inform?
- What am I trying to tell the reader?
- Who will read the document?
- What is the reader's background and experience?
- How much does he know about the subject?
- What is the reader's interest in the document?
- What order of writing sequence is best suited for the subject—chronological, spatial, or geographical?
- Should the paper be written in decreasing or increasing importance?
- What are my writing objectives?
- What information do I need from other sources?

After the writer has answered these questions, he should prepare his outline, which may be just a preliminary outline, the object of which is to get the writer started and in which he jots down the objectives of the writing assignment. As the first draft progresses and as more material is researched, the writer can alter his outline into its final form.

If the writing assignment is larger than a few pages, or is a difficult report to prepare, a conference with the supervisor may save time and changes later. A conference on the writing objectives is useful to the supervisor and to the writer. The supervisor can tell from the outline whether the writer understands the writing assignment; the writer will gain a clear idea of what is required.

The outline is a tool to keep the writer on the main track. It is only a working sketch and not a schematic. Its purpose is to keep the writing objectives before the writer. The writer may start at the ending or the middle or the beginning of the outline; he should not feel that he must follow what is on the outline in a rigid order. As the writer develops his draft, he may find himself writing on ideas or topics not listed on the outline. The outline should not hinder the creative flow of ideas. It is a guide: use it as a checklist to make sure that all topics are covered in a logical order.

The writer should keep the writing objectives before him during the writing assignment. This will prevent him from straying from the subject. By sticking to the writing plan and following the suggestions contained in the rest of this chapter, the technical writer will be able to produce a clearly written document.

GETTING STARTED

Getting started is the most difficult part of writing. If the writer has organized his material and prepared an outline well, getting started is just a matter of picking a topic —and starting to write. Start on the easiest topic of the outline. It is not necessary to start with the first topic. Pick the topic that you are most comfortable with at the moment. It may be the last topic or the third on the outline. After the first draft has been typed the topics can be realigned.

The main concern is to get started. If a writer's thinking is not organized, he will have a hard time getting started; he may make a dozen starts before he gets his first idea on paper. Organize your ideas in your mind and start writing. Write everything you know about that topic. Remember, this is the first draft of that topic. Let your thoughts pour forth onto the paper. Write fast. Do not worry about the grammar or punctuation—just write. These things will iron themselves out later in the writing process.

In the first draft, you should not worry about grammar or punctuation or paragraph and sub-paragraph structuring. If you pause to worry about the grammar or logical order of the writing, you may lose some valuable ideas that were ready to flow forth. Do not get *braincramped* while writing. Let your fingers suffer the agony—but write.

The writing assignment may require that you write an introduction. If you tackle the introduction first, you may be bogged down for hours. It may be better to write the introduction last. The writer will have a better idea of what the introduction should be after he has completed the first draft.

The main purpose of the introduction is to introduce the document and say something about it. The introduction should catch the reader's attention and create an interest in reading the document. The introduction may contain some background information.

Depending on the writing assignment, there are several ways of getting started:

- · A brief statement on the main ideas.
- · Your opinion on the subject.
- · Your solution to the problem.
- · A statement of the purpose for the document.
- · Your recommendation on the subject.
- · Background on the subject.

WRITE FOR YOURSELF

One of the most difficult problems of technical writing is trying to write like someone else thinks. Do not try to copy someone else's style of writing. Be yourself. Use simple, everyday language, and straight-forward writing. Write the way you talk— almost. There are several ways to correctly express an idea or write a sentence. The technical writer should develop his own writing style. Do *not* try to write the way the supervisor does. No two people think alike, nor do they write alike. A good supervisor knows this and will not insist upon it. But the informed supervisor should insist that the technical writer write in a clear, natural, straight-forward and factual manner.

LIMIT THE FIRST DRAFT

Do not try to do too much in the first draft. Leave the reviewing and polishing for later. If the writer tries to produce a final written piece with the first writing, he will find it frustrating. He will be jumping around in his writing, redrafting and relocating ideas and statements. He will be more concerned with grammar, clarity, and the logical order of his writing than he will be with the *free flow* of words and ideas.

It is unusual when a writer can turn out an acceptable written piece with the first writing. It is usually caught by the supervisor and returned for rewriting. After stopping the free flow of words and the trend of thought, the writer may forget what he wanted to write next. He will spend much time rereading what he has written, rewriting the paragraph or sentence, and consulting his outline—but he cannot recapture the words or idea. The perfectness of the words or ideas that are lost will cause him agonizing moments.

AVOID INTERRUPTIONS

The writer should avoid interruptions. If he does not have a private office, he should seek a quiet area for his writing. As anyone who writes, whether it be general correspondence or large documents, can attest, interruptions disrupt unity of writing by breaking the trend of thought.

Depending on the length of the interruptions, the writer may spend hours trying to pick up where he left off. If he is under pressure to complete a writing assignment, he should close the door to his office or seek the privacy of a closed office, asking that he not be disturbed and that his phone calls be held until the assignment is complete—or until he takes a break or quits for the day.

If the writer must pause, he should try to do so at the end of a paragraph and finish the paragraph with a transitional sentence. This will make it easier for him to pick up where he left off without too much hesitation.

REVISING

After the first draft is complete, the technical writer should not attempt to revise the draft immediately. This is not the time for him to be critical of his writing. He must give himself time to forget the writing process so he can be fair and objective in his reviewing process.

Reviewing and writing require different moods or frames of mind. Revising requires an objective and critical review. The writer should wait awhile before he starts to revise the draft. The length of the document and the writing experience of the individual should determine how long he waits before revising. If the document is short, the writer may wait only as long as it takes to have the draft typed, but if the document is long, he should wait overnight or over a weekend.

Revising is hard work. It requires patience and an objective approach. It must be reviewed diligently. Not only should the writer be in a different frame of mind for reviewing, but he should look at the draft through the *eyes* and *mind* of the reader. Some people are poor writers, not because they cannot write but because they will not revise. Writers should feel relieved and proud when they have finished the first draft. It took hard work to complete it. But in the first draft the writer poured out everything that he knew, and no doubt more than he should. The following sentence is an exercise in verbosity:

> The purpose of this is understood in that the assignment of an individual to a special project does cost the developing organization in time unavailable for its primary mission; however, this category of work should be handled conventionally as either unavailable time if the type of special project meets the criteria of the definition of unavailable time in AFM 25-5 or perhaps as some other category.

The writer of this sentence was not concerned with brevity. Had the writer been concerned with clarity and brevity, he would have condensed this 66-word sentence to something similar to the following:

> This is understood. A person assigned to a special project is not available for his primary duty. Special project work should be recorded as unavailable time, or as another category, as defined in AFM 25-5.

The rewrite consists of three short, but clear, sentences containing 34 words.

The key to improving your writing is revision. The time spent on revising and polishing is a matter of individual judgment. The technical writer should consider the reader rather than himself when making this judgment.

The art of writing is in condensing. Here the writer should strive for *clarity* and *brevity*. The technical writer who discards his own writing in search of clarity and brevity will soon discipline himself to the art of clear writing.

Much of our writing could be reduced, particularly government writing, if writers wrote in a clear, simple, brief, and direct way.

> In short, too much of writing fails to get its message across quickly and easily because the writer forgets his responsibility to the reader. The reader doesn't get meaning; instead, he gets GOBBLEDYGOOK. This catch word means that the writer uses:
>
> · Many words to say what could be said just as well in a few.
> · Unfamiliar words.

- Words of three or four syllables when simpler words would give the same idea.
- Jargon and trite, overworked phrases.
- Long and involved sentences.
- Foreign expressions.
- Jumbled, unrelated, illogical ideas.

This kind of writing is inexcusable. It wastes manhours, money, and material —and it still doesn't get the job done. In fact, it seriously interferes with the mission.[1]

The technical writer's purpose is to write a clear, brief, and technically correct EDP document, rather than prose to persuade or convince. Usually, EDP documents can be polished to clear, brief and accurate documents in three revisions and several readings.

First Revision:

In the first revision, the technical writer should check for technical *content* and *concept*. It may require several readings to do this. While making these reading passes through the first draft, the writer should ask the following questions:

- Are the concepts and suggestions clear—do they make sense?
- Are they well organized?
- Is the distinction between facts and opinions clear?
- Are the instructions, procedures, and facts correct?
- Does the document contain all the information the reader needs?
- Do the instructions, procedures and facts need more interpretation?
- Are the sources for the facts the best obtainable?
- Is the document too detailed—or not detailed enough?
- Have I included enough information—or too much?

After correcting any content and concept weakness, the first draft should be retyped for the second revision editing.

Second Revision:

During the second revision, the technical writer should concentrate on *clarity* and *brevity*. This is not easy to achieve. The writer should look for unnecessary words, big words, and ambiguous writing. Technical writing should contain only meaningful and necessary words to make the writing clear. The writer may have to make several reading passes through the second revision to condense the paper to a clear and concise document.

Deadwood in writing: In the first reading, the writer should look for *deadwood*. Meaningless and superflous words are deadwood. They take up space but add nothing

---

[1] "Guide for Air Force Writing," Air Force pamphlet 10-1, published by the Superintendent of Documents, U.S. Government Printing Office, Washington, D.C., 20402, p. 2.

to the meaning of the sentence. Put the deadwood words to the chopping block. Seek them out, cross out, and cut out. Substitute little words for big ones, when possible.

To show how deadwood and meaningless prepositional phrases clutter up our writing, study the following example.

Example 1:   *"Therefore, our approach to* this study *has shifted toward developing a system that* can be used as a *scheduling* tool, *and will at the same time* generate *the needed historical* manhour utilization data."

Rewrite: "This study can be used as a tool (to) generate manhour utilization data."

Example 2:   *"It is essential that* errors in design and coding must be *identified and* corrected as early as possible *to prevent the compounding of such errors. Seemingly insignificant* programming errors, if not promptly *detected,* can cause *numerous* manhours to be wasted and *result in* a slippage of the *entire* project."

Rewrite 1:   "Errors in design and coding must be corrected as early as possible. Small programming errors, if not detected, can cause wasted manhours and slippage of the project.

Rewrite 2:   "Errors in design and coding must be corrected as early as possible, or the completion date for the project will not be met."

The italicized words are deadwood. In the first example, by removing 22 dead words and adding a word (*to*), the original sentence of 32 words has been rewritten in 13 words. In the second example, by removing 21 dead words the original paragraph of 49 words has been rewritten in 28 words. The first rewrite has been further reduced to 23 words. If the authors of these two examples had taken the time to chop away at the deadwood, they would not have let the original writing stand.

The following are examples of deadwood and circumlocution [2] prepositional phrases. Look for and remove them from your writing.

Do You Write	*Instead of:*
In an effort to improve	To improve
All programmers	Programmers
Any programmer	Programmers
In the event that	If
In view of the fact that	Because, since
In order to	To
In a manner similar to	Like
In the case of	If
Despite the fact that	Although
At the present time	Now
Until such time as	Until
In the majority of instances	Usually
In a number of cases	Some
On a few occasions	Occasionally
Accounted for by the fact that	Due to; caused by

---

[2] Webster's Seventh New Collegiate Dictionary defines circumlocution as "—1: The use of an unnecessarily large number of words to express an idea."

Do You Write	*Instead of:*
Afford an opportunity	Allow, permit
A great deal of	Much
An example of this is the fact that	For example; as an example
A number of	Several; many
As of now	Now
The majority of	Most
In my next communication	In my next letter
During the time	While
In connection with	About
In close proximity	Near
In reference to	About
In the event of	If
It is incumbent on me	I must
It is often the case that	Often
For the reason that	Because; since
It would not be unreasonable to assume	I assume; we assume or think
Leaving out of consideration	Disregarding
Necessitate	Require; need
Of considerable magnitude	Big; large
Of very minor importance	Unimportant
Prior to	Before
Relative to this	About this
As a general rule	Generally
By the use of	By
Resultant effect	Effect
In the range of	About
Currently being	Being
And will at the same time	Will
The only difference being that	Few
There is very little doubt that	Doubtless; no doubt
By means of	With; by
In the near future	Soon
Past history	History (History *is* past.)
Check on	Check
Merged together	Merged
Surrounding circumstances	Circumstances
Debate about	Debate
Within the realm of possibility	Possible; possibly
Assuming that	If
In rare cases	Rarely
If at all possible	If possible
In the vicinity of	Near
With this in mind	Therefore
With the exception of	Except
To summarize the above	In summary
On grounds that	Because
It is my personal opinion	It is my opinion

Do You Write	*Instead of:*
Few in number	Few
When and if	If
Are desirous of	Want to
In a manner similar to	Like
It is recommended that consideration be given to	We recommend that you consider
Take appropriate measures	Take action
The fullest possible extent	The most
With due regard for	For

BIG WORDS VS. LITTLE WORDS

Do You Use Big Words	*Instead of Little Words*
Subsequently	Later
Approximately	About
Component	Part
Configuration	Pattern
Disseminate	Spread
Illustrate	Show
Operational	Working
Optimum	Best
Paramount	Main, grave, serious
Terminate	End
Voluminous	Bulky; large; big
Compensation	Pay
Encounter	Meet
Presently	Now
Modification	Change
Accomplish	Do
Aforementioned	Above
Inexpensive	Cheap
Incalculable	Infinite
Incapacitate	Disable
Indecipherable	Illegible
Inoperable	Stalled; out; dead
Illuminate	Clarify
Elucidate	Explain
Expedite	Rush
Facilitate	Aid
Objective	Aim
Compatible	Agree

Hedgewords: In the second reading the EDP technical writer should look for *hedgewords.* Hedgewords are loopholes in writing. Sometimes an "out" must be retained in our writing, as in feasibility studies and general correspondence. But when writing an EDP technical document to give precise instructions or to state a cause and affect relationship, hedgewords should not be used. When a writer is not sure or is doubtful to certain information, he gives himself a loophole by hedging. This way, he hopes to escape from that statement. He does not want to be pinned down or have to defend it.

In writing a document that requires technical accuracy, hedgewords should never be used. Some hedgewords are legitimate. Sometimes a technical writer should use hedgewords to show caution, but the statement should be so written that it cannot be interpreted any other way. Too frequent use of hedgewords will not project a good image of the writer and the reader will not place much confidence in the document.

The following are examples of hedgewords when used in a certain context:

Generally	Seems
Normally	Might
May	Possibly
Occasionally	Usually
Ordinarily	Seldom
Apparently	If
Perhaps	Should
Probably	Rarely
I believe	Most

When the writer finds these and similar hedgewords in his writing, he should ask the following questions:

· Is the word necessary to show caution?
· Is the word needed for clarity?
· Is the information factual? If it is, eliminate the hedgeword.
· Is the procedure, method, concept, or instruction correct? If it is, remove the hedgeword.
· Will something happen due to a cause and affect relationship? If it will, eliminate the hedgeword.

If the sentence or statement where a hedgeword is found falls in one of the above categories, the hedgeword should be removed. Consider the cause and affect relationship in the following example:

When the EDP technical writer writes: "Generally, it is assumed that when the console command CORDUMPA is entered, Module 'A' should be printed from memory" . . . he is hedging.

Will the reader know for sure what will happen when CORDUMPA is entered? No. Check the hedgewords "generally," "assumed," and "should." Let's remove these hedgewords in the rewrite of the sentence:

"When the console command CORDUMPA is entered, Module 'A' will be printed from memory."

There is no doubt what will happen when the hedgewords are removed. Do not write in a way that can be interpreted another way by the reader.

After the EDP technical writer has eliminated the deadwood and corrected the grammar, the document should be retyped.

Third Revision:

During the third revision the EDP technical writer should concentrate on the *technical accuracy* and *style*. The writer may make several reading passes through the second typing to isolate inaccurate information and inconsistent style. The writer should doublecheck the accuracy of the facts, instructions, and procedures. He should make sure that they are current and pertinent to the writing objectives.

Most EDP technical documents will be typed in a paragraph numbering structure as discussed in Chapter Twelve, Appendix A. The writer should make sure that the numbering sequence is adequate to achieve good style in paragraph structuring and that it will aid referencing and updating.

The technical writer should check for good organization and layout of the document. Technical writing does not lend itself to sentence or paragraph transition as easily as administrative writing. When writing and revising general administrative documents or feasibility studies, the technical writer should look for faulty transitions and lack of coherence in his writing.

The technical writer should make needed changes and carefully read the updated copy. The paper is then ready for final typing. Before the paper is given to the typist, the writer should make a final read through and consider the following questions:

- Is the document effectively organized?
- Are words specific and concrete, rather than vague and abstract?
- Is the document consistent in style and organization?
- Does the document describe the data, test, instructions and facts with clarity and accuracy?
- Is the level of writing appropriate for the reader?
- Is it:
  —too technical?
  —too detailed?
  —too concise?
- Are unfamiliar abbreviations and terms explained?
- Are the recommendations and assumptions pertinent and valid?
- Are the illustrations, tables, etc., identified and near the data they support?
- Are topics and sub-topics identified with headings?
- Have all deadwood and hedgewords been removed?
- Is the document clear, concise, and complete?
- Is the information in the document complete and accurate?

Proofreading: After the final typing is complete, the EDP technical writer should proofread, with the secretary, the typed copy against the draft. Because of the technical nature and content makeup (often a combination of alpha-numeric characters and programming symbols) of documentation, EDP technical writing lends itself to typing errors more than does general correspondence. Because of this, proofreading should not be neglected.

REVISING AND EDITING OTHER PEOPLE'S WRITING

Some writers are sensitive about their writing. They get emotionally upset when their writing is criticised. Writers take criticism as a reflection on their personality. If corrections are untidy and made in large writing on a page, the writer is insulted. But if changes are neatly made between the lines and margins, they are less likely to upset the writer. No writer likes to see his work covered with sprawling pencil marks. Oftentimes a programmer or analyst may defend or support a poorly worded sentence, or one full of deadwood. But when an error or unnecessary coding in a program is pointed out to them, they will not hesitate to correct it.

Some people who approve other people's writing have no technical writing training or experience in technical editing or supervising the writing of others. Some are poor writers.

Supervisors who approve the writing of others should use tact when editing and critiquing a subordinate's writing. Writers will appreciate corrections of facts and sloppy grammar. But when a different style of writing is suggested, or when the editing and criticism is based on semantics, the writer can become uncooperative. The writer may be justified in his uncooperative attitude.

A person who approves or supervises the writing of others should express complimentary remarks either in writing or in conference with the writer. A good supervisor can always find something about which to compliment the writer. A tactful supervisor will concede a point now and then to a writer. Decisions about how something is written, other than the rules of grammar, are matters of taste and writing style. The supervisor should not *force* his writing taste or style on the writer.

When suggesting changes, the supervisor should give sound reasons why the change is needed. He should not write or say "I don't like this," or "This is not a correct sentence." The supervisor should tell why he does not like the writing or what is wrong with a particular sentence or paragraph.

When correcting grammar infractions, the supervisor should explain the grammar rule. He should convince the writer by reason and not expect the writer to be convinced by such haughty arguments as: "This is the way I want it," or "I never saw it written this way," or "I like it this way because it reads better." The supervisor must be well informed about the subject material and the rules for grammar if he is to make decisions and give advice about writing.

Educated people realize that an idea may be correctly expressed several ways. "There is often more than one acceptable way of phrasing an idea. If a writer's expression is satisfactory, he should not have to change it. And good supervisors remember that editing can be too fussy; there is little point in caviling over unimportant matters, and a sensible person recognizes the occasion on which he should not correct." [3] When an EDP supervisor tries to be an expert in all aspects of documentation writing—grammar, writing style, formating, organization, printing and reproduction—he looses the respect of the writer.

The EDP manager should leave these things to the technical writer. He should leave the grammar to the secretary and the technical writer. Too often, the secretary is used as a human robot. She types, files and fetches coffee. Secretaries should be encouraged to be on guard for grammatical errors—even the boss's errors. Most experienced secretaries are usually better grammarians than their bosses. They make their living staying close to the rules of the English language. Use them for this purpose.

A supervisor does not have to be an English major to recognize good writing. If the writing is clear, easy to read, and coherently written, good writing principles have been used. This does not mean that the supervisor or reader must be able to understand the details and concepts of *what* is being written. Some supervisors may try to hide this lack of knowledge by pedantic insistence on their own expressions and semantics. When this happens, the technical writer may give up trying to write simply and coherently and write in a style to please the boss. The style may be Victorian, pompous and full of deadwood.

Constructive writing advice and editing based on reason and grammar rules can be beneficial to the technical writer. The supervisor may have more knowledge on the subject than the writer, and may be a good writer. The technical writer should try to improve his writing skill. He should pay attention and ask questions and apply the advice that seems reasonable. By doing so, the writer will develop a rapport with his supervisor and improve his writing skill.

The technical writer should not take writing criticism personally. The writer should not use a writing conference with his supervisor to demonstrate his debating skill, or to display bad temper and ignorance. The writer should study the penciled notes on his paper. He should weigh the advice and try to improve his next writing assignment.

Appendix A contains certain proofreader's marks.

---

[3] H. J. Tichy, *Effective Writing*, copyright by John Wiley and Sons, Inc., New York, N.Y., p. 314.

APPENDIX A

PROOFREADER'S MARKS

WHAT IS TO BE DONE	MARGINAL NOTATION Showing WhAT is to be done	NOTATION IN TEXT Showing WHERE it is to be done	ILLUSTRATION	
PUNCTUATION				
Insert period	⊙	∧ or /	⊙	press∧ The learned correct
Insert comma	⋏	∧ or /	⋏	However / the necessity of a
Insert apostrophe	⋎	∧ or /	⋎	purely printers errors, and
Insert colon	⊙	∧ or /	⊙	of the following∧pencils,
Insert semi-colon	;/	∧ or /	;/	other days / there is no rea
Insert quotation marks	⋎ or ⋎	∧ or /	⋎ ⋎	The word∧not∧was omitted by
Insert hyphen	=/	∧ or /	=/	open to non∧members only.
Insert question mark	?/	∧ or /	?/	how will they know/ That is
Insert exclamation point	!/	∧ or /	!/	a terrific climax/ Naturally
Insert parentheses	( )	∧ or /	( )	on Page 37∧which see∧ Here
Insert brackets	[ ]	∧ or /	[ ]	"These∧the free-silver Demo
Insert en dash	/en/	∧ or /	/en/	were employed∧men who first
Insert em dash	/—/	∧ or /	/—/	opinion∧their experience will
SPACING				
Push down this space	⊥	/	⊥	upon/the best arrangement
Space evenly	✓✓✓	∧	✓✓✓	I have∧talked∧with∧many a
Insert space	#	∧	#	and almost∧immediately associ
Less space	⌣	⌣	⌣	one unconsciously⌣calls up
Close up entirely	⌒	⌒	⌒	may be neces⌒sary but, the
Insert em quad space (Indent one em)	□	∧	□	under construction∧Twenty
Take out character and close up	ℰ	ℐ	ℰ	they w/ere rather what we
Take out lead	ℰld	—	ℰld	with considerable regularity were previously used on the
Insert lead between lines	ld>	>	ld>	naturally could not be resp state or province as the

PROOFREADER'S MARKS (Continued)

	WHAT IS TO BE DONE	MARGINAL NOTATION *Showing* WHAT *is to be done*	NOTATION IN TEXT *Showing* WHERE *it is to be done*	ILLUSTRATION
POSITION CHANGE	Move to left	[	⬭	[⊢ (Life Underwriting)
	Move to right	]	⬭	] (Life Underwriting) ⊣
	Lower	⊔	none	⊔ Supply ᴅepartment
	Raise	⊓	none	⊓ Supplᵧ ᴅepartment
	Paragraph	¶	∧	¶ and of everything. ₐIt was
	No paragraph	*no* ¶	none	*no* ¶ cannot be transferred. A new call must be made
	Transpose letters or words . . .	*tr*	⊓	*tr* When branch opᴇꞧator answer
TYPE	Change defective letter	X	○	X most cf theⓜhave been prac
	Change to proper style of type (wrong font) . . .	*wf*	○	*wf* or could just use ⓣⓗe exerc
	Set in capitals	*caps*	≡	*caps* the <u>major</u> provisions of the
	Set in small capitals	*s.c.*	≡	*s.c.* the <u>MAJOR</u> provisions of the
	Set in lower case	*l.c.*	/	*l.c.* the ȴower half of the region
	Set in Roman	*Rom.*	○	*Rom.* the(lower)half of the region
	Set in Italic	*ital*	—	*ital* the <u>lower</u> half of the region
	Set in bold face	*bf*	⌇⌇⌇	*bf* the <u>lower</u> half of the region
	Set in bold face Italic	*bf ital*	≈	*bf ital* the <u>lower</u> half of the region
	Use ligature (fi, fl, ff, ffl)	f̂i	⌒	f̂i tiring to the f̂ingers. Natu
	Letter upside down; reverse . . .	℗	○	℗ Any opꞁꞁꞇor will have prio
DELETION	Take out; delete	℈	⬭	℈ emphasized this(this)point
	Take out character and close up . .	℈̑	ⵣ	℈̑ emphas̑ized this point in a
REINSTATEMENT	Retain crossed-out word or letter; let it stand . .	*stet*	—	*stet* that a ~~complete~~ survey can
	Retain only crossed-out words under which dots appear . .	*stet*	. . . .	*stet* ~~when and cost~~ removed from

Courtesy of General Services Administration National Archives and Records Service Office of Records Management; Federal Stock Number 7610–753–4771; for sale by The Superintendent of Documents, U.S. Government Printing Office, Washington, D.C. 20402.

12

Effective EDP Documentation Writing

I write as I walk because I want to get somewhere, and I write as straight as I can, just as I walk as straight as I can, because that is the best way to get there.

H. G. Wells

A technical document should have one objective—to convey information that is clear in meaning to the reader and in as few words as possible. It should be presented in a logical order and be easy to follow.

Technical information should be clear, concise, complete and written in simple everyday words, familiar to the reader. There should be but one purpose—to make contact with the person who will read what is written. Too much EDP technical writing is full of verbosity and nonessential preliminaries. It is more impressive than expressive.

For some people, there seems to be something about writing that brings out unfamiliar or long words, the most complex sentences, and very formal writing style. This was the style for all writing in the Victorian era, but in the technical and "real" world of today, such writing is considered stilted, pompous, and showy. The writer does not communicate with the reader. He confuses him. The reader will give up because he will not bother to figure out this mumbo-jumbo writing.

We should write as we talk—almost. We don't speak in a formal way. If we did, we would be laughed at. So why write that way? We use brevity in our conversations. When we talk, we usually straighten out the sentence structure, make our sentences clear, complete and short. Our spoken words are familiar to the other person. To get our message across, we use slang and colloquial words at times.

In EDP technical writing, it would be difficult, at times, to convey information without using technical jargon and colloquial terms. It is better to use such writing habits than to fragment a sentence with formal and verbose writing, just to obviate the use of jargon, or colloquial terms, or to avoid ending a sentence with a preposition.

Example:

· After many errors appeared and after considerable study, it was discovered that a software deficiency existed in the read Module of the MCRI software package. Why not say:
· A bug was discovered in the read Module of the MCRI program.

The use of jargon or colloquial terms should be kept to a minimum. EDP technical writing can be effective without the overuse of such terms.

The reader often is a busy person with stacks of papers or documents he needs to read. Most documents can be reduced one-third to a half if the writer thinks about what he is to write. The technical writer should refrain from including useless details and wordy phrases. The reader must be given credit for being intelligent. If the writer has done his "homework," he will know something of the reader's scope of experience and know just how detailed to get.

The writer should bear in mind two points: (1) the reader is busy—write just to inform, leave out the wordy phrases; and (2) assume the reader has average intelligence—leave out the details. If these two factors are kept in mind, the reader will not have to struggle with wordy sentences or scan over insignificant details.

EDP technical writing should contain short sentences and common everyday words. The sentence length and word difficulty are the most important factors in measuring readability. Words that the reader can easily understand should be put in short and uncomplicated sentences. Technical writing that is easy to read is usually easy to understand. Some readers may feel the writing is oriented to junior high school level, but they will not complain that it is too easy to understand or to read. Most of the non-scientific periodicals have a reading level of high school or below. Consider the following: [1]

Reading Material	Reading Level
Westerns and *True Story*	5th grade
Look, Life, and *Ladies Home Journal*	6th—8th grade
Reader's Digest, Time	8th—10th grade
Harper's, New Yorker, Business Week	11th—12th grade
Professional, Technological, and Scientific Journals	16th grade or above

This is not to suggest that all EDP technical documents be written at or below high school levels. The technical writer must be flexible in his writing. He must write for his reader.

Verbosity replaces brevity when the reader has to glean through lots of words which have little to do with the real meaning of the sentence. If he fills paragraphs with a number of wordy sentences that contain just a little meaning, the writer has wasted the reader's time. Each word in a sentence should advance the meaning of that sentence.

---

[1] "Guide for Air Force Writing," Air Force Pamphlet 10-1, published by the Superintendent of Documents, U. S. Government Printing Office, Washington, D.C., 20402, p. 153.

Each sentence in a paragraph should advance the thought of that paragraph. Each paragraph should advance the purpose of the document.

NONESSENTIAL PRELIMINARIES

Writing should be direct. The writer should let the reader know immediately what each sentence and paragraph is about. Nonessential preliminaries have no place in EDP technical writing. It is the writer's responsibility to ensure that every word, every statement, is important enough to be included. It is easy to test this. Consider the following two examples:

Example One:

· *All programmers taking advantage of the* record *overflow/*track overflow feature *available* on all 2314/2321 devices *at this center* must supply contiguous parameters at space allocation time.

All words in italics are nonessential and unimportant words. They add nothing to the meaning of the sentence. Study the rewrite for brevity and clarity of thought:

· The contiguous parameter must be supplied when using record and track overflow features on the 2314 and 2321 devices.

The sentence has been rearranged and rewritten. The rewrite contains 18 words. The nonessential words have been dropped. Each remaining word except for the first "the" has a definite role in the sentence. To remove any one of them would make the sentence unclear.

The following paragraph is an exercise in verbosity, fuzzy and vague writing:

Example Two:

· The program problem status report provides a record of each problem experienced in the system from detection to resolution. This report, as a management tool, will be only as good as the information received and used for its composition; therefore, local unit managers and supervisory personnel must instill in operating personnel the need to recognize and accurately report all problems they experience. The effective use of the progress requests, timely achievement of customer command short and long range objectives, and problem status reports will accelerate our goals and provide customer satisfaction.

This writer probably felt that the length of the paragraph and preliminaries would convince the reader of the importance of the paragraph. A paragraph should lead the reader clearly and smoothly through each line. If the writer of this paragraph had thought through what he was going to write, he might have written something similar to the following:

· The report provides a record of problems experienced in the system and serves as
a management tool. Supervisors are requested to accurately report all problems.
The objective of the report is to provide better service to our customers.

To obtain brevity, our writing must be direct, clear, concise and complete. However, clarity should not be sacrificed for brevity. A paragraph or document written in a direct, clear and concise manner appeals to the reader much more than writing full of trite expressions, space-filling nonessentials, and repetition of words having the same or nearly the same meaning.

Let's go back and examine the original writing of Example Two for these attributes. In the first sentence, the writer didn't give the reader much credit for having any intelligence. What does "from detection to resolution" say that "provide a record of each problem experienced in the system" didn't say? The words "a record" imply a chronological history and relate the past events of a problem—from "detection to resolution." What competent individual would give only half of a record?

In the second sentence, the writer further insulted the readers by not giving them credit for being able to understand the significance of "management." The writer could have said, "This report is a management tool." But instead, he subordinated "management," the word that gave meaning to the sentence, as a parenthetical expression, and rambled on in gobbledygook for another three dozen words.

Most readers probably gave up on this paragraph when they got to the third sentence. The writer starts the third sentence with a new subject, "progress requests," but ends it talking about the subject he introduced at the beginning of the paragraph, the "problem status reports."

Vagueness and wordiness are hard to tell apart. Unnecessary words tend to obscure meaning. Consider the third sentence in the original writing of example two. Vague and abstract writing fails to convey clearly the writer's meaning. The writer should have three objectives in mind when he writes: to make his writing *clear, concise* and *complete*. These three factors should guide him in his writing. What may appear clear, concise, and complete to the writer may not to the reader.

EXPRESSION IN DOCUMENTATION WRITING—MAKE THE UNFAMILIAR FAMILIAR

In literary and creative writing, the writer is free to compose as he wishes. He may alter facts, ideas and concepts as he sees fit. Such freedom is not permitted in EDP documentation writing. Unlike literary prose, figurative writing has no place in EDP documentation writing. The writing should be impersonal in tone. Generally, pronouns should be avoided.

The documentation writer should write to inform and not to impress. Too often our writing is more impressive than informative. Consider the following examples:

Example One:

· Effective immediately, all personnel engaged in creating volume parameters are reminded that VOLUME=PRIVATE is no longer needed on any tape DD card; therefore, since its use may result in superfluous operation "KEEP" messages, it is imperative that it be avoided.

Compare the rewrite:

· VOLUME=PRIVATE is no longer needed on tape DD cards. Its use should be avoided because it will generate excessive "KEEP" messages.

The first statement with these words, "effective immediately," "engaged in," "are reminded," "therefore," "superfluous," and "imperative," has nothing to do with conveying the main idea of the statement. It took twice as long to write and to read the first statement as it did the second. The reader had to read a third of the way through before he reached the pertinent information. He had to read another third of the way through to find out that he was not to use this parameter.

Another word the writer used that may have caused some readers to question the need for the statement was "may." As used in this example, this is a hedge word. Hedge words should be avoided in technical writing. By use of the word "may," the writer was admitting (although not realizing it) that he was not sure that "KEEP" messages would be generated.

The rewrite informed the reader in 21 words what it took the first writer 41 to do. You will note, too, that the "imperative" tone has been changed. The word "should" was substituted for imperative. It is a show of arrogance and in bad taste to use dictatorial phrases and statements in technical documents. Such writing may be useful in the training of young military recruits, but it has no place in a technical profession. You will note also that the positive word "will" was substituted for "may." This leaves no doubt in the reader's mind what will happen if VOLUME=PRIVATE is used.

Example Two:

· The programming office will perform an evaluation or system study, as discussed in previous paragraphs, on each requirement or recommendation to provide the headquarters staff directorate information to render managerial decisions on the validity of each requirement.

Let's examine the second example in detail for repetition of words with the same or nearly the same meaning and for words and phrases used to impress rather than inform. This type of writing is clumsy and is known as redundance or tautology. What is the difference between "evaluation" and "study," or "requirement" and "recommendation"? What is the difference between "headquarters staff directorate" and "headquarters"? "Staff directorate" does not identify the exact office or person at "headquarters" who is to receive the information and it tells us no more than "headquarters." Why confuse the reader by adding it? When a person "evaluates," he also "studies." A "requirement" is also a "recommendation."

Consider the impressive statement "headquarters staff directorate . . . render managerial decision on the validity." This is redundant writing and adds nothing to the meaning of the sentence. Headquarters implies management where "decisions" are made.

Compare the rewrite:

· The programming office will perform a study on each requirement and furnish headquarters information of their findings.

EDP DOCUMENTATION WRITING STYLE

When EDP systems were small environments with a total EDP force of a few programmers, the style and presentation format for documentation didn't matter very much. Most documentation was retained in the programmer's head or on pieces of scrap paper in a desk drawer. Often, the programmer was a combination analyst, programmer, computer operator, and documentation writer. Writing was considered an unnecessary burden and little emphasis was placed on the quality of documentation. If a documentation gap existed, it could be bridged over a cup of coffee.

This concept is no longer true. Large computer systems with a multitude of I/O devices and comprised of a number of operations and programming sections, all relying on interface work areas, must have accurate, complete and clear documentation to function as an effective EDP organization.

The two foremost qualities of EDP documentation are its clarity and accuracy. If the statements of an EDP document are so worded as to confuse and mislead, the time and effort of preparing the documentation will be of little value. Clarity of documentation is enhanced with a uniform style arrangement. Verbosity, coupled with a poor style layout, will discourage people from reading a technical document.

Organization, style and presentation methods are the prerogative of the technical writer. Good grammar, accuracy of terminology, and adherence to company policy are vital characteristics of all documentation. However, the style and paragraph structure in EDP documentation must be arranged to accomplish the following:

· Aid rapid reading.
· Convey the exact meaning.
· Ease of reference and document maintenance.

Aid Rapid Reading: Too often the reverse is true. The writer writes rapidly without giving too much thought to what is being written. His only thought, it seems, is to get what he is thinking down on paper. As a consequence, phrases and clauses in a sentence are linked together with commas or semicolons, making the reading difficult. It is not the number of words that make a sentence difficult to read. It is the way the sentence is put together.

This concept of writing is the way the first draft should be written. But too often the first draft is the final draft. It is rare, indeed, when a writer can produce a clear and concise written piece involving more than a few sentences in one writing. It is just as rare when a programmer can write an error-free program the first try. The following are two examples that hinder rapid reading:

Example One:

· We can quickly determine from the chart that, similarly, with three physical records per track, BLOCK CONTAINS 11 RECORDS, therefore, 33 logical records per track; with 2 physical records per track, BLOCK CONTAINS 17 RECORDS, therefore, 34 logical records per track; and with 1 physical record per track, BLOCK CONTAINS 36 RECORDS, therefore, 36 logical records per track.

Test the rewrite for rapid reading:

· The chart indicates:

—3 physical records per track, using BLOCK CONTAINS 11 RECORDS, would give 33 logical records.
—2 physical records per track, using BLOCK CONTAINS 17 RECORDS, would give 34 logical records.
—1 physical record per track, using BLOCK CONTAINS 36 RECORDS, would give 36 logical records.

The original write-up comprised one sentence, containing 58 words tied together with commas and semicolons. The author of this statement was a competent programmer, an expert in his speciality. But he failed to demonstrate the same proficiency as a writer. The writer was using literary prose and figurative language to communicate a technical process. The document that the sentence came from was written to familiarize less knowledgeable programmers with a complex programming technique.

The programmer did not consider his "audience," the reader. He wrote on a level that only equally experienced programmers would have readily understood; but only because they would understand the techniques and not be bothered with trying to understand the poor sentence. The writer should consider the reader's scope of experience and his educational level of the subject.

The writer should bear in mind the purpose of the document. Is it to inform less experienced personnel? If this is the case, the writer may have to include more details and "write down" in a simple straightforward manner. If the document is historical rather than instructional, and directed to equally experienced technicians, the writer may write on a higher level, omitting details. Regardless of the reading level, the document should be clear, direct and free of figurative language.

The rewrite of the example contains three sentences and is arranged to permit rapid reading. The reader can read through this technical process one sentence at a time. He doesn't have to glean through figurative language, commas or semicolons to get to the heart of the statement. Here is another example that is not clear and hinders rapid reading:

Example Two:

· After final completion of the program requirements and test/validation, computer implementation instructions and hardware configuration, with the change patch documentation, are prepared and forwarded to the applicable agency for implementation according to existing procedures and directives which govern the system programs.

Compare the rewrite:

· Programs that have been validated will be sent to the user with implementation instructions for implementing according to existing procedures.

The rewrite contains 20 words while the original sentence contained 41. The rewrite could be further reduced by eliminating the last six words. The purpose of the sentence was to give instructions on what to do with programs after they are developed and tested. Let's say that by eliminating those six words:

· Programs that have been validated will be sent to the user with implementation instructions.

What the writer said in 41 words could have been said in 14. Was it necessary to remind the sender "for implementing acording to existing procedures"? The sender will not be implementing the program. The user or receiver knows how to implement programs because he obviously has the "existing procedures."

Convey the Exact Meaning: To convey the exact meaning, the writer must first "think" of what he is to write and then communicate these thoughts on paper in simple language and terms that the reader can interpret and translate to his thought processes. A technical document should be written using the words that are familiar to the reader. How will a writer know this? By finding out the reader's experience level and knowledge of the subject.

The act of communication, whether written or oral, requires three elements: (1) a communicator who should have something meaningful to express; (2) words and symbols that convey the meaning; (3) an audience or readers who receive the words and translate them into meaning in their minds. In writing, no "meeting of the minds" occurs unless the reader is able to understand what has been written.

In the EDP field, the greatest barrier to effective communication is the lack of a common experience level between writer and reader. The written words, terms, symbols, and phrases must be within the reader's scope of experience. Too often a word or term may not convey the same meaning to the reader as it does to the writer. Association and experience are the ways most people become knowledgeable of the EDP field. For example: A writer may write "an off-line storage device" is needed to run a certain job. To some persons it may mean magnetic tape, to others it may mean drums, and to still others it may mean disc packs or data cells.

As we know, words convey different meanings to different people. Most words have several meanings or synonyms. The reader will interpret a word based on his experience or association. To convey true meaning, the writer should use "concrete" words and specific terms commonly known within the EDP environment about which he is writing.

Concrete words and specific terms convey meanings of human experiences. They are words that have a tangible affect on the five senses.

Abstract words and uncommon terms cannot be immediately associated with direct experiences. The meaning becomes vague and unclear. When this happens, the reader attaches a different meaning than that which the writer intended.

EDP technical writing, dealing with "program" documentation, does not lend itself to abstract words and terms as does general correspondence or prose writing. However, at times the inexperienced EDP writer will switch from a concrete word to an abstract word. Consider the words "programmer" and "user" in the second sentence of the following example.

- When a programmer makes available a value that has not been previously supplied by the symbolic parameter value, that value will be used instead of the procedure default value. When a programmer uses PARM.COMP= to override the parameter list, only those values supplied by the user are passed to the computer. Any parameter not specified by the user then defaults to the SYSGEN default. If the size parameter defaults to its SYSGEN default and a region of 120K, as in catalog procedures is used, an 804 abend will occur.

In this example, the writer did not "think" through what he wanted to convey or did not take the time to edit (debug) what he wrote.

Has the programmer conveyed the exact meaning? Yes. But it is misleading and lost in a maze of gobbledygook. It will take time to figure out the writer's meaning.

In the first sentence, what "value" does the writer mean? In the second sentence, the writer started talking about the "programmer" but ended up talking about the "user." Whose "values," the programmer's or the user's, will be passed to the compiler?

Consider the rewrite for clarity of meaning:

- When a programmer supplies a value for a symbolic parameter, that value is used instead of the procedure default value. When a programmer uses PARM. COMP=, the complete parameter list is overridden and only those values supplied by the programmer are passed to the compiler. Any parameter not specified by the programmer reverts to the SYSGEN default value. If the size parameter reverts to its SYSGEN default value and a region of 120K is used, an 804 abend will occur.

The rewrite becomes clear. The deadwood is removed and the abstract word "user" is replaced with the concrete word "programmer." We now know whose "value" will be passed to the compiler. (More about concrete and abstract writing later on in this Chapter.)

We would not need to write documentation to inform if all individuals in an EDP environment had equal experience and knowledge of the subject as the programmers. However, some programmers write as if this were true. This is similar to asking for a Utopia. We may have been closer to a Utopia in EDP knowledge in the days when there was the "one manual that contained all that had to be known" that James Martin spoke of in Chapter Ten.

The writer should write simply and clearly with sufficient detail to insure that what is being written will be understood by people involved in that subject or work function. Consider the following instructions:

> · On June 20, 1970, RJE /*/ MSG cards will be routed to SYSOUT for all non-spool jobs. This is accomplished by internally changing the /*/ to a JCL comment card //* and associating the "MSG" cards with the JCL job card immediately preceding them.
>
> There are no changes in the format of the RJE (*) MSG cards. They will continue to be printed on the operator's console at the time they are received. To insure that they are associated with the correct job, the MSG cards should be placed after the complete job card.

```
Example:    //     JOB (XXXXX), "XXXXX," X
            //     MSGCLASS=
            /*/ MSG "THIS IS THE CORRECT PLACEMENT
            /*/ MSG OF THE MSG CARDS."
```

The instructions and example are concise and "technically" correct—but not clear in meaning. When the programmer who wrote the instructions was asked for clarification, he said anyone familiar with RJE would understand the instructions. However, the Programming Manager and a programming instructor, who were "familiar" with RJE, had difficulty understanding the instructions. The question was asked: "Isn't the example contrary to the second sentence in the first paragraph? Shouldn't //* precede MSG in the example rather than /*/?"

By inserting a word and deleting symbols in the second sentence, the meaning becomes clear. Test the rewrite of the sentence and its effect on the example.

> · This is accomplished by JOB R internally changing the /*/ to a JCL comment card and associating the "MSG" cards with the JCL job card immediately preceding them.

The instructions were written for computer operators and some, if not all, might have asked the same question the Manager and instructor did, had the instructions reached them in the original write-up.

Ease of Reference and Document Maintenance:

Technical documents intended as reference material and subject to frequent changes should be written in a manner that will facilitate reference and document maintenance.

Consider the style layout and paragraph and sentence numbering in the following example for difficulty of referencing and document maintenance:

1   This subroutine was carefully planned and was cataloged to enable programmers to read data sets containing variable length blocks into core for subsequent processing.

2   The format of the calling sequence of this program is according to the following:

A   In order to use this subroutine, CALL READV (dsrn, dssn, address value1, address value2, address value3)

B   Where:
   (1)   "dsrn" is the data set reference number.
    (a)   Must be an integer constant.
   (2)   "dssn" is the data set sequence number.
    (a)   Must be an integer constant.
   (3)   "address value1" is an integer variable in which the block length (in bytes) of the data return will be stored.
   (4)   "address value2" is a subscripted array name and is the first variable of the list.
   (5)   "address value3" is an integer variable for end-of-data and/or error indicators to programmer.
    (a)   0 if normal
                                                     1 if at end-of-data.

3   RECFM in the DD statement of the JCL must be specified as U (undefined) for. . . .

A document containing several pages arranged in this paragraph numbering sequence would be difficult to reference and update. It appears to have been thrown together with each paragraph or statement assigned a numeric or alpha character, with no order of style or presentation format. Unless the presentation of a document is easy to follow, making reference to portions of the document and updating becomes confusing and difficult.

Compare the following presentation of the same information against the original write up:

A.   This subroutine has been developed to enable programmers to read data sets containing variable length blocks.

B.   CALL READV (dsrn, dssn, address value1, address value2, address value3).
   1. "dsrn" is the data set reference number.
   2. "dssn" is the data set sequence number and must be an integer constant.
   3. "address value1" is an integer variable in which the block length (in bytes) of data return will be stored.
   4. "address value2" is a subscripted array name and is the first location into which the data is read. Data must be read into contiguous storage locations.

5. "address value3" is an integer variable for end-of-data or error indicator to programmer.

C.   RECFM in the DD statement of the JCL must be specified as U (undefined) for . . .

The rewrite has been edited and unnecessary wording (deadwood) removed. Paragraphs and statements are numbered in a manner that will make referencing and updating easier.

CONCRETE AND ABSTRACT WORDS

Clarity and brevity are aided by the use of concrete words. Concrete words that deal with life, action, sight, sound, and direct human experiences have meaning to most people. The parables of the Bible relate only to things that can be touched or seen. Even St. Paul, the writer of the Biblical Corinthians, was concerned with the use of concrete words. In his message to the first Corinthians, he expressed in Chapter 14, Verse 9, these words: ". . . except ye utter by the tongue words easy to be understood, how shall it be known what is spoken? For ye shall speak into the air."

Clearcut definitions of terms, features, symbols, and key words must be expressed in concrete words. The reader must know what the writer is discussing before he can understand the meaning. Words such as "systems," "timely implemented," "computer education," "telecommunications," "magnetic storage device," may mean different things to different people. Senseless arguments arise because people fail to agree on meaning. Instructions have not been carried out because the reader did not know what the writer meant.

The writer must be specific. What is a system—what system? What does "timely" mean? What if instructions were written: "The inventory job will be received from Warehouse #4 via telecommunications and written to storage"? Would the operator understand? Chances are he would not. But if the instructions had been written: "The inventory job will be received from Warehouse 4 over the data circuit 2 and written to the 123 disc storage device," there would be no doubt in the operator's mind as to *what* circuit the job would be received over, or *what* storage device the job would be written to. The word "storage" takes on many connotations. It could be paper storage, tape or EAM cards; or it could be magnetic storage, tape, cell, drum, or disc. EDP technical writing will gain strength and clarity if concrete rather than abstract words or terms are used.

Abstract words make technical writing unclear, uncertain, and cumbersome. If it is necessary to use an abstract term, it should be defined in words that will clarify the term to the reader. Consider the following two examples:

· *Network:* Anything reticulated or decussated, at equal distances, with interstices between the intersections.[2]

---

[2] Glenn Leggett, C. David Mead, William Charvat, *Handbook for Writers,* third edition, Prentice-Hall, Englewood Cliffs, N.J., p. 296.

· *Network:* A series of points interconnected by communications channels, or the interconnection of electrical components.[3]

It is obvious which of these two definitions will have the greatest impact on understanding to a greater number of people.

When a technical document contains abstract writing, the writer is leaving himself open to be misunderstood, misquoted, and misjudged—and his readers will be misguided. Abstract words stand for ideas, concepts, and theories that may be so far removed from the reader's experience that a precise mental image cannot be formed. "Some language experts describe words in terms of an abstraction ladder. The lower ranges of the ladder represent the concrete terms for which the reader can readily identify the reference. As you go up the ladder, each word becomes more abstract than the one below it. At the same time the reference becomes more vague and therefore open to debate." [4]

This theory is demonstrated in the following diagram:

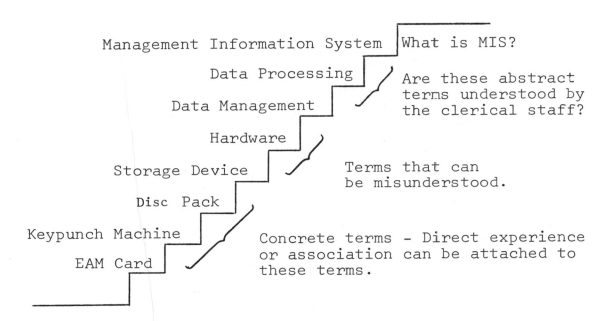

Abstract terms and words similar to those at the top of the stairs may be useful in writing program or system abstracts, announcements, or briefs for management on EDP projects or problem areas. But such terms frequently used in EDP technical documents

---

[3] Edgar C. Gentle, Jr., *Data Communications in Business,* AT&T Co., 1965, New York, N.Y., published by Publishers Service Company, Room 600, 75 Varick St., New York, N.Y. 10012 (in Glossary), pp. 149–150.

[4] "Guide for Air Force Writing," Air Force Pamphlet 10-1, published by the Superintendent of Documents, U.S. Government Printing Office, Washington, D.C., 20402, p. 128.

and operating instructions will confuse the reader and not convey the same meaning that the writer intended. When abstract statements are used, they should be followed with examples or illustrations. Abstract words make reading difficult, while concrete words make reading easy.

The technical writer should not overly concern himself with the rules of grammar. "Grammar, of course, aims at clearer speech and writing. And so long as it clarifies communication it deserves respect. But meaning overshadows grammar in importance. The first step of grammar is to center your attention on the meaning you wish to convey. . . . Take care to make your meaning clear and, for the most part, your grammar will take care of itself." [5]

The technical writer's main concern should be the *clarity, conciseness, completeness,* and *accuracy* of the writing. However, to achieve this, certain elementary grammatical rules should be followed.

WRITING ACCEPTABLE ENGLISH

The technical writer will find it easier to meet his objective, to write clearly, concisely, completely and accurately if he will follow certain grammatical rules.

The writer should not "lock" himself onto these rules and neglect the clear thought processes of his writing. To communicate a technical process clearly, in as few words as possible, words must be arranged in a certain order within a sentence. Very seldom are technical processes communicated by using individual words. But an abstract expression or idea with vague meaning may be. The arrangement of words forms an idea or invokes a thought process in the reader's mind. Words must be linked together in an acceptable manner so that the idea is recognizable and conveys meaning to the reader.

This is where the rules come in. They set up the pattern for the writer to follow in writing acceptable English. "A good many of these rules of writing English are merely conventions. Logic alone does not justify them; they represent . . . traditional practices. . . . We observe them . . . because generations of readers have come to expect writers to observe them. . . . To be ignorant of these conventions, or to violate them, is by no means to commit a cardinal sin. . . . During the eighteenth century, English grammarians devised a host of elaborate and artificial rules to govern the use of English. . . . This ' eighteenth-century ' attitude has passed in the subconsciousness of the . . . American people and makes it difficult to discuss the ' standards ' of modern English realistically." [6]

The intention of this chapter is not to discuss the merits of these standards or to present complicated formulas for writing. Acceptable English should follow the actual usage of present-day "technical" speaking and writing habits. There may be some grammatical purists left, but most people in writing business correspondence use simple

---

[5] Robert Gunning, *The Technique of Clear Writing,* revised edition 1968, McGraw-Hill Book Company, Inc., N.Y., p. 11, 330 W. 42d St., New York, N.Y. 10036.

[6] Glenn Leggett, C. David Mead, William Charvat, *Handbook for Writers,* third edition, Prentice-Hall, Englewood Cliffs, N.J., pp. 6 and 13.

English, small words, and straightforward talk. Simple English doesn't mean "simple-minded."

"Writing is an art, ultimately, and there is no set of rules that will guarantee success, nor can the writer hope to reach perfection. One must know the rules of usage, grammar, sentence structure; but one never knows for sure how all the rules are to be applied in a particular case. The final product must be a matter of individual judgment. . . ." [7]

EDP documentation should be written in simple English for practical purposes—to convey exact meaning and aid rapid reading. Writing is readable if it easily communicates thoughts to the reader. To do this, the writing must be clear, concise, complete and simply written. Simplicity is the key to technical writing. It is not easy to write simply; it requires common sense and good judgment, and short sentences.

THE SENTENCE STRUCTURE

The word order or position of the words conveys the meaning of a sentence. The arrangement of the words determines if the meaning of the sentence is clear. Most writers can usually arrange these words according to their significance or the function that they are to perform in the sentence. This is usually done without regard to the grammatical relationship of other words being written by the writer.

A documentation writer may be able to write grammatically correct sentences without being able to identify the various parts of speech, other than the subject and verb. It is not a prerequisite to writing clear sentences that the writer be able to memorize the parts of speech or the complicated grammatical rules for their use. Clear sentences are a prerequisite to good documentation. Knowing the elementary rules of writing and the common use of the parts of speech wil make the process of writing easier.

Grammarians have classified sentences in four categories: simple, compound, complex, and compound complex.

- · A simple sentence has a subject, verb, object, and maybe some modifying words.
  It is a complete thought or clause.

Example: The computer has 65K storage capacity.

- · A compound sentence has two or more main clauses.

Example: The computer has 65K storage capacity, and it has the fastest memory of any computer on the market.

- · A complex sentence has one main clause and one or more subordinate clauses.

Example: The computer has 65K storage capacity and 16 input and output channels, each capable of transmitting data at 5,000 bits per second.

---

[7] Ritchie R. Ward, *Practical Technical Writing*, published by Alfred A. Knopf, New York, N.Y., p. 39.

· A compound complex sentence has two or more main clauses and one or more subordinate clauses.

Example: The computer has 65K storage capacity; and because of its integrated circuits, it has faster memory cycling capability than any other computer on the market; and it can accommodate up to 16 input and output devices, each capable of transmitting 5,000 bits per second.

Being able to identify the type of sentence by its word length will not improve our writing. The arrangement of words, sentence length, and how the parts of speech are used will improve the readability. The writer should stay away from long and involved sentences. Experts recommend an average sentence length of 15 to 20 words. Some sentences may be as long as forty words, some as few as three. It is not the number of words that makes a sentence difficult or easy to read. It's the way the words are arranged in the sentence.

Long sentences and long words seem to go together. Usually, the writer who uses long and involved sentences will use long and unfamiliar words. This is not the mark of a writer who writes to inform, but the mark of one who writes to impress.

Good sentence structure demands from the writer the following attributes:

· Short sentences.
· Subject, verb, and object relationship.
· Familiar words instead of unfamiliar words.
· Concrete words instead of abstract words.
· Modifiers placed close to the word or statement they modify.
· Think before writing.
· Be accurate, complete, and thorough.
· Write in a direct, straightforward manner.
· Edit the sentence, cross out dead words (words that do not add to the meaning of the sentence).

The main ingredients for a sentence are the subject and predicate, or subject, verb, and object. The subject is a noun, pronoun, or a word or group of words used as a noun. The predicate consists of the verb and its modifiers, object or complement. The predicate describes the subject. The first step in recognizing a sentence is to identify the subject and verb. For directness and clarity in writing, the inexperienced writer should use the subject, verb, object order, and stick to simple or compound sentences. As the writer advances in skill, he may be comfortable with longer complex sentences with the verb and object coming ahead of the subject.

Most people may be able to recite the parts of speech but have forgotten the rules for using them. Thus, our writing habits have become a natural order of our talking habits. Most of our writing follows the subject, verb, object order that we use in our conversation. In talking, we use gestures, facial expressions, and a change in voice tone to make ourselves clear and to emphasize our main idea. It doesn't matter too much how long the sentences are because we can make ourselves understood through our "body English." But in writing, a different method for clarity and emphasis is needed.

The parts of speech and how they are used in a sentence are the writer's only tools for clarity of expression and emphasis of ideas.

RECOGNIZING THE PARTS OF SPEECH

"In modern English, we recognize eight parts of speech. There are three bases for classifying a word as a particular part of speech:

· Its grammatical function, such as subject or modifier.
· Its grammatical form, such as the " 's" of a possessive noun.
· Its type of meaning, such as the name of a person or the statement of an action.

The most logical way of identifying a part of speech correctly is to identify the function of the word in its particular sentence context." [8]

Noun: A noun is the name of a place, person, or thing. To show the possessive form, we add an apostrophe (') if the noun ends in an (s); if not, an ('s) is added to the word. The subject of a sentence is a noun or pronoun, or a word or phrase used as a noun.

Pronoun: A pronoun takes the place of a noun and refers indirectly to people, places and things; e.g., you, me, she, he, I, who, it, which, anyone, etc.

Adjective: An adjective modifies a noun or pronoun. For example: *large* computer; he is *aggressive.* Adjectives are words that point out or indicate a certain quality of a noun or pronoun; e.g., *your* computer; *round* disc pack; *inoperable* computer. Adjectives may be formed also by adding *able, ly, ing, ese, ful, ish, ous, y,* etc.

Verb or Verbal: A verb expresses action or indicates a state of being or feeling. The purpose of the verb is to say something about the subject. A verb may be one word or several. Example: The disc pack *fell.* The computer *should have been dismantled* yesterday. A verbal is a word derived from a verb but used as other parts of speech. Example: *Adjective*—It was time *to leave* the computer room. *Noun—Programming* is exciting.

Adverb: An adverb modifies a verb, an adjective, another adverb, or an entire clause or sentence. The adverb tells how, where, when, or to what degree acts were performed, or indicates a degree of quality; e.g., slowly, fast, yesterday, small, etc. Adverbs may also be formed by adding *ly.*

Preposition: A preposition relates to a noun, pronoun, or phrase by showing the relationship between them; e.g., at, about, to, for, by, in, etc. Example: The program is *about* finished. I gave the documentation *to* the analyst. The cards were placed *in* the card reader.

---

[8] Glenn Leggett, C. David Mead, William Charvat, *Handbook for Writers,* third edition, Prentice-Hall, Englewood Cliffs, N.J., p. 30.

Conjunction: A conjunction is a word used to join words, phrases, or clauses; e.g., because, and, nor, or, as, since, but, for, if, when, where, however, therefore, etc.

Interjection: An interjection is an exclamatory word that expresses emotion. (The interjection would seldom, if ever, be used in EDP documentation writing.)

Some of our words can serve as more than one part of speech. They may be used as nouns, adjectives, and verbs without changing the spelling.

Example:

· Noun—Programming requires patience.
· Verb—The analyst is programming.
· Adjective—He destroyed the programming sheets.

MISPLACED MODIFIERS

Modifiers are words or phrases that limit or restrict the meaning of the subject (noun). Placing the modifiers close to the words that they modify makes a sentence clear and easy to understand. A sentence of less than twenty words may be grammatically correct but difficult to read. This is because the modifiers are placed too far from the words that they modify. When we talk, it doesn't matter too much where the modifiers are because we can make ourselves understood. It is easier to speak clear sentences than it is to write clear sentences. A spoken sentence or word can be withdrawn and another word used or we can say it in another way. A written document is usually directed to people whom the writer cannot conveniently talk with. Thus, the writer cannot easily change a word or phrase once it is in the hands of the reader. The writer cannot study the reader's puzzled look, or see him straining to understand what he is reading. Usually this difficulty in reading can be traced to misplaced modifiers.

Misplaced modifiers may raise questions in the reader's mind. Consider the following sentence:

· The tape canister on the table with a broken top must not be used.

Although this sentence is grammatically correct, it is awkwardly written and may raise questions in the reader's mind. What has a broken top? The tape canister or the table? What must not be used? The tape canister or the table?

The awkwardness has been removed and the questions eliminated in the rewrite by placing the modifying phrase "with the broken top" next to the word that it modifies.

· The tape canister with the broken top on the table must not be used.

In long sentences, if modifiers are widely separated from the words they modify, the reader will be confused. Study the following sentence:

· Cost accounting and payroll update programs developed will not be written to an overlay area in modular form larger than 250K.

The modifiers in the sentence are too far removed from the word (program) that they modify. The meaning of the sentence is not clear. Must the reader have "an overlay area" less than 250K before the program is written to overlay? Or does the "modular form" require less than 250K? The sentence has been rewritten and the modifiers placed close to the word they modify. Compare the two sentences.

- Cost accounting and payroll update programs larger than 250K developed in modular form will not be written to an overlay area.

Misplaced modifiers make it easy for the reader to "read in" some other meaning than what the writer intended. A sentence contains more than just the subject, verb, and object. Other words are added to clarify, describe, or elaborate on these three elements. They are known as modifiers. Modifiers must be placed as close as possible to the words they modify. If the writer will get to know his modifiers and keep them close to the words they modify, he will be following one of the most fundamental rules of effective technical writing.

Some modifiers can play tricks on the reader and change the meaning of a sentence. Consider the elusive adverb modifier "only" in the following sentences:

- The analyst asked to be considered for this job only.
- The analyst asked to be considered for this only job.
- The analyst asked to be considered for only this job.
- The analyst asked to be considered only for this job.
- The analyst asked to be only considered for this job.
- The analyst asked to only be considered for this job.
- The analyst asked only to be considered for this job.
- The only analyst asked to be considered for this job.
- Only the analyst asked to be considered for this job.

The position of modifiers is important because they can change the sentence meaning. Placing the modifier "only" at different positions in the sentence above changed the meaning of the sentence. Examine the first sentence. By placing "only" at the end of the sentence, it is implied that there are several jobs. By placing the modifier ahead of the word "job" in the second sentence, it is implied that there is only one job. In the fifth sentence, the analyst is asking that only he be considered for the job. Sentence eight implies that there is only one analyst.

It can be determined by this demonstration of the modifier "only" that the position of words and the simple rules for their use play an important role in the writer's ability to write a clear and meaningful sentence. The same disciplines that apply to writing clear sentences will enable the writer to write clear and coherent paragraphs.

SENTENCE PUNCTUATION

Punctuation is used to clarify and aid the reader in obtaining the meaning of a sentence. Punctuation should be used with restraint. If the wording is good and the writer uses short sentences, punctuation will not be a problem.

There are certain fundamental rules that will aid the writer in punctuation.

Brackets: Use brackets ([]) to set off a word or explanatory phrase that has been added to quoted material. This lets the reader know that the writer inserted comments of his own.

Example: "The first computer programmed by this author [Martin] had one manual of operation. . . ."

Colon: The colon should be used to introduce something that is to follow, such as an enumerated list or an explanation. The colon is also used to introduce a long quotation in the body of a document.

Comma: There are many rules for the use of the comma. The following are the most common uses:

· to separate main clauses that are joined with a coordinating conjunction—and, but, or, nor, for, etc. In short compound sentences, the comma may be omitted;
· to separate long introductory phrases and clauses from a main clause;
· to set off parenthetical or non-restrictive elements a word or a group of words that is added to the sentence, but does not alter the basic meaning);
· to separate three or more words, phrases or clauses in a sentence;
· to separate cities and states in addresses; and
· to separate a name from a title or degree.

Parentheses or dashes: The use of parentheses or dashes is usually a personal matter. Normally, the parentheses or dashes are used instead of a comma when an afterthought is inserted that is loosely connected and does not alter the main thought of the sentence. Parentheses are recommended to introduce an abbreviation or ACRONYM for the first time in a document on a particular subject.

Example: The central processing unit (CPU). American National Standards Institute, Inc. (ANSII).

Quotation Marks: Use quotation marks to set off direct quotations of words whether written or spoken and to set off titles of published material. A period or comma should be placed inside the closing quotation marks. Single quotation marks are used with a quotation within a quotation.

Semicolon: As with the comma, there are several rules for using the semicolon. The following rules are recommended:

· Use a semicolon to separate main clauses not joined with a coordinating conjunction.
· Use a semicolon to separate a series of items that contain commas.
· Use a semicolon to separate main clauses joined with such words as *however, therefore, nevertheless, consequently,* etc.

Period: Other than to indicate the end of a sentence or used after an abbreviation, the period is used to indicate an ellipsis (. . .) within a sentence. The omission of words from quoted material is indicated by an ellipsis of three periods. If the omitted words come at the end of a sentence, the ellipsis should contain four periods (. . . .).

There is disagreement among grammarians on the correct use of punctuation. Other than in the use of the period, question or quotation marks, punctuation is more or less a personal choice. "In questions of punctuation, there is often no absolute standard . . . to which you can turn for a 'correct' answer. But there are two general rules that serve as reliable guides: first, remember punctuation is an aid to and not a substitute for clear and orderly sentence structure. Before you can punctuate a sentence properly, you must have constructed it properly. No number of commas, semicolons, or dashes will redeem a poorly written sentence. Second, observe conventional practices in punctuation. Though many of the rules are not hard and fast, still there is a community of agreement about punctuating sentences. . . ." [9]

THE PARAGRAPH STRUCTURE

The majority of EDP documentation writing involves writing long documents with several paragraphs or pages. Each paragraph in the document should relate to the previous one in a logical order. The paragraph represents the writer's thinking on a particular subject, idea or statement of fact. A paragraph is a group of sentences logically related to each other. They should form an *effective* paragraph in the development of an entire document.

To be *effective,* a paragraph must be developed around a topic sentence. The topic sentence should contain the central idea of the paragraph. In EDP documentation, the topic sentence should be the opening sentence of the paragraph. This will enable the busy reader to read the first sentence of a paragraph and get the idea and information that is contained in a document. If the reader wishes more detail, he can read the supporting sentences. To demonstrate this point, just read the underscored sentences on these pages to get the *main idea* of the "paragraph structure."

To get the reader's attention, the *idea* should be stated immediately. Each subsequent sentence in the paragraph should support the topic sentence. The purpose of the supporting sentences is to describe, explain, prove, or lend supporting information to what was said in the topic sentence. To insure that the main idea is clear and is supported by other sentences, the paragraph must have *unity, coherence,* and good organization.

A paragraph is a *unified and logically* related group of sentences whose main purpose is to express an idea or subject. Experts recommend an average length of eight to ten sentences. A paragraph, like a sentence, should be short with *transitional words* or phrases.

To transfer the trend of thought from one paragraph to another, the writer should use *transitional words or phrases.* Transitional words will lead the reader through an idea, from paragraph to paragraph, without losing his trend of thought. When using a transitional word or phrase, the writer should make sure that it logically shares a relationship between the paragraphs that are being connected.

---

[9] Glenn Leggett, C. David Mead, William Charvat, *Handbook for Writers,* third edition, Prentice-Hall, Englewood Cliffs, N.J., pp. 123–124.

Transitional words or phrases may be related to preceding paragraphs or to the overall subject of the document.

One way to use *transitions* in a new paragraph is to repeat key words or phrases previously used. The purpose of the transtion is to move the reader from point to point. To demonstrate how transitional keywords and phrases will guide a reader from one paragraph to another, study the words in italics. Note how the italic word "effective" in the last sentence in the first paragraph relates to the italic phrase "to be effective" in the first sentence of the second paragraph. The italic phrase "main idea" of the last sentence of the second paragraph relates to the italic phrase "idea should" in the first sentence of the third paragraph, and so on for the rest of the discussion on "paragraph structure."

Other examples of transitional words or phrases are: conversely, finally, so, next, therefore, however, now, first, on the other hand, in the second place, another point to consider, a second method, etc.

In developing a paragraph, the EDP documentation writer should keep in mind the following rules:

- Use a topic sentence.
- Confine one idea or subject to a paragraph.
- Keep paragraphs short.
- Use transitional words or phrases.

PARAGRAPH NUMBERING

There are several paragraph numbering methods that may be used. Paragraph numbering is the prerogative of the writer. The paragraph layout and numbering should permit easy reading and referencing. For documents used as a reference and subject to frequent changes, each paragraph and sub-paragraph should be numbered. The following are two examples recommended for EDP technical writing.

Paragraph Structure Using Arabic Numbers: This type of paragraph numbering is recommended when writing a specification document or instruction manual. Each subject (paragraph and sub-paragraph) is given a sequential number derived from the section (or volume) number.

Paragraph Structure Using Arabic Numbers and Alphabet: This type of paragraph numbering may be used for specification documents and instruction (user) manuals, but it is recommended for EDP summaries, abstracts, studies and general correspondence. This type of paragraph structuring allows for five sub-paragraph levels. All these levels may not be used. Their use and indentation depends on the writer and the type of document he is writing. For example: General correspondence and short EDP summaries would not require sectioning nor would the capital letters of the alphabet (major topics) be required.

Appendix A depicts the above paragraph numbering structure. Appendix B contains commonly used mathematical and programming symbols.

APPENDIX A

EXAMPLE OF ARABIC NUMBERS USED IN PARAGRAPH STRUCTURING

SECTION THREE

3.1 (First paragraph of Section Three) _____

_____.

3.2 (Second paragraph) _____

_____.

3.2.1 (First sub-paragraph of paragraph 3.2) _____

_____.

3.2.1.1 (Second sub-paragraph of sub-paragraph 3.2.1) _____

_____.

3.2.1.1.4 (Fourth sub-paragraph of sub-paragraph 3.2.1.1) _____

_____.

3.2.2 (Second sub-paragraph of paragraph 3.2) _____

_____.

3.3 _____

_____.

3.5.2.1 (First sub-paragraph of sub-paragraph 3.5.2—not listed—) ___

_____.

SECTION FOUR

4.1 _____

_____.

4.1.1 _____

_____.

4.3.2 _____

_____.

4.3.3.12 _____

_____.

4.5 _____

_____.

4.5.1 _____

_____.

4.5.1.1 _____

_____.

EXAMPLE OF ALPHABET AND ARABIC NUMERALS IN PARAGRAPH STRUCTURING

SECTION I

A. (Major topic) _____

_____ .

    1. (Paragraph) _____

_____ .

        (1) *(When a main paragraph is interrupted with a colon (:) to enumerate items or clarify certain points, these items or points should be assigned on arabic number enclosed in parentheses. Example: . . . the two levels of documentation are defined as:*
           (1) _____

_____ .

           (2) _____

_____ .

        a. (Sub-paragraph) _____

_____ .

           (1) (Sub-paragraph of paragraph 1.a.) _____

_____ .

              (a) (Sub-paragraph of paragraph 1.a.(1)) _____

_____ .

                 1 (Sub-paragraph of paragraph 1.a.(1)(a)) ___

_____ .

                    a (Sub-paragraph of paragraph 1.a.(1)(a)1 ___

_____ .

                    b _____

_____ .

                 2 _____

_____ .

              (b) _____

_____ .

           (2) _____

_____ .

        b. _____

_____ .

    2. _____

_____ .

B. _____

_____ .

APPENDIX B

∞	Infinity
∂	Partial Derivation
$\mp$	Minus or Plus
$\pm$	Plus or Minus
$<$	Less Than
$>$	Greater Than
$\geqslant$	Greater Than or Equal To
$\leqslant$	Less Than or Equal To
$\triangle$	Delta
$\therefore$	Therefore
$\because$	Since or Because
$\approx$	Is Approximately Equal To
$\int$	Integral Symbol
$\simeq$	Is Similarly Ordered
$\sim$	The Difference Between or Is Similar To
$\%$	Percent

	Approaches as the Limit or Indicate Data Flow
$\sum$	Algebraic Sum Symbol
$\sqrt{}$	Square Root Symbol
$\gg$	Is Very Much Greater Than
$\ll$	Is Very Much Less Than
[ ]	Brackets
( )	Parentheses
$\equiv$	Is Identical With
π	Pi
{ }	Braces
$+$	Plus or Positive
$-$	Minus or Negative
$\times$	Multiply
$\div$ or /	Divide
$\doteq$	Equals
$\neq$	Not Equal
	Communications Link
$\cong$	Incongruent To

13

How to Create a Written Piece[1]

Use plain, simple language, short words, and brief sentences. That is the way to write English. It is the modern way, and the best way. Stick to it; don't let fluff and flowers and verbosity creep in.

Mark Twain

The Assignment.   What triggered your writing job? Was it a problem? Did you select the job? Or did it come from your boss, from top management . . . or from a customer or client? Whatever the source, you do know the other end of the process, a written piece of some kind. It may be a proposal, a report, an article, a speech.

THE CREATION PROCESS

This chapter has a single aim: to guide you through a process that starts with an assignment and ends with an excellent written piece that does its job. The process we'll describe is not the only way. But it does work. If you follow it you'll produce an effective written piece.

Objective? Write it out. The process is a documentary one . . . in which you pin information down in black and white on paper . . . so you'd write down (1) the subject, (2) the problem, or (3) the assignment. Describe the task you're tackling. Any activity needs a "handle," so grab a working title for now. You can develop the final title later.

---

[1] A note about this chapter. I was given permission by Systemation, Inc., and Mr. Leslie H. Matthies, copyright owner, Colorado Springs, Colo. 80901, to use "How to Create a Written Piece" in this book.

Part II of this book is directed at personnel who write about EDP systems. However, this chapter is also addressed to those individuals who are not involved in writing EDP documentation but seek information in "capsule form" to aid them in writing. The chapter is skillfully written, and gets to the heart of good writing practices. The material has been slightly edited.

The information that you'll present to your reader already exists in some form . . . probably in great bulk. The facts, the data, are scattered around . . . out there, somewhere. Your job is to search out these raw facts, and once you have them to refine them (through a mental process) so they will be significant to your intended reader. Like the gold miner, you may have to process 5 tons of raw material to come up with 5 ounces of valuable substance.

You'll go through large quantities of information, data, charts, and statistics. After processing this bulk through your own mind you'll produce a written piece containing a small quantity of information. Therein lies the value of your work. The data in its bulk form wasn't usable. Now, in your written piece, it will be useful.

GATHERING THE FACTS

Writing is a technique and it is just one step in the process of creating a writtten piece. To apply the technique you need raw material . . . bulk information. Where do you get the information, the raw materials? You'll consider such sources as:

- · Your own experience
- · The experience (and knowledge) of other people
- · Documents

Avoid Swivel Chair Flavor:

Be aware that there are 2 definite dangers that can threaten the value of your written piece. Let these 2 dangers wave like red flags so that you're aware of their existence, and, being aware, avoid them. They are:

- · Swivel chair flavor
- · Inaccurate factual data

Consider the swivel chair flavor. It can come because you try to do the job the lazy way. You base your work only on your experience, and make little effort to update your knowledge. Other people can contribute some swivel chair flavor if they provide you with their opinions, which are rarely accurate. The swivel chair flavor will disgust the discriminating reader. Avoid it.

Inaccurate factual data is worse. Somebody tells you that the company sends out 300 invoices a day. Your study involves the production of these documents. You could be in trouble if you take that "fact" (300 invoices) as correct. It may be accurate. It may not. It may be 100 invoices—or 500.

One incorrect fact will throw doubt on the other information you put in the written piece . . . if a top executive or staff man checks this one item and finds that "300 invoices a day" is not factual. Thus the value of your written piece evaporates.

Don't reject information offhand, however, even though you suspect its validity.

Take it in. But take it in with the thought, "I must get a verification of this fact." (From a different source, of course.) You may do the job by talking to people, by going through the files, by recalling your own experiences. You'll rake in a lot of data. However, because you did some preliminary thinking (resulting in the written piece objective), you'll know what data may be useful. This will cut down the gathering phase enormously.

SORTING THE DATA

You can sort data in one of 2 ways: (1) you can sort out the data in your head . . . or (2) you can sort out data on paper. It's easier to use paper. That's what we recommend.

How do you do it? To do data sorting, you must convert all information into written form. Even the information in your own head must come on paper. If you have ideas of your own, scribble them out, type them, or dictate them. Oral or unwritten information won't do, even yours.

Convert all data into writing so you can sort it, so you can place it in a number of stacks which represent various classifications you're going to use to develop your written piece. Did you have some interviews? Type or write out the data the people gave you. Did you take notes? Finish these.

Your next step is to scan all the material you've gathered. Don't try to sort now. Read it rapidly. Better yet, have someone else read it to you. With a clipboard on your knee, make notes as the reader reads. Some documents may contain data that falls into several classifications. Example: You have the minutes from a top level staff meeting and they contain data that falls under several classes. Do you have a copy machine handy? Then make an extra copy or two of these minutes. Mark the different classifications on each copy. Then sort these copies by each classification.

Now take a little time to write out the answer to this question:

· What is my written piece supposed to achieve?
· What is its OBJECT?

When you answer that question, put it down IN WRITING. In arriving at the answer you'll consider your reader. What does he know about the subject? What doesn't he know? Remember that in this process, you're the refiner. All the facts that your reader needs were there . . . somewhere. But you did (1) a gathering job, and now you'll do (2) a condensing job. It's your job to provide just the key information in a form that is useful to someone else. You'll sort the raw, bulk information, of course, into selected classifications. How do you decide on classifications?

Select the Idea Packages:

Think first in terms of packages of ideas. Next consider the right sequence for presenting the entire idea. Here's a typical packaging of ideas, and a logical sequence:

- The Background Situation
- The Symptoms
- The Real Problem
- Poor Results Now Suffered
- Possible Methods of Correction
- The Recommended Method
- What Results to Expect
- What Will It Cost?
- How Long Will It Take?

Those idea packages will become sections in your written piece. If you write down the objective of your written piece, these packages of ideas will come easier. So will the sequence.

Logical sequence is essential. The best packages alone aren't necessarily the answer. Example: If you present the section on "BACKGROUND SITUATION" at the last, then you'd be guilty of poor sequencing. But in certain instances your sequence of ideas should start out like this:

- The problem
- The losses
- What can be done . . . etc.

Now you're ready to capture all the ideas . . . anything that has any relationship to any one of your idea packages.

THE FIRST DRAFT

Now that you know your classifications, as well as the objective of your written piece, you put all the pertinent information into those groups. Then your next step is to capture the information in "your own words."

By now you have nothing that hasn't been typed, scribbled out, or captured in some written form. Be sure of that. Now do a quick sorting job on your desk to get the documents into stacks according to your classifications. If you have 7 classes, you'll now have at least 7 stacks of papers. You're in the process of developing the sections of your final written piece.

Sort all the documents into the classes that you've selected. Notice that at this time you don't try for any particular order within the packages. You just sort all papers into stacks. Label the stacks using a large sheet of paper which has the classification, such as "SYMPTOMS," hand printed in bold ink at the bottom. Or fold over some heavy cardboard as a nameplate.

You'll have some papers that won't sort, that is, they won't seem to fit into any of your 7 "packages." Set these aside in a separate stack. You'll look these over later. Now you're ready to shape up the material by running it all through the world's best and most creative computer—your own mind.

You can draft/capture your ideas in one of 3 ways:

· Handwrite it
· Type it
· Dictate it to a machine or steno

We recommend that you dictate to a machine. That's the best method. If you take any other path, you'll have to find a slower way as best you can at this point in the process. Dictating to a machine gives you time to think as you compose.

You're not going to repeat just what is in the documents. You're going to use a mental digesting process. Here's the sequence of work at this stage:

· Look at the write-up covering the objective of your written piece. Keep it in front of you.
· Pick up the stack of documents in the first classification, such as those on the BACK-GROUND SITUATION.
· Sort the documents into the most sensible sequence within the classification stack.
· Read each document quickly to get your own thoughts flowing.
· Dictate your thoughts.
· Ask the typist to give you a quick, rough draft.

Work Fast but Work Freely:

Talk about the subject, with no inhibitions. Don't concern yourself about grammar, spelling, punctuation, or anything else. Just talk away. You're now filtering the raw material from the documents through your own mind. By filtering the information through your mind you'll improve it, aim it at its purpose!

Sure, you'll get some foreign matter (non-pertinent data) mixed in, or some stuff that belongs in another classification. But don't let that stop you. Don't wait for anything now. Capture the ideas quickly. You'll notice that this activity is self-stimulating. But also expect that much of what you turn out will be so much dross or waste. That happens when you're using the quick draft method.

Remember the movie maker. He may expose 90,000 feet of film, but he'll show only 5,000 feet in the theater (85,000 feet was also dross, waste, imperfect, or non-pertinent). The 5,000-foot picture taken from 90,000 feet of exposed film is now worth seeing.

Did you set aside a "miscellaneous" stack? Review the documents here. Do you need another classification? Should you drop this information? Parts of it? None of it? Decide at this time.

Pass on the quick draft idea to the typist. Tell her: "This is just a draft. Allow a lot of space around the edges. Double-space it. Bang it out. Don't worry about strike-overs. Get it back to me quickly."

When you've finished dictating Section 1, go on to Section 2.

KNEADING THE MATERIAL

Let's review. You wrote out the objective of your written piece. After thinking about "packages" of information, you gathered it. You talked to people. You wrote up your own experiences. When every bit of information was in writing, you sorted it into sections or packages. Then you read through this mass quickly. Next, you dictated your version of the information, stack by stack. Now all the data is in "your own words." During all this you kept the objective of the written piece in front of you.

The Second Sequencing:

The drafts are now back on your desk. They're rough, but the copy is all double-spaced and there is lots of white space on the paper. Now you're ready to run the material through the mental mill (your own mind) a second time. This is another step in the refining process.

Take the first section. Blue pencil a number out in the left in front of each paragraph. Numbers? What for? They're handles, just as your section (classification) titles are handles. Such handles enable you to manipulate the information as you work it over. Regarding subheads, we suggest you use at least one to every page.

Now read through the draft copy on Section 1. Your next job is to put the paragraphs in a logical sequence. You may feel that paragraph 26 should be first. Indicate this on a separate sheet of blank paper. Then pick the paragraph, perhaps 13, you think should be second, and then the next, and next. Take a separate sheet of paper. List the sections by number and title such as:

- SITUATION
  (Leave lots of space here)
- SYMPTOMS
  (Space)
- PROBLEM
  (Space)

If you have 7 sections (packages) list them on the sheet, but spread out so you have about an inch of space (6 lines) under each section. As you think of the sequence you want, jot the paragraph number down under the section. At this point you can take one of 2 paths: (1) have the material retyped in the sequence you've selected, or (2) do a snip and staple job.

Retype by the Numbers:

If you decide to retype, tell the steno: "Retype the material in the paragraph sequence shown on this separate sheet." Whether the steno redrafts or you do it, always put a blue diagonal line across the old copy. This is a handy signal. It tells you: "This has been redrafted."

In this process you've undoubtedly run across material you don't want to use at all, perhaps a lot of it. Or, you may run across some paragraphs that don't, on second thought, belong in this section. Move them over into the section where you think they do belong. All through this process, slash around with your blue pencil. Always improve the copy as you go, but your major problem now is to:

· Select and eliminate paragraphs
· Improve the sequences

How about the second path of resequencing, if you're shy of stenographic help? Take some blank sheets of paper. Cut all the paragraphs apart. Staple the paragraph strips onto the blank paper in the order in which you want them.

Use Marginal Notes:

You've been revising the material as you resort it. You may need "reminders" at some points in the copy. That is, you may need to insert a page number that you can't know at this time. Write it in like this: "This point is covered in more detail under Section 4—ALTERNATE METHODS. See page . . . . . ." Then out in the margin put this note: "Fill in page number when known."

You might want to remind yourself of something else that you must do later. Use the margins for this purpose. Instruct the typist to type the note in the margin. Here are typical notes that authors use:

· Pix 16-A will go here.
· Asterisk here.
· Give page number of final copy when layout is complete.
· Full-page table (Exhibit 23) follows this page.

The picture (pix) can, of course, be a chart, photograph, or drawing.

Recognize that you're using a manufacturing (reshaping) process. Compare it with a manufacturing process that leaves a slag heap—piles of scrap, and articles spoiled or not used. In the same way, as you create your written piece, you must eventually reject the majority of the material you gathered.

Start getting a bit hard-boiled at this point. If a bit of writing doesn't fit in, even though it is well-written, get rid of it. How can you tell? You can . . . IF you've kept the writing objective in front of you. Now you've got the second version back, with the paragraphs sorted in reasonably good sequence.

THE BOIL DOWN

The redraft (or the snip and staple job) is now on your desk. Now you really get tough on the copy. Whatever form the draft is in now, whether it is a series of stapled strips on a sheet of paper, or a typewritten redraft . . . you are ready to boil down the copy to its essence.

How many pages should the final (with copy single-spaced) written piece be? 5 pages? 8 pages? 10? Let's say 10. How many (double-spaced copy) pages do you have now? 40? If it's 40, then you must boil down 60% of your present copy. (Consider the spacing factor . . . from double to single.) Remember: You never unload all the verbal collection on your reader. If you did, he wouldn't read it. And you wouldn't achieve your objective.

The Telegraphic Stage:

How many sections do you have, 7? If so, write 7 telegrams. Don't gasp. Sure, you've been told that writing is easy. It isn't. It is hard work.

Do the job this way: Reread the section and then turn it over. Next take a blank sheet of paper and write (from what you have just read) the essence of the section *as a telegram*. This work is not easy. You must stretch your brain. But it will improve your final written piece immensely.

Seek the key words. Leave out most of the non-essential adjectives, adverbs, conjunctions, articles. Concentrate on 2 grammatical elements . . . nouns and verbs. Under Section 1: "BACKGROUND SITUATION"—your telegram may read something like this: Changed receiving dock location requires 500-foot trip for inspectors when specialty articles arrive. Result: severe hold-ups on dock.

Now list the nouns you find there: location . . . trip . . . inspectors . . . articles . . . hold-ups . . . dock. It's necessary to modify the first noun, "location," so you pinpoint it. You place the words "changed receiving dock" in front of "location." You may slip a bit and wind up with a 25-word telegram. No one will be the wiser, except you. If you can't do the job in 20 words, have you really captured the essence of the section? Write such a telegram on each section. Then you'll be ready to go into the semifinal phase of the work.

The Compression Job:

Whether you call this next work step boil down, compression, or selection . . . it is the stage at which you must eliminate from 60 to 80% of the material you first drafted. If you gathered very little information, your written piece will be a poverty-stricken product. The richness and power of your written piece will come when you have plenty of material to draw from.

If you didn't gather and draft at least 4 times as much material as you'll finally use, be assured that your written piece will be weak. So now you go back to work on the copy, keeping 3 documents in front of you:

· The objective of the written piece.
· The section plan.
· Your telegram covering the section you're going to boil down first.

The telegram will tell you what copy you should keep. At this stage you'll drop most of the copy and boil down and smooth out what you retain.

This will probably be pencil work. With your pencil you'll slash, rearrange, make notes, and perhaps even add information here and there. But mostly you'll be condensing and compressing, always following the 20 words in your telegram. Perhaps you did such a good job with your telegram that it is all you need. But usually the telegram is a little spare and bony. It needs a few words to fill out its flesh.

THE SEMIFINAL DRAFT

After dictating the boil down, which you based on your 20-word telegrams on each section, you now have the newest draft on your desk. This cleaned up copy helps you to see where you are now. There will still be some roughness in the copy from which you will prepare the semifinal draft. Do the job with a pencil, blue preferred. However, if you're skilled at dictation, you can even talk out this semifinal version.

Work Section by Section:

Now you read through each of the sections, one at a time and very critically. You have in front of you, of course, that all important guide . . . the objective of your written piece. Examine the material for sequence. Is it sensible? Logical? You now examine every sentence for good writing. This is the time to correct misspelled words, poor grammar, or any lack of agreement between subjects and predicates. You're still in the double-spaced typing stage so you have room to work over the copy.

Do you have enough subheads sprinkled through? At least one subhead on each page will increase the readability of your copy. A sprinkling of applicable pictures, charts, or exhibits will help.

You're getting ready for the finish; for the completion of your task. Rarely can you go from the boil down draft to the final. You'll require a semifinal draft. Don't be discouraged. Many writers go through 6 or 7 drafts to shape up an important document.

THE FINAL COPY

You go from the semifinal draft to the final and now you have the written piece. In the semifinal draft you did everything that must be done to improve the effectiveness of the writing. You checked the grammar, the punctuation and the spelling. You tucked in any loose ends, such as notes, references, illustrations, or charts. You looked at the exhibits, the pictures, the references, the asterisks, and the footnotes . . . to be sure everything was in good order. As soon as the semifinal draft is back, read it carefully.

Now is the time to proof all figures. Go back to the original sources. Don't trust figures redrafted from previous drafts. Someone may have made an error somewhere along the line. So be sure to proof all numerical data against original sources.

If you make changes on the semifinal draft, make them neatly. Hand print such changes. No handwritten scrawl. Then the typist will be able to go right to your final copy.

Do you believe in copy variation? It adds to the readability and the appearance of the final printed piece. Then mark the variations you want. Variations include:

· Underlining
· Words in capital letters for emphasis
· The indentation of significant points to make them stand out

Will your printed piece be set in type? Then you can add more variations such as bold-face (most of the copy will be in lightface), italics, different sizes of type . . . and type features such as stars, circles, arrows, or pointing hands. But probably your final written piece will be typewritten. Will you need a number of copies?

You can produce carbon copies, but we'd recommend (if the document is important enough) that you have the typist make just one carbon copy (for your files) and get other sets of copies from the copying machine. Be certain that these copies are sharp and black. Don't spoil the whole job by accepting weak, faded, or washed out copies.

The Change in Typing Specifications:

Previous to this you were working with drafts, even the semifinal draft. But now the typing specifications change. Tell the steno:

· Now single-space the copy, double-spacing between paragraphs. Triple-space above the subheads.
· Place 4 line spaces between sections. Center the numbers and section titles.
· Cut the subheads "into the line." Type these in caps and lower case, underlined. Then continue on the same line with the sentence that follows.
· Make the margins the same on the top and sides of the sheet (1⅛ inches). But at the bottom of the sheet, have a 1½-inch margin. Indent each paragraph 5 spaces (unless your organization's style guide calls for block paragraphs).
· This is a final. Make one original and one carbon. It must be perfect copy. So see that it is typed accurately. Correct any errors on the original sheet, plus the carbon.

Investigate your typist's typewriter. Are the keys clean? Have the final typing done on an electric machine, one with sharp, clean typefaces, and a paper carbon ribbon. Then your copy will be sharper.

The width of line should be between 6 and 6¼ inches. (The outer margins of the sheet, if you're using standard 8½ x 11 paper, will be 1⅛ inches.) For greater readability, we recommend margins of 1½ inches, giving you a 5½-inch typed line. The closer you get to a 5-inch line width, the more readable the line will be.

Check a Sample Page:

To be sure the typist is doing the job, ask her to type one page and bring it to you for checking. She may have forgotten to single space, or follow some of the other specifications.

On the first page, you'll want the final title. Leave the upper ⅓ of the page clear, providing lots of white space "flowing around" the title itself. All other pages will start 1⅛ inches down from the top edge of the paper. Give some attention to the paper. Use 20-lb. white bond or heavier. If you want the piece to be really beautiful, get white rag content paper, with some texture. Avoid colors. Use white paper.

Now, when the typist finishes, you'll have your final written piece . . . a written document that you created and that will serve an important purpose in your organization.

THE TECHNIQUE OF WRITING

We are not attempting here to teach you how to write. Our aim is to explain a process you can use to create a useful written piece. Example: You're assigned to study problems of "costs and peak loads" relating to telephone traffic between people in your organization and their outside contacts. The information about this activity is voluminous. The problems are many.

As the writer, it's your job to condense this and in so doing, to reshape information. You'll bring the problem into sharp focus. It may take you many hours of hard work.

But an executive may be able to read your written piece in perhaps 20 minutes. He can then make a decision. Let's say that your job—the creation of the written piece—took a full month. This gives us a "manufacturing process" time of 173 hours. This would be 519 twenty-minute periods. So this gives a ratio of 519 of creative 20-minute periods (yours) to one "consuming" 20-minute period (your executive's).

Are several executives interested? Four or 5 executives couldn't personally give an entire month to this problem. They are engaged in too many other activities. That's the importance of an effective written piece. It can provide time-leverage ratios like our 519 to 1 example. Much value there.

Reforming Habits:

In this chapter we are carrying you through the process of creating a written piece. It seems like a lot of steps. And it is. But take heart! After you've followed the process 3 or 4 times, it becomes much easier, but recognize this: Creating an effective written piece requires work. It requires mental effort, patience, analysis, meditation, guidance, and push, push, push. It also requires a knowledge of the process that leads you to the final product . . . the written piece.

Consider a Writing Jag:

Is the job a big one? Would your boss consider it important enough for you to spend an entire month of 173 hours on it, and do nothing else? You can do it in less than a month if you go on a writing jag. You can compress time. You can get the written piece ready in 3 weeks or even in 2 . . . instead of 4.

How Do You Do It?   You get the facts and information, do the interviewing, get every bit of information down in draft form. You collect related documents. Then, as you start through the process of creating the written piece, you forget regular working hours. You work night and day. Get out of the office. Escape. Take a pleasant hotel or motel room.

Take your dictating equipment, office paraphernalia like scissors, staplers, tape, and all your written material. Arrange for someone to pick up your tapes for typing and then bring the drafts back to you. Cut off all other contact with your office. Give your phone number only to your family and your boss.

The writing jag gives you tremendous momentum. You'll feel a personal enthusiasm. You may work a full 2 shifts; perhaps into the early hours of the morning. You drop into bed only when you're exhausted.

As soon as you're refreshed, showered, shaved, and coffeed, you're ready to go at it again. You go through the exact process that we describe in this booklet but you go through the steps quickly. You won't have to pick up and review what you did the day before. You'll find your continuity tremendously improved.

WHAT IS WRITING?

Writing is a technical skill, a discipline. By itself writing skill has no value. But writing skill does have value as a transforming technique. But of course there must be something to transform. Knowledge. Subject matter.

You're going to produce a written piece. It will have both a purpose and a form. You are the only one who can spell out its purpose or objective. But its form may fall into a category. Here are some forms of a written piece.

- A report
- An article
- A chapter in a book
- A speech
- A paper (technical)
- A complex letter
- A proposal
- An explanation

Your writing needs a specific aim. Otherwise it will not be strong, purposeful writing. If you try to use one piece of writing for several purposes, you'll fail to achieve the other purposes.

Index